Wo

Luton Sixth Form College

with

Support Staff

SCHOOL LEADERSHIP AND MANAGEMENT SERIES

Series Editors: Brent Davies and John West-Burnham

Working with

Support Staff WITHDRAWN

Their roles and effective management in schools

Professor Trevor Kerry

An imprint of PEARSON EDUCATION

Harlow, England · London · New York · Reading, Massachusetts · San Francisco · Toronto · Don Mills, Ontario · Sydney · Tokyo · Singapore · Hong Kong · Seoul · Taipei · Cape Town · Madrid · Mexico City · Amsterdam · Munich · Paris · Milan

PEARSON EDUCATION LIMITED

Head Office:
Edinburgh Gate
Harlow CM20 2JE
Tel: +44 (0)1279 623623
Fax: +44 (0)1279 431059

London Office:
128 Long Acre,
London WC2E 9AN
Tel: +44 (0)20 7447 2000
Fax: +44 (0)20 7240 5771
Website: www.educationminds.com

First published in Great Britain 2001

© Pearson Education Limited 2001

The right of Trevor Kerry to be identified as author
of this Work has been asserted by him in accordance
with the Copyright, Designs and Patents Act, 1988.

ISBN 0 273 65423 3

British Library Cataloguing in Publication Data
A CIP catalogue record for this book can be obtained from the British Library.

10 9 8 7 6 5 4 3 2 1

Typeset by Pantek Arts, Maidstone, Kent.
Printed and bound in Great Britain by Bell & Bain Ltd., Glasgow

The Publishers' policy is to use paper manufactured from sustainable forests.

About the author

■ ■ ■

Professor Trevor Kerry is Professor and Senior Vice President of the College of Teachers; Visiting Professor in the International Institute for Educational Leadership, University of Lincolnshire & Humberside; Visiting Fellow in Education, UEA; former senior manager in FE/HE/ITT; former Senior Adviser for Norfolk LEA; former primary and secondary teacher; part-time SENCO (primary); former primary inspector, Ofsted. Former Staff Tutor and currently External Examiner for STA courses.

He is an author of more than 20 titles including: *Questioning & Explaining in Classrooms* (Hodder); *Teaching in FE* (Blackwell); *Topic Teaching in the Primary School* (Routledge). His most recent book for Pearson Education, *Mastering Deputy Headship* (2000), was published within the Leadership Skills in Education Management series, for which Professor Kerry is the Series Editor.

About the contributors

■ ■ ■

Carolle Kerry has wide experience of research in schools and of school governorship. A former Clerk to Governors, she has been Vice Chair of Governors in a large primary school and is currently an LEA governor in a rural primary. She has worked for Local Authorities in various roles, including special education and public relations. A co-author of the *Blackwell Handbook of Education* (1995), she has also written a number of journal articles in the areas of minority education and educating able pupils. Carolle is a social scientist by training, and holds the first Fellowship of the College of Teachers to be awarded to a school governor. She is currently engaged in doctoral studies.

Pat Foulkes is a Senior Lecturer in Education Studies at the University of Luton. She currently manages the BA Education Studies and the Specialist Teacher Assistants' courses at the University of Luton, both of which offer in-service training and development for experienced paraprofessionals in schools. She has a special interest in the role of teaching assistants and nursery nurses, particularly in recognising the contribution they make to supporting learning and in facilitating their progression into a teaching career. She has considerable experience as a consultant in supporting schools with employment-based teacher training schemes, the Graduate and Registered Teacher programmes. She also works closely with a number of School-Centred Initial Teacher Training consortia in supporting their PGCE courses.

Contents

■ ■ ■

Acknowledgements

■   ■   ■

The author would like to thank the following, who gave 'expert testimony' regarding the various support staff roles and their management that are featured in this book:

David Baxter, Karen Blakey, Sue Brewster, Pat Buck, Chris Child, Sandra Childs, David Cobb, Linda Coombes, Amanda Cooper, Judy Davison, Michelle Feather, Carol Flanagan, Lynn Garnett, Brian Garton, Karen Henry, Sue Hill, Albert Hudspeth, Andrew Kerry, Margaret King, Ann Knapp, Jillian Mack, Husek Miloslav, Julie Newton, Simon Nicholson, Jane Pluta, Angela Radjenovic, Angela Reast, Christine Robinson, William Rose, Judy Shaw, Tony Sheppard, Kelvin Simmonds, Debbie Simpson, Henk Sligte, Ginni Smith, Patricia Temple-Fielder, Meurig Thomas, Patricia Van Reet, Marleen Vanderpoorten, David Warbrick, Joanna Watkins, James Welsh, Mandy Wilding, Rita Williamson, Sue Witton.

The International Institute for Educational Leadership (Head: Fergus O'Sullivan) at the University of Lincolnshire and Humberside funded a consultative conference for support staff in January 2001. The following acted as facilitators on the day: Debbie Betteridge (doctoral student IIEL, and consultant), Alison Johnston (Professional Association of Teachers), Carolle Kerry (TK Consultancy, contributing author), Professor Ray Page (CEO, College of Teachers), Elizabeth Wood (IIEL, Head of Bursars' courses); Catherine King and Dawn Hunt administered the conference.

Introduction

∎ ∎ ∎

However one looks at the future, there can be little doubt that schools are changing, and that they will continue to change rapidly over the next two decades. We are witnessing what, in retrospect, may turn out to be one of the most rapid and fundamental periods of upheaval that formal education has ever witnessed. As this book is being written debates are in progress about all of the following issues:

- performance-related pay for teachers;
- new calendar structures such as the five-term and six-term years;
- a modified inspection system;
- a plethora of funded government initiatives such as Excellence in Cities;
- the growth and implications of Information and Communications Technology (ICT);
- the establishment of City Learning Centres;
- changes to the GCSE and A level examination systems;
- private funding initiatives for schools;
- revisions to the National Curriculum.

Every one of these debates has far-reaching implications of its own. Together they make up something approaching a revolution. The time-scale against which this change is happening is significant, too. No longer can education mould itself through quiet evolution. In the political climate of the early 21st century change tends to be rapid, brutish and politically absolute.

But there are subtler changes, too. Over the last few years the emphasis in schools has moved away from teachers and teaching and towards learners and learning. This is an inevitable outcome of the drive towards measurement – of quality, standards and attainment. Input has given way to output, to use a commercial metaphor. It is also a result of ICT. The myth that learning can be achieved only by students attending at set times, in designated places, for specific periods of time has been fatally eroded by access to learning on the Intranet and Internet.

This book is set against this context of rapid change. It looks at a critical issue that underlies much of what has been implied already: the emerging roles of staff employed by schools. The cardinal thesis here is that, just as organisations change, so their staffing has to change to meet the new shapes; and the management of those staff has to rise to the challenges of the new situation.

So this is a book that looks at those who support learning in schools but who are not 'qualified teachers' in any technical sense. The intention is to examine the many varied roles that support staff play in both primary and secondary schools from a particular perspective. How do heads, teachers and others charged with leadership roles in schools, manage the work of these support staff to maximise their effectiveness in bringing about student learning?

Who are the support staff whose management is covered by this text? A look at the literature about support staff suggests there may be some 20 roles that are now widely recognised in schools. This book covers the majority of these generic roles, paid and unpaid, trained and untrained, that support students' learning. Thus, individual chapters or parts of chapters cover the roles and management of:

- classroom (also called teaching or learning) assistants;
- special educational needs teaching assistants;
- laboratory technicians;
- technical officers;
- administrative staff (secretaries/receptionists);
- bursars;
- volunteer helpers;
- school governors;

as well as

- resource/library technicians;
- nursery nurses;
- other non-professional support staff (e.g. mid-day supervisors);
- counsellors;
- other professional staff working in school contexts (psychologists, medical staff, careers officers, health professionals etc.).

We decry the tendency for these staff to be called 'teaching assistants'. We shall argue that they do indeed support learning in varying degrees – a function which is often undervalued by society and underplayed by teachers. But the heart of schooling, we maintain, is learning not teaching.

Before looking at these support roles and their management in some detail, the book begins with three more general surveys. Thus in Part One, Chapter 1 explores in a little more detail the growing roles of support staff and provides some context for their work. Chapter 2 examines some selected international perspectives on the use of support staff. Chapter 3 examines aspects of leadership and management as they relate to managing the work of support staff to maximise their contributions to student learning. These opening chapters are followed in Part Two by others about the first eight individual roles listed above. In Part Two, chapters are paired: a case study of each role is followed by one about the management issues as they relate to that support role. The book ends with a reflection on the role of support staff generally and their management in the education service of the future.

In compiling this book I have drawn on the experiences of a number of support staff and their managers: their contributions are recognised in the Acknowledgements. I have also been fortunate in being able to make use of the specialist contributions of two 'guest authors' of individual chapters: Pat Foulkes of the University of Luton for the chapters on specialist teacher assistants and their management; and Carolle Kerry of TK Consultancy for the chapter on international issues and the two chapters on school governors and their management. In the chapters on bursars I have been given unlimited access to work by my colleagues at the University of Lincoln: Fergus O'Sullivan, Elizabeth Wood and Professor Angela Thody.

As this book goes to print the government is promising 20,000 new 'teaching assistants' by 2002 – some full-time, some part-time. New qualifications structures are promised, and a national pay scale (Gold 2001). But the key issue is still that 'teaching staff need training in how to manage adults [i.e. support staff] in the classroom' (p. 7). It is this issue that much of the book is designed to address.

Reference

Gold, K. (2001) 'New wave of support', *Times Educational Supplement*, 6 April 2001, pp. 6–7.

About this book and how to use it

■ ■ ■

The first purpose of this book is to encourage those heads and teaching staff in schools who manage support personnel to take a more pro-active stance in managing their work. In particular, the thesis of this book is that support staff, along with teachers, are part of the 'learning team'. For these staff to be used to maximum effect, their impact on pupils' learning needs to be recognised, analysed, utilised and managed efficiently.

The second purpose of this text is to help support staff themselves to re-assess their own job roles and to take a detached look at these roles and how effectively they are managed. We hope that this book will encourage support staff to take a fuller place in the learning team of the school and will give them the confidence they sometimes lack to undertake professional development in their roles.

For the purpose of this book, support staff are defined as comprising both employees who are paid to undertake specific school-based functions, and also volunteers (such as parent-helpers and school governors) who are unpaid, but who make significant contributions to pupils' learning nonetheless (a view justified at various points throughout the book). We have tried to cover the main roles in detail throughout the text, though inevitably a number of the many different roles can be afforded only a brief mention.

The book is in two parts. Part One is comprised of three chapters. Chapter 1 looks at the various roles that paid and unpaid support staff occupy in the lives of schools. In Chapter 2, the scene moves to some international perspectives that throw some light on support staff roles elsewhere in the world. In particular, we look for examples of good practice that can be applied in this country. Chapter 3 sets out the underlying management theory on which this book is developed, its purpose being to underpin management decisions about the management of the job roles of support staff.

Part Two looks at specific support roles, chosen because they are the most widespread in schools:

- early years support staff;
- special needs support staff;
- laboratory assistants;
- ICT technical officers;
- school secretaries/receptionists;
- bursars;
- parent-helpers; and
- school governors.

In the case of each of these job roles there is a chapter using data collected from the appropriate post-holders describing the role and their vision of it and a chapter looking at the management of the role with suggested Management Strategies that managers might care to use to review or improve their management.

The book is intended for use by a variety of readers, and can be used in different ways. The readership might include:

- school heads and teacher-managers;
- support staff of the kinds listed above, both paid and unpaid;
- LEA and similar education administrators;
- those studying for degrees or higher degrees in education and education management.

Uses might include the following:

- The text can be read straight through as a straightforward source of information.
- Part One of the book might be accessed as source material for assignments for those studying for professional qualifications; in this context Part One is substantially referenced.
- Part Two might be read by individual groups of support staff to throw greater light on their particular roles and how they might be managed.
- The management chapters in Part Two might be used in a number of ways by school-based managers to strengthen and review their own procedures.
- The whole text might provide guidelines and food for thought for education administrators, inspectors etc. when reviewing provisions in individual schools or in groups of schools.

The advantage of texts such as this is not only the variety of uses to which they can be put, but also their essentially practical nature. This book is very much in the tradition of applied research, and has a high utilitarian purpose in the 'real world' of schools. It can be dipped into as required and used as a reference text.

A note on the research underpinning this book

■ ■ ■

The place of research in this book

The data that underpins this book was not plucked out of the air. Every quotation and every case cited is real. All the management strategies are elicited from post-holders themselves and from the literature of support staff in schools.

To ensure that the book was based on sound data we adopted a number of different research approaches each appropriate to specific groups of support staff.

Much of the book is based on data gleaned from a cross-section of support staff who attended a conference hosted by the International Institute for Educational Leadership at the University of Lincolnshire and Humberside. This event was advertised as a consultative conference, and was many times over-subscribed – itself an indication of the hunger of support staff for some kind of training and recognition. Six kinds of support personnel were invited: classroom assistants (early years), special needs teaching assistants, laboratory assistants, technical officers, school secretary/receptionists and parent helpers. Places were filled on a first-come-first-served basis. In pure research terms, the sample used for the research may have been skewed by two factors: the attendees were volunteers and they were employed in schools that were prepared to release them (not all were, as correspondence with us indicated).

Colleagues from the IIEL, along with several invitees whose work is referred to in the Acknowledgements, acted as group facilitators for the day. These facilitators were each chosen to have skills and knowledge in the area covered by the work of the attendees to whom they were assigned. The author explained the purpose of the conference and set up the activities that were designed to collect the data about support staff roles and their management. The research instruments were guided by the kinds of insights provided by the literature that is reported in Chapter 1 of this book. Most of the conference day was spent in the four group-based research exercises that form Tables R.1–R.4 at the end of this chapter. The author then gave a short talk about the future development of education and the potential roles of support staff within those developments.

This method of research was basically a self-report form of case study. Data were generated by group discussion prompted by the facilitator (Tables R.1 and R.4); by free writing (Table R.2); and by completing a semi-structured questionnaire (Table R.3). In addition, attendees were required to bring other evidence about their jobs to the conference and to contribute them to the research: their CVs, their job descriptions, and an assessment of the accuracy of those job descriptions to the jobs that they actually did.

Bursars were not included among the paid support staff in the consultative conference; governors were also excluded among non-paid support personnel. These were deliberate decisions. By excluding these post-holders we were able to invite larger numbers from other groups as we already had research data on the excluded groups. At the IIEL, colleagues O'Sullivan, Wood and Thody had carried out detailed research on bursars – described at page 161. The same was true of governors to an extent: we were able to draw on Thody's work, and this was augmented by specific research for this volume on governor roles and their management, by Carolle Kerry described at page 192.

The material relating to classroom assistants has been augmented using case studies of trainee and trained classroom assistants at work in local schools with qualified teachers. These have been collected by Pat Foulkes of the University of Luton as part of the work of the Specialist Teacher Assistants course there.

Other data has been gathered opportunistically. IIEL research on issues such as the use of ICT in schools gave us access to interviews with technical officers. We have used quotations from these interviews to augment the text. Carolle Kerry has used material gathered during a study visit to Portugal in the chapter on international perspectives; and she used a specially-devised e-mail questionnaire to gather other sections of this data (see Chapter 2).

We received some unsolicited letters from support staff who had seen our advertising for the consultative conference but were unable to attend; some told stories of their own jobs and these have been used where appropriate.

Summary

This is a book based on sound research data culled from several sources using different approaches. This method helps to provide the reader with the 'living voice' of support staff in schools – though it may not satisfy the purist researcher. The book, however, is not intended to be a piece of research into support staff and their roles but rather an analysis of support staff, their roles and management, based on research that provides credibility and practical insight.

Table R.1 Sharing pleasures and problems

Notes for leaders

In this session you are asked to elicit initial information from your group of delegates and to pull together their thoughts onto a flip chart sheet (with which you will be supplied on the day). The questions fall into three sections. Please keep an eye on the time and cover them all.

It is important that you keep the delegates on task, and don't let them wander off into general discussion. To this end, below are some notes to help you form a structure for the session (30 minutes).

*

Get the delegates to introduce themselves, and to say in two or three sentences something about themselves and their locations. Keep this brief.

Collect the information they have been asked to bring with them – job description, notes on the job descriptions, and CV: these need to be put into the appropriate box file.

Then ask them to identify (and you record on the flip chart) the following:

1. What are the five most important aspects of their work and its contribution to what happens in school? (Leader listens to the discussion, the group lists the aspects and the leader records the agreed list.)

2. How does their work contribute to pupils' learning? (You may need to explore this carefully – we need to discover, e.g.:
   what kinds of things pupils learn from support staff;
   how their work meshes with that of teachers;
   in what circumstances they might actually 'teach' pupils (if at all);
   whether they feel their work is concerned with, e.g. setting an example, the ethos of the school, social skills etc.

(The leader needs to record on the flip chart all the suggestions offered.)

3. What hinders the work of your delegates? Try to elicit as many suggestions as possible. Make a list of all of them. Are there any items that are especially important? (You might star these.) Why are these items important?

Table R.2 Personal writing: a case study of your role

In this 45-minute session we would like you to write freely about your job (or, in the case of parents and volunteer helpers, your role). You can write whatever you choose, the things you think are most important for us to know.

It is important that what you write are YOUR OWN THOUGHTS AND FEELINGS so please do not discuss this exercise with others in your group.

Your writing may be quoted in whole or part in the proposed book.

We have given you some questions for guidance, but you are not confined only to writing about these.

Please put your name and role at the top of your writing (these will not be quoted in the book, so no individual school will be identified and you can write in confidence).

- What does a 'typical' day look like?
- What qualities do you need in order to do your job/role well?
- What motivates you to undertake this job/role?
- How do you *feel* about your job/role?
- Most importantly, how do you contribute to pupils' learning?
- What would make your job/role easier, more pleasant?
- Can you describe one of the most difficult incidents you have faced in your job/role? How did you deal with it?
- Can you describe an incident that gave you a great deal of satisfaction in your job/role? Why was this so important?
- What particular contribution do you think you have brought to your school?
- How do you see your job/role developing in the future?
- Is this how you would like it to develop?
- What is the particular or distinctive contribution that your job/role can make to the school?

Table R.3 A management questionnaire

Instructions to leaders re: the management questionnaire

Please give out the questionnaire and ask delegates to complete it. Stress that this section of the data collection is one of the two most critical in the day. Emphasise the need to answer page one quickly, and pages two and three reflectively.

The group should be able to do this in 30 minutes (please keep an eye on the time), which will leave you with about 10 minutes spare.

Now you will need to make a judgement:

- If the group needs more time, let them keep going for the full 45 minutes;
- If the group finishes, ask them to share some outcomes – those to questions 11 and 12 might be least personal and less likely to break any confidentiality, because they are speculative.

The management questionnaire

Introduction

In this session we are asking you to complete a questionnaire. The time-scale for this is 30 minutes. At the end of this time your group leader will ask you to share with others in your group some of the responses you have made. However, the questionnaire itself is anonymous, so that your school will not be identified if any material is quoted directly in the book.

Instructions

This questionnaire consists of 13 questions. Questions 1–5 simply collect information about you/your job/role and can be answered very quickly. The remaining questions ask you to think about how your job/role is, or should be, managed. We ask you to write as fully as you can about each of these questions.

Your help, and attention to detail, will be much appreciated.

ABOUT YOU AND YOUR JOB/ROLE

1. What is your job title or role in the school?

2. How long have you occupied this role?

3. What is your main/most advanced qualification (if any)?

4. Please indicate gender (M or F) here.

5. Please rate your current level of job/role satisfaction on the following scale (1 = high satisfaction, 7 = low satisfaction).
   [Circle one number thus: ⑦]:

$$1 \quad 2 \quad 3 \quad 4 \quad 5 \quad 6 \quad 7$$

ABOUT YOUR MANAGEMENT

6. What is the job title of your line manager (e.g. head, class teacher, bursar etc.)?

7. Please describe the process through which your job is managed by answering the following questions:
   (a) When do you meet up with your manager?
   (b) How often do you meet your manager?
   (c) How are management decisions communicated to you, and how is your work guided by your manager? (Please give examples if possible.)

8. What are your opinions about the effectiveness of your management in your job/role?

9. Reflect back on your answer to question 8. Try to identify any STRENGTHS (up to four) in the way in which your job/role is managed, and list them here:

10. Still reflecting on your answer to question 8, try to identify any WEAKNESSES (up to four) in the management of your job/role, and list them here:

11. In the best of all worlds what changes would you like to see in the way in which your job/role is managed in your present situation?

12. What do you feel are the three main characteristics of a good manager in your situation?

13. Finally, if there is anything else you would like to say about the management of your role, please write it here:

Table R.4 What kind of training and development do you need?

This is another group exercise: the group discusses the issue, prompted by the leader, while the leader notes down on the flip chart the points made.

The starting point of this discussion is that teacher professionals in schools have a requirement for a minimum of five days' training, and many undertake much more than this voluntarily. For support staff the situation is less clear. Try to get the delegates to articulate (and you record) their thoughts about:

- The training opportunities that currently exist for their job/role – give specific examples if possible.
- Whether they access these. If so, how easily, and what are the problems?
- If no/few opportunities, then what would they like to see? [This is the key point, so pursue this fairly hard.]
- Would preferred training opportunities be:
  Compulsory/voluntary?
  In or out of school time? When?
  How funded?
  Accredited? What kinds/levels of accreditation?
- What kinds of things might be covered in the training? What skills? Knowledge? Understanding?
- Who would be the most appropriate trainers?
- What would be the ideal career path for the job/role?

Part One

■ ■ ■

Research
and theoretical
underpinning

1

■ ■ ■

The changing role of support staff

Introduction

The use of support staff in schools is not new. The sight of the lab assistant trundling around with disgusting-looking specimens in jars of foul-smelling liquid has turned the stomachs of most who attended a secondary school and were not destined for careers as *avant-garde* artists. Apart from spasmodic research on individual support roles, however, little has been published on the topic of support staff in schools since Mortimore, Mortimore and Thomas (1994).

What has changed in that time is the variety of tasks that are now carried out by such employees as they move towards a more significant status – as paraprofessionals, or the agents of learning support. (As far back as December 1998, BBC News reported that up to 25 per cent of support staff held qualifications in learning support.) What will also continue to change is the centrality of these roles to the learning of students. In 1994, Shifflett (1994) was reporting on a rural primary school in Virginia where unpaid volunteers alone gave 112 hours of time a week and where more than 80 per cent of the staff felt that this assistance had increased significantly the amount of time the professionals were able to spend with individual pupils.

On the other side of the coin the teacher recruitment crisis, in the UK in the year 2001, may force government to look harder at how traditional 'teaching' roles can be spread to other kinds of employees. Kelly (2000) reports a two-year government initiative in ten Education Action Zones to draft in undergraduates as 'teaching associates'. Even such a respected figure as Tim Brighouse has gone on record recently saying that in ten years' time teachers may be paid twice as much but there will be half as many of them (Brighouse, 2000). While it is important to understand that not all support staff will provide any form of 'teaching', many can and do provide learning support – much of that directly in classrooms, face-to-face with pupils and students. David Blunkett recently re-affirmed a commitment to providing support staff (BBC News 2001b), and pledged £400 million. This commitment accorded with a previous statement in which he 'would introduce adult assistants into secondary schools working under qualified teachers or "learning managers"' (BBC News 2001a). It was a commitment fuelled by a vision of the future:

We are not talking about less teachers but we are talking about using them more effectively. Seeing them as professionals, taking a 21st century view of the classroom, and a school of the future…we are asking the teaching profession to take that leap of faith with us…

Needless to say, this proposal was met by 19th century responses from the NAS/UWT's Nigel de Gruchy (BBC News 2001a), who described it as 'a policy of despair'.

In contrast to de Gruchy's anachronisms, this book looks at a number of different kinds of staff who provide, in one way or another, learning support. There are those who hold paid employment in primary schools; those who hold paid posts in secondary schools; those who hold paid posts which may operate similarly across both phases; and those who are not paid, such as volunteer helpers and school governors. For the purposes of this book we shall regard them all as 'support staff' because they all – in one way or another – support and promote learning. In this chapter we shall begin by surveying the eight roles that will form the core chapters in Part Two (classroom assistants, special needs teaching assistants, laboratory assistants, technical officers, secretaries/receptionists, bursars, volunteers and governors); and then we shall look briefly at some other support roles to which we do not devote specific chapters.

Some of the roles have been quite carefully researched by others, for example those of classroom assistant by Lee and Mawson (1998) and of the bursar by O'Sullivan, Wood and Thody (2000c). Other roles are relatively unsung. But, though this book will examine the roles themselves, our primary concern is how to manage the roles to maximise benefit to schools and individual students. This has received scant attention in the literature.

Chapter 1 attempts a brief review of the main kinds of support staff commonly encountered in schools, their roles and how these have evolved.

A survey of support roles considered in detail in Part Two

Classroom assistants (teaching assistants, learning assistants)

If one were to use the phrase 'support staff' when speaking to a lay audience, the most likely vision to be conjured up would be that of those invaluable women who carry out 'general duties' in primary schools. They are almost always women – Lee and Mawson (op cit.) found 99 per cent to be female as the Plowden Report (1967) predicted they would be. Their numbers are considerable. Nine out of ten schools employ at least one; some larger schools many more. They may be full-time or part-time. Their ranks are often swelled by trainees, for example from agencies that carry out BTEC child care courses and it is not uncommon to find one or more, employed or trainee support assistant in every classroom of a larger (usually primary) school. Their duties are often, but by no means exclusively, targeted towards pupils with special educational needs.

Conscious of the need for adult help in classrooms, the Government established a training course in 1994/5 for such support staff – the Specialist Teacher Assistant Course (STAC). The products of such courses are known for convenience as STAs. The purpose of STAC (Ofsted, 1997) was to provide staff who could support teachers in delivering basic skills (reading, writing and mathematics) at Key Stage 1. It has to be noted, though, that schools often deploy such trained personnel more widely. The original proposals for such courses required Higher Education Institutions and Local Education Authorities to work closely together to devise suitable courses and recruit suitable candidates.

Proposals for STA courses met with considerable opposition, teachers' unions in some areas coming out vociferously against them. The controversy of the time was known as the 'Mum's Army' debate. The fear was that these semi-trained adults would eventually usurp the qualified teacher's role with Key Stage 1 pupils. The fear was grounded in the context of a government that made it clear that its view of teaching was of a technician-based profession and that training for teaching was on the apprenticeship model: practise a few competencies, get a craftsman to sign them off and get a certificate to prove your ability. The teacher as technician, and the competence model of the teaching profession, are inadequate bases for professionalism and can be dismissed for the purposes of this book. A summary of the issues can be found in Maynard and Furlong (1993).

In August 1998, the 'Mum's Army' debate re-surfaced when it was reported that the unemployed were being allocated to classrooms (though only in Wales) as teachers' aides, and that it was hoped that 'some would go on and train for teaching' (according to a TV news report of the time). The resulting exchanges between politicians and teachers' unions were somewhat acrimonious (Barnard, 1998).

There was some irony in all of this, since the concept of the classroom assistant was nothing new. Lady Plowden had proposed the role in the Report that bore her name. She had challenged the 'Mum's Army' objections of the time, recommended training for her proposed assistants, conceived of teachers as their managers, suggested their rationale was to raise standards (para. 921), saw them being recruited in their thousands and argued that they should permeate the junior as well as infant years (Plowden Report, 1967).

The roles of this group of support staff have remained relatively suppressed, and Mercer (2000) has argued that, despite increasing numbers in the role, status and opportunities for advancement are still 'appalling'. There are probably several reasons for this. Most are employed in primary schools, which in the eyes of the public have lower status than secondaries. They are poorly paid. Some have STAC training, but most do not. Their job titles are many and various. Lee and Mawson (1998) list:

- classroom assistant;
- learning support assistant;
- special needs assistant;
- non-teaching assistant;
- ancillary;
- welfare assistant;
- child support assistant;
- general assistant;
- education care officer;
- specialist teaching assistant;
- primary helper;
- nursery nurse.

One of the weaknesses of the Lee and Mawson paper is that it lumps a number of disparate roles together and surveys the whole population. This was an act of convenience based on the way in which the employing schools themselves behave. Clearly, the job titles need some sorting out for the purposes of this text. In this book the following strategy will be adopted. Reference will be made to:

- *Specialist teacher assistants (STAs)* – those who have successfully completed a course of training as specified by the STAC but working in any school context in a paid capacity.
- *Learning support assistants* – people carrying out the kinds of job occupied by STAs in any school context in a paid capacity but who have either no formal qualifications or qualifications other than STAC.
- *Special needs teaching assistants (SNTAs)* – those who are paid to support the work of one or more children with special learning needs (whether statemented or not) and whether or not they are qualified.

- *Nursery nurses* – paid employees who hold a qualification in child care from the National Nursery Education Board (NNEB), or an equivalent qualification (such as BTEC).
- *Voluntary assistants or volunteers* – unpaid, casual classroom helpers, such as parents, whether or not they hold any formal qualifications.

Each of these groups will be referred to separately throughout this text with the exception of the first two (specialist teacher assistants and learning support assistants). These roles will be considered together under the generic title *classroom assistants*, except where distinctions are signalled by the use of the individual titles. Readers should note that some schools use the title 'learning support assistants' – the Government's preferred option is 'teaching assistants'. Our view is that these staff support learning; the title 'teaching assistant' is not always welcomed by the profession – the generic term 'classroom assistant' is less contentious.

There is a very real sense in which classroom assistants are the 'poor bloody infantry' of the school world. Without statutory training, employed piecemeal, paid a pittance (in Lee and Mawson's 1998 survey less than 1 per cent has reached a Senior Officer salary scale and 79 per cent earned under £7,000 a year), in insecure full- or part-time jobs, without paid support for training sessions, and lacking a promotion structure or enhanced pay commensurate with qualifications. This is not an appealing role for the upwardly mobile. Yet many seek such employment, motivated overtly by job satisfaction, and covertly by the pay (however low) and the working year (which fits in with their own children's holidays). A recent Open University survey (Hancock, Marr and Swann, 2000) found, however, that many classroom assistants are 'directly' involved in classroom learning 'albeit with groups' rather than classes. Gold (2001) promises better conditions of service shortly.

Classroom assistants are the extra pair of hands that every teacher needs to maximise his/her specialist skills and time. It is a role that operates at the front-line of learning: face-to-face with the child at a formative age. It is, therefore, a role that needs effective management – a theme to which we return later in the book (see page 77). However, it seems opportune to mention here another group of support staff – nursery nurses.

Nursery nurses

Nursery nurses are the group of classroom assistants most readily recognised as having a separate, quasi-professional identity. This is almost certainly because for decades they have been trained by a professional body with a recognisable name: the Nursery Nurse Education Board. In the private sector they have often been uniformed (we shall not consider the private sector role here), and qualified NNEBs have used the post-nominal letters and have been entitled to a badge indicating qualification. We consider their role and management here but do not include a separate section on them in Part Two, since almost all of what is said generically about classroom assistants would apply to them and their management.

Other courses, such as BTEC care courses, were added in the 1990s as routes into this sector of employment. At the time of writing, the work of training was in the hands of an agency: CACHE. This body offers a Certificate in Child Care and Education (CCE for nursery assistants) and a Diploma (DCE). The award structure also includes access to the STA certificate and an advanced diploma (ADCE) giving management skills for nursery managers. Some professional up-dating opportunities exist through short courses known as professional development awards (PDAs).

The nature of the work of nursery nurses as assistants in reception and other school groups is well known to parents and the community. NNEBs and those similarly qualified have also formed their own professional associations (such as the Professional Association of Nursery Nurses (PANN)) can access the new post-qualifying training and have some specialist magazines devoted to their kind of work.

Like other classroom assistants, nursery nurses are almost exclusively women. This is doubtless because vastly more women than men are interested in training for work with children in the age-bracket covered (0–7 years); but may also be because of the enormous social pressure that excludes men from the care of young children (except in their home-based roles as fathers).

Generally, the nursery nurse profession is not very well served with specialist research and professional journals to back up its work (in comparison to early years' teachers, for example). In a Scottish study of more than 400 nursery nurses at 175 schools Hall and Powney (1995) found that parents were very happy with the work of these support professionals. Suggested improvements in nursery nurse provision were related to parents' requests for:

- more places in nursery classes to be available; and
- children to spend more time in the nursery setting.

The benefits of contact with nursery provision were seen to be:

- young children having a chance to mix with others;
- good preparation for school; and
- sound preparation for later educational experiences.

This last cluster of views accords with research in the 1980s where, in the longitudinal Child Health and Education Study conducted by a Bristol-based team of researchers, it was established that early educational experiences (i.e. pre-school) continued to have effects into the teenage years (Osborn and Millbank, 1987). This pioneering study and its implications have been under-utilised by policy-makers despite living up to the cover blurb.

This is the first British study to show conclusive evidence of the long-term educational advantages of nursery schools and playgroups, and its findings have far-reaching implications....

The work of nursery nurses is essentially practical in nature, but it has to be based on a sound theory of child-care. In some research of my own with nursery nurses in training (Kerry, 1993), they identified how they thought they learned their practical skills and gave some indication of the relative importance (in rank order) of each learning strategy (*see* Table 1.1).

Table 1.1 Factors in learning practical skills on nursery nurse courses

Practical skills in nursery nurse training are brought about by:

- Carrying out one's own planned activities in the training placement.
- Observing the work of experienced others.
- Taking unsolicited advice available in the training placement.
- Asking for advice in the training placement.
- Attending practical sessions in college.
- Chatting informally with staff in the training placement.
- Learning by example from the teaching methods of college tutors.
- Attending theory lectures in college.
- Receiving visits and advice from college tutors in the training placement.
- Receiving advice from friends and relatives with young children.
- Watching TV or listening to radio programmes.
- Reading texts and other sources.
- Visiting a range of nurseries.
- Talking to other nursery nurse students.
- Spending time with children's relatives, carers.
- Listening to specialist speakers.

The work of nursery nurses was seen by the Hall and Powney study to have inter-agency dimensions through contacts with other educational professionals such as speech therapists and psychologists. Areas of in-service training in need of expansion were dealing with special needs' children and parents.

More recently, Johnston and Pritchard (1999) called nursery nurses 'the invisible professionals' because they felt that employers and others failed to recognise and give weight to their training and skills. They identified the following key duties and responsibilities as endemic to the role:

- Planning, implementing and evaluating activities to promote children's learning.
- Interacting with children's play to extend it into learning.
- Assisting in the display of children's work.

- Caring for children's physical needs.
- Dealing with safety issues.
- Maintaining resources for learning.
- Contributing to all aspects of pastoral care and oversight of young children.
- Establishing positive contacts with parents and other carers.
- Observing, assessing and recording progress.
- Maintaining professional contact with other health and education professionals.

Johnston and Pritchard (1999: 4, 5) conclude:

> *This comprehensive range of duties and responsibilities fulfilled by nursery nurses demonstrates the depth of quality and experience required…They put in a lot of hard work and dedication for little financial reward and are often left feeling under-valued with lack of recognition by colleagues.*

Special needs teaching assistants

The history of special educational needs teaching assistants as we know them really begins with the adoption of a Code of Practice for special needs (DFE 1994). This brought into play the now familiar five-stage model in which stage five was the issuing of a formal statement of special needs that set out provisions that needed to be made by LEAs and schools to support a child's specific learning or other need.

This Code of Practice opened the way for statemented children to receive help in the form of 'occasional support from a non-teaching assistant' or 'daily support from a non-teaching assistant' (op cit.: 81). These provisions opened the way for the two main special needs assistant roles that are currently played in schools (Shuttleworth, 2000).

The first role of SNTAs tends to be where these individuals are assigned to a specific pupil. For example, a pupil whose special need is mobility may need a full-time carer while in school. If the child is statemented, the LEA is required to pay for this care and schools often are happy to take on staff to assist individual pupils.

The second role is where a school with several or more children with various kinds and levels of special need, often learning need, decides to employ a classroom assistant to support the learning of those children specifically and of other children, through more general duties. Since the learning needs of such children are often in the basic skills of reading, writing and number work, schools frequently employ STAC qualified staff to fulfil this role (these are emphasised in the STAC training) even though the pupils may be in the junior, or even secondary, phases of education.

Shuttleworth (2000: 123) is right to point out the potential conflicts in managing these staff and advises the SENCO to work closely with the head teacher to resolve them. This issue will be re-visited at an appropriate point in the book. Interestingly, the references to the non-teaching support for learning provided under the Code are sparse within the document itself, confined to the two roles discussed at page 10. The role is not even listed in the index to the Code. Yet the non-teaching assistant's role has become a critical one for many children and in many schools. It might be worth speculating for a moment about why this should be.

The answer almost certainly lies in the debate about inclusion or exclusion: in other words, about whether children with special needs should be educated inside or outside mainstream schools. Social context now sees it as more politically correct for students with special needs to be educated alongside their peers in normal schools. In order for this to happen these youngsters need learning support. The issue has been visited many times. I noted the ambivalence of schools on this issue two decades ago (Kerry, 1981) and a good modern summary for primary issues can be found in Swann (1995) or in Webster (1999). The DfEE regarded the issue important enough to sponsor a CD-Rom for schools explaining the concept and its workings (Visser, 2000). Prior to the Code, some had argued for locational integration (education on the same site) but against educational integration (Hornby, 1992), but Wedell speculates that inclusion will be a watch-word for the next 25 years (Wedell, 1994). The debate will not go away, as many of the problems are intractable in practice. However, the broad principle has been established that all learners must benefit from whatever organisational structure is adopted at any given time (Florian, 1998). The notion of learning support in an integrated context has often included a qualified special needs' teacher working alongside the regular teacher in the normal classroom. The cost of this solution and the problems it may cause in terms of potential conflict between the styles and views of two professional equals, may have made it less attractive than the option to replace the teacher with a non-teaching assistant. Roles of the non-teaching assistant typically include:

- supporting the learning of individuals and groups as directed by the teacher;
- keeping records of children's progress;
- communicating with the class teacher, SENCO, and in some instances with parents;
- planning learning alongside the teacher;
- acting flexibly in supporting the overall work of the class.

So, special needs' assistants have found favour, not least in the secondary sector, as a cost-effective means by which to achieve learning gains. John Evans, a head teacher, expands on the theme in conversation with Peter

Ribbins (Rayner and Ribbins, 1999): 'We probably spend more on ancillaries [sic] than the county ratio' (p. 174). This is a proud boast in context, and it is meant to be – it is the shape of things to come (Gold, 2001).

Laboratory technicians

Next to no significant research appears to be available in this country to illuminate the role of laboratory technicians, though many are employed by secondary schools nationwide. It is hoped this text may shed a little light on this role and its management.

Technical officers

Some kinds of support staff (such as librarians and laboratory technicians) have always been with us, others hold roles that are new and still developing. This is the case for what this text labels technical officers. A definition is in order.

For the present purposes, technical officers are fundamentally seen as those support staff who have responsibility for the implementation and maintenance of ICT systems in schools. The role tends to have two main aspects: those whose job it is to supply, maintain and repair the hardware of school information systems and those with the technical expertise to install and keep the essential hardware of ICT running. They are fundamental to the maintenance of the learning systems, but play little part in the learning itself.

However, as ICT systems have found their way closer to the heart of learning, this 'person-with-a-screwdriver' technician has evolved into the person with programming and creative expertise. The skills of the new breed of technical officer include:

- finding the right software systems to deliver learning;
- knowing what servers and technical back-up are needed to run systems efficiently;
- understanding how to set up and operate an Intranet for the school;
- being able to translate teacher-generated learning materials into a user-friendly programme format.

Such people need a deep insight into learning – they cross the boundaries between teacher and technician. They need to:

- understand the learning needs of pupils;
- have a basic curriculum knowledge;
- appreciate what makes learning easier or more difficult;
- act as a very real bridge and channel of communication between the teacher and the teacher's materials on the one hand, and the student on the other.

Technical officers with these skills are not, as yet, being trained; they are evolving out of either the technician or the teaching force. However, one can envisage a time when this specific support role becomes the focus of specific training.

Certainly the ICT learning support technician is a role that is going to mushroom and develop over the next decade. It may be optimistic to say that every school will have one by 2010; but it is likely that most secondary schools will and that other schools will have access to one through an LEA or some other consortium arrangement. To think otherwise is to suggest that computer-based learning will not grow in scope and popularity – this is inconceivable. When Dettman (1997) wrote about putting laptops on every pupil's desk it was a novelty. By 2000, Microsoft had declared its *Anytime, Anywhere* learning intentions (Hallett, 2000). It is not uncommon in what would like to be considered 'cutting edge' schools, for considerable work to have been done on laptop learning; the signs are that it is proving effective in raising thinking levels in classrooms – a real test of success (Taylor, 2000). Nor is there any doubt about its popularity with pupils, and it is one of the positives in raising boys' levels of interest in school work (TES, 1998). Even assessment may go on-line, thus gaining in flexibility and becoming less of a burden to teachers and pupils (Newman, 2000).

By 2010, it is possible that a far greater proportion of the teaching force will be able to play this kind of role for themselves. At present, most teachers are of a generation that is significantly less familiar with technology than their pupils and not just with how to operate it (Gillmon, 1998). This situation is true not only in this country but has been true even in the USA, though the situation would appear to be changing among newly trained teachers. Abbott and Faris (2000) found that technology was well received and its use well integrated into the work of trainee teachers when the work was integrated into literacy courses. (The real questions here are how technology can underpin learning as opposed to using computers as word processors. Usually, it is only teachers trained within the last five years who really have a feel for this issue.) We predict that those who occupy the role of ICT technical officer in relation to schools – whether they come through teacher training or a more technical route – will become key players in the learning business.

Some of the issues that have to be addressed here include:

- What kinds of support are needed for students who are increasingly using home computers to facilitate homework or distance learning? (Lauman, 2000.)
- The effects computing will have on relative learning by girls and boys (Young, 2000).
- The role of parents supporting (or not supporting) computer based learning (Taylor, 2000).

Administrative staff (secretaries and receptionists)

This section discusses those members of the school support staff who occupy jobs related to secretarial and reception duties (but not to financial administration, which is dealt with under the heading of bursars). These administrative staff are the equivalent of the personal assistants of business and commerce, and of the hotel front desk staff. They are found equally across both the primary and secondary sectors, although smaller primary schools may only have a part-time secretary and no reception staff. For convenience, the two roles shall be distinguished as 'secretaries' and 'receptionists', though a single individual often carry out both roles.

This group of support staff have two roles that make their work critical to every school. They are often the public face (or on the telephone, the public voice) of the school. They are often the people with crucial knowledge (they handle appointments, confidential issues, filing of documents, keeping of records and so on) and may wield significant power. Each of these issues is considered in turn.

The marketing of schools, a phenomenon that spawned and escalated during the Conservative administration of the 1980s, put the administrator/receptionist in a situation of considerable influence. All the literature of marketing and marketism emphasises the need for all staff in the school (indeed, all governors and pupils) to share the school's vision and mission (*see* Chapter 3). The administrative staff also share this vision.

So, the vision of Offside school might include a welcoming ethos, in which legitimate information about the school is freely available, where the head and year staff are accessible and in which promotion of the agreed virtues of the school is a role attributable to everyone. Into this situation comes a parent of a prospective pupil. The parent appears at the reception desk; she is ignored for a full three minutes while the administrator finishes the print run on the copier. Then a brusque enquiry seeks her business. The parent explains the situation: the family is moving into the area and she would like a school brochure. The receptionist says that this is a waste of time, the school is full. Our parent refuses to be put off; the receptionist eventually capitulates. The parent can have a brochure but 'as you can see, we've run out because people keep coming in for them and I'm just running some off. If you want to wait I'll staple some, but it will take a time because I might get interrupted by the phone.' The parent sits down in the only obvious chair and stares at the wall while the receptionist staples 20 brochures. Eventually she calls the parent back to the reception counter and gives her one, with a repeated warning about the school being full.

This is not a fantasy, this is a true story of events repeated at two schools on the same afternoon. Clearly the receptionist did not share the welcoming ethos of the school, did not promote its virtues and put up barriers rather than providing legitimate information. All over the country, bank tellers, shop workers, and garage service departments are repeating this scenario even as we read. Yet what the head had hoped for was closer to the assertion of Davies and Ellison (1997):

> Clients expect to be treated seriously, courteously, with concern and with problem-solving, rather than blame-attaching attitudes…(they) do not expect to be told there are so many internal problems that prevent a solution.

B. Davies, and L. Ellison *Strategic Marketing for Schools*.

A similar situation occurs in many schools when the administrator adopts the role of personal assistant (PA) but then either assumes the guise of watchdog by banning access to the head, or uses confidential power in political ways to control the running of the school. A guileful administrator may feed selective information to key members of staff, or retain, e.g. resource information so that a weak head has to rely totally on her expertise. One such administrator was able to influence the way staff were perceived in the school by controlling the amount of help and support she gave to each (for example, when copying learning materials), thus making some look efficient and others inept.

Of course, most administrators do not do these things: they are efficient, polite, helpful, discreet, tactful and highly professional. The role of receptionist is a critical 'front of house' role, and critical in the external perception of the school. The PA role is less public, but fundamental to achieving genuine efficiency across the school and its senior management. Yet few substantial studies of these roles have been undertaken.

Bursars and school business managers

The role of the bursar is currently a burgeoning one in schools and has been the subject of detailed study by a team from the University of Lincolnshire and Humberside (ULH). Their work is featured in some detail in Chapters 14 and 15. For the moment the intention is to draw out some background points from their various research.

The ULH team produced two Working Papers, referred to here as WP 37 and WP 38 (O'Sullivan, Thody and Wood, 2000a, b). The first of these (WP 37) surveyed the extant literature on bursarship and set out the research methods by which the team investigated bursarship. Interestingly, they discovered (as we have noted about other support roles in schools) a 'virtual non-literature' (WP 37: 17). While they find the bursar 'an elusive butterfly', they do feel they can trace an evolution in the role, which is shown in Table 1.2.

The Lincoln team also investigated what roles bursars played in their schools (O'Sullivan *et al.*, 2000b). WP 38 lists six areas of operation:

- finance;
- human resources;

Table 1.2 Evolution of the bursar 'butterfly'

Caterpillar

The bursar as outside the senior management team (SMT), regarded as an administrator servicing the needs of teaching staff on request. Bursars are regarded as unable to understand learning processes because they are not teachers though they may be able to provide information pertinent to educational decisions.

Pupa

The bursar as a member of the SMT but still seen as subordinate to teaching staff; in such schools, there are battles being fought over the establishment of status for bursars.

Chrysalis

The bursar as a fully functional and accepted part of the SMT, operating as part of the strategic direction team, attending all meetings and making a valuable contribution to all school management processes through offering alternative perspectives.

Reengineered butterfly

A new species of educational leader, emerging from a background previously little expected to operate successfully in senior school posts.

Source: WP 37: 18 (amended).

- premises;
- information technology;
- pupil services;
- marketing.

It is in the fourth and fifth areas above that bursars become most inextricably bound up with issues impinging on students' learning. The relationship between administrator and learning supporter is perhaps more clearly recognised in the USA (*see* Chapter 2). Thus ERIC Digest 135 (2000) and Donovan (1999) remind us that 'technology is not an end in itself'; while 'administrators should discuss with [teaching] staff how technology can best be used to enhance teaching and learning'. The same process can be observed in the jobs of bursars attending the specialist courses now available at ULH.

In the same way, bursars are no longer seen as merely the sources and providers of cash with which to promote students' learning through appropriate purchases. More and more, bursars are seen to have a part to play and some expertise, in identifying what resources are appropriate for students. Even indirect provisions, such as time-effective travel arrangements, have a bearing on the learning opportunities for students. The boundaries are being obfuscated even as I write, and you read, this page. Bursars are often the managers of support staff (WP 37: 22). We have argued in this text that support staff are a learning resource, so bursars must be seen in a context that takes some account of their role in students' learning.

O'Sullivan, Thody and Wood (2000a, b) argue that the bursar has moved on to being the school business manager. They suggest that some senior teachers have become bursars (often with the status of deputy head); and ask why the opposite should not happen. They see bursars as 'leaders with experience', while teachers' experience may be limited (school – university – school); and they note 'the challenges to traditional patterns of authority and power in schools posed by these possibilities' (WP 38: 8).

Parents and volunteers

In January 2000 the *Times Educational Supplement* trailed a headline: 'Doubt over value of volunteers' (Budge, 2000). This item reported the outcome of a piece of research conducted at the University of Sunderland by Julian Elliott, Jane Arthurs and Robert Williams. The thrust of this item was that pre- and post-tests on the children supported in reading by parent volunteers showed that the subjective view that progress had been made by the youngsters was disproved by the scores. The outcome had 'given ammunition to critics of the Government's drive to recruit thousands of classroom helpers'.

Of course, there have always been some problems with voluntary classroom helpers. They have been utilised mainly in primary schools, and often in the younger age-groups of pupils. They are typically mothers who give up some time to assist children once their own are all at school. They often seek placements in the classes of their own children. They are usually untrained. If they are untrained and are used for anything other than the most menial tasks they attract the criticism of the more militant teachers and unions. Even some specialist texts (for example, Crozier, 2000) about the relationships between parents and schools are disappointing in ignoring the parental role as volunteers, concentrating on their place in the 'consumerism' that now dominates the political education agenda. It is ironic that this text was published after a period when, during the Clinton administration in the USA, there had been increased pressure to involve parents in schools (e.g. Goals 2000: Educate America Act), and these roles were being linked directly to functions that supported learning. Thus the Strong Families, Strong Schools movement was advocating (Ballen and Moles, 2000):

- parental involvement at both elementary and secondary levels;
- specific support through monitoring homework and encouraging extra-curricular activity;
- monitoring children's out-of-school activities for learning;
- checking on coursework delivery;
- using TV wisely;
- engaging in conversation with children;
- communicating sound social behaviours;
- helping to make learning relevant to life; and
- using technology to support learning.

In the UK, despite resistance, these helpers are valued in many schools and it is not hard to see why. They often save teachers a lot of time carrying out non-teaching duties: the proverbial 'washing the paint pots', taking children to the toilet, encouraging individuals who lack concentration, stock taking, covering books, looking after the library, cataloguing resources and a thousand other jobs that have to be done.

The key to their effectiveness is deployment. Budge's (2000) TES résumé of research about their role in supporting literacy may have missed the point: volunteers are not teachers and should not be used as such. The failure of the children in the reported study to make progress in reading and spelling under the guidance of volunteers is not the fault of the volunteers but rather the fault of their management by the host school. This kind of issue is discussed in Chapters 16 and 17.

In Britain, volunteers operate mainly in primary schools and their work appears to be generally valued. International research (*see* Chapter 2) supports this view. Shifflett (1994) discovered that American primary teachers in a small-scale rural study felt that the use of volunteers provided:

- help with school trips;
- assistance with school functions and events;
- routine grading of tests;
- clerical and library support;
- contributions to an enrichment curriculum.

Some of these roles might offend English susceptibilities – though one might legitimately ask why they should. But the key finding from this study was that volunteers freed up the teachers to spend more (learning) time with the pupils. Maybe this is why the USA looked seriously at senior citizens as school volunteers (Lipson, 2000).

Obviously, the use of volunteers has to be hedged around with safeguards. Some volunteers may have more advanced skills than others. But once again – and appropriately – this directs us to the other key theme of this book: the management of support staff. The effectiveness of volunteers is in direct proportion to how they are managed.

Governors

One might ask why governors should be given a place in a book like this, since they are not staff and, unlike parents or volunteers, they do not (necessarily) work directly in classrooms. We have included both parents and governors because, though they are not paid staff, they often give significant amounts of unpaid time and the latter clearly render support to the school in their Ofsted-favoured role as critical friends. Ensuring that learning is effective is a requirement of the role. Their power and influence makes them crucial to the functioning of schools.

The history of school governors (in secondary schools) and managers (in primary schools) can trace its origins back to at least the 1940s. However, it is the recent history that needs to occupy us in this book. The establishment of the role of governors for schools in both phases was due to the Education Act of 1986, which laid down that LEAs must put in place an Instrument and Article of Governance for all schools. The requirements were strengthened in legislation in 1988 and in 1998.

Every school, including Church schools and City Technology Colleges (though slightly different rules apply to their governing bodies) must establish a governing body, with a membership that includes parent and teacher governors as well as governors appointed by the County, district or other local government body (who may, therefore, represent a specific political persuasion). Co-opted governors include those members of the local business and commercial community who are able to make a significant contribution to the school. Governing bodies of schools must meet at least once per term, and while they may establish sub-committees to advance specific pieces of business such as financial or curriculum matters, the decisions of import must be made by the whole governing body.

The roles and responsibilities of governors include:

- admission of pupils;
- annual reports and meetings of parents;

- appointments of staff;
- charging policies for school activities;
- collective worship and religious education;
- financial management;
- grievances and dismissals;
- health and safety;
- overseeing conduct;
- overseeing the curriculum;
- publishing a statement about the ethos and values of the school in the school brochure and for the school brochure itself; and
- control of school premises.

This list is only the tip of the iceberg: the most recent guidance (DfEE, 2000) lists some 80-plus job roles for LEA governors. Clearly, the vast majority of school governors are lay people, with little if any specialist knowledge of the education system or of teaching. Yet the power that they wield is considerable. Their existence was born out of a philosophy of marketism espoused by the Conservative administrations of the 1980s, and has not been rejected by subsequent administrations to date. The underlying view was that communities should have the schools they wanted, and to achieve this a mechanism had to be found to subject the management of schools to community scrutiny. Further, since schools 'owned' by their communities would be successful schools, those schools that resisted such ownership by failing to listen to the messages of governance would become 'unchosen' by their local populations and face inevitable extinction – the victims of market forces.

How governors interpret their roles has a dramatic bearing on how a governing body works and what it sees as its major concerns. Bradbury (2000) notes that the intentions of governors may vary as disparately as to:

- improve examination results;
- improve discipline;
- create a specific school 'image' (e.g. via school uniforms);
- promote the interests of their own children;
- promote their own careers.

It is not surprising, given the summary above, that governors are often spoken of in the literature in political, quasi-political or industrial terms. Deem *et al.* (1995), label them 'state volunteers', Adams (2001) discusses the appropriateness of labelling them 'non-executive directors' and Thody (1999), wants to call them 'political servants'. Their roles are certainly contentious. They have taken over considerable management responsibility for schools (as shown above), and there are often conflicts between the head and the governors about the extent to which this area of 'responsibility' for issues is translated into 'direct action' to further the issues.

Governors are also involved in the micro-politics of schools. Governors' meetings may involve considerable jockeying for power. Some decisions will be seen through the party political perspectives of those who appointed them. In their other roles (as local councillors or members of the business community, for example) they may pursue agendas that are less related to education and more towards policy or profit. Some see governors as major source of stress for head teachers (Hardcastle, 2000).

Two groups of governors may have a particular penchant for bias in the power business, in the view of some: parent governors and teacher governors.

Felicity Taylor (Taylor, 1997: 116) makes some sound points about parent governors. She recognises the fact that they are largely committed to their schools through vested interest, even if they cannot necessarily take a longer-term view. Nevertheless, it is not all plain sailing:

> *The recruitment of parent governors has improved steadily, although it is still patchy. There are inner city schools with a high proportion of parents for whom English is a second language and who, despite the linguistic complication, provide excellent models for involving parents. There are other schools, many in more affluent areas, who may have abandoned the classic 'No parents beyond this point' notice in material form but still have it written in their hearts.*

Parent governors can be a positive force for change, but are not parental 'delegates' and cannot speak for the collective body of parents. One significant task that the head and the chair of governors has to achieve is to persuade inexperienced parent governors that their first concern is the welfare of the school as a whole and not that of their own children. Demographic changes mean that more parents (especially mothers) work and cannot afford the time for this role; there is a real danger that many parents stay uninvolved on the basis of what might be called 'the apathy of contentment', leaving the door open for the non-representative discontents to take over. Heads themselves report significant stress levels caused by governors or governing bodies.

Teacher governors, elected by teaching staff, also feel under pressure. They may be relatively junior members of the staff, yet are party to confidential knowledge otherwise shared only by the senior management team. Sometimes, other governors bypass the senior managers and approach the teacher governor direct on controversial issues, adding to a sense of alienation (Shepherd, 1992). Some teacher governors respond to the internal conflict by not participating effectively in the debates of the governing body (New, 1993). Like parent governors, teacher governors must see themselves as their 'own people' and are not the delegates of their colleagues.

Nowadays, governing bodies have members elected by the non-teaching support staff. The same kinds of issues may relate to these appointees and they may attract some hostile attitudes from teachers who still find it odd that support staff should be managing 'their' schools.

What cannot be doubted are the key roles of governors within schools. Nowhere is this more powerfully illustrated than in their roles in relation to inspection of the school by the Office for Standards in Education (Ofsted). Work by Ferguson *et al.* (2000) suggests that governing bodies are expected to:

- provide a strategic view for the school;
- make policy;
- be a critical friend;
- ensure accountability;
- set targets for pupil attainment;
- provide 'specialist' governors (e.g. in relation to special needs, finance etc.) who can answer inspectors' questions;
- provide support to staff before, during and after the Ofsted inspection;
- receive the Ofsted report;
- implement the resulting action plan;
- monitor the school's performance (both within and outside the classroom);
- provide an overall framework for school improvement.

Governors occupy positions of considerable power. Some would like to extend those powers into the professional heart of the school in order to monitor the quality of teaching in classrooms. This is resisted within the teaching profession. Ofsted flirted with the idea of scoring the performance of governors (like that of teachers and lessons) using a seven point scale (Ofsted, 1997). This process implies, at the very least, that governors are seen as 'responsible' for the 'management' of the school's 'success' and 'standards'.

Thody's (1999: 42–3) very controversial view is that the power of governors should be increased:

> *The outward and visible sign of the changes should be that governors acquire letters after their name, such as MGB (Member of a Governing Body). Other citizens operating for the democratic state acquire titles that confer status, such as Justice of the Peace (JP), Councillors (in local government), MP (Member of Parliament), MLA (Member of the Legislative Assembly) or MEP (Member of the European Parliament). . . .It is worth remembering that powerful school governors are in their infancy. This should be a learning period in which school professionals can help governors develop. This is uncomfortable for professionals who are being asked to relinquish some more of their powers to governors very soon after they have had to surrender power to central government. In doing so, however, they are likely to create governors who strongly support teachers.*

While many teachers might want to stop short of Thody's picture, there is sufficient goodwill to include governors in whatever is happening in the school (Russell, 1995). The current danger for governors (and for a government that wants to maintain such a democratic system) is that governorship is becoming increasingly demanding and time-consuming. Thus Thornton (2000) reported that the National Association of Governors and Managers' recent research had said that many respondents asserted that the Government should either reduce their responsibilities, or pay for the time and work that these responsibilities consumed. This view may be reflected in the statistics relating to vacancies on governing bodies: in 1999, 25 per cent of governing bodies had vacancies, many of them for LEA governors. Retention of governors was also proving difficult with 58 per cent of schools reporting governors failing to see out their terms of office (Phillips, 1999).

Some support roles not included in Part Two

Resource and library staff

The image of the school librarian, cob-web encrusted among dusty paper, eternally crying 'Hush', has probably vanished totally in today's world. After a period of 'broadening' the role to embrace a variety of materials in various audio-visual media, for which many traditional librarians were ill-equipped, the revolution on learning technology has now bitten deep. Today's librarian is probably a talented multi-media manager who unlocks the gates of learning with nearly as much panache as AOL's fantasy helper, Connie.

Of course, school libraries are staffed by people with a variety of backgrounds. In addition to the trained and specialist school librarians, there are those who have

- traded a public library job for a school setting;
- no formal training but have learned 'on the job';
- trained in more technically-orientated fields such as ICT; and there are
- the volunteer supporters (turned up as volunteers to classify a few books under guidance).

Parent helpers are dealt with at page 176. Here, we concern ourselves with the changing face of supporting learning through employment in a library/resource centre.

In secondary schools across the country the staffing picture is varied. Some LEAs have traditionally required school librarians to be trained staff; others have not, and in these strapped-for-cash times are happy to pay at non-qualified rates. We have even come across, in rural areas, trained librarians taking non-qualified rates of pay for staffing school libraries simply in order to hold on to a local job. Training for the few is through specialist college courses, but there is also a plethora of qualifications such as post-graduate certificates and NVQs that afford specific levels of expertise. The Library Association provides a chartered librarian qualification (the Associateship, ALA) based on experience and a collection of assignment-style papers or logs, as well as an advanced qualification (the Fellowship, FLA) that competes with higher degrees in the subject. Many secondary school librarians have learned what they know from working in a library and learning on-the-job.

The situation in primary schools is bleaker, with few qualified staff. Often the role falls to an English teacher, or a drama specialist; and sometimes there is volunteer back-up, maybe for classifying new books or for stock control or issuing.

Library provision is variable – some schools remain traditionally book-based, while others are trying desperately to abandon this concept in favour of the virtual library based entirely in computers (Internet and CD-Rom). Many are at some half-way house. The best equipped are probably that small minority that also serves a community purpose, i.e. they are open to the public.

Many librarians – trained or untrained – are definitely supporters of learning in the sense in which we have employed it in this text. They do not merely issue books or other media; they are involved in teaching the students how to use the library. Some LEAs still have centrally-based support staff who may teach children as young as those in the infant school the rudiments of library use. The extent to which librarians may act as supporters of students' learning beyond this role is variable. There are undoubtedly many who are engaged in encouraging study skills and healthy study patterns, who are active in pursuing knowledge with younger pupils especially, who help older pupils to extract information and reference their work, and so on.

What is clear is that the importance of global information will increase in the future. Libraries in schools will be part of the system for accessing that information. Libraries of all kinds are also very costly to establish and maintain, so efficiency and effectiveness are critical. Librarians will carry a considerable responsibility for supporting learning and the quality of that learning may well depend on their skills. While it is possible that their job will be redefined to take account of the technological revolution, and even the job title may change, the function will remain central to learning.

Lunchtime and school meals supervisors

An obvious objection might be raised at this point. Lunchtime and school meals supervisors (SMS for short) may be employees of the school, but they hardly qualify for inclusion as supporters of learning, one might assert. Yet is this true?

Naylor (1999), in a wide-ranging piece of research, challenged this assumption. He asked SMS to identify the job-roles that related to their work, and he noted those that had a direct relationship to children's learning. Table 1.3 is

Table 1.3 Job roles of lunchtime and school meals supervisors, and their relationships to children's learning

- Serve dinners, cut up food.
- Teach children to use utensils and to eat properly.*
- Patrol the playground.
- Organise and join in games.*
- Maintain discipline.*
- Listen to pupils.*
- Ensure safety.
- Administer first aid.
- Oversee personal hygiene.*
- Nurse sick pupils.
- Complete necessary paperwork.
- Organise movement around the school.
- Mop up, wipe tables, move furniture.
- Supervise indoor activities (in the wet).*
- Lead prayers/grace.*
- Liaise with teaching staff about children.*
- Cope with visitors to the school premises.

* items directly related to pupils' learning

based upon Naylor's work, though some of the order and wording are adjusted for the present purposes.

The SMS group in Naylor's study were under no illusions – they contributed to learning. Of course, most of this learning was very specific:

- social skills (how to eat properly, good manners);
- affective skills (how to mix and play with other children);
- skills of self-discipline (how to work and play without anger, aggression);
- behavioural skills (how to act as a monitor).

SMS frequently complain of being the butt of poor pupil behaviour, usually because they do not have – in the children's eyes – the status of teachers. A few no doubt contribute to their own downfall by chatting in groups in the playground, for example, rather than mingling with the children and doing their appointed tasks. However, some SMS have specific skills, such as play leadership, which are put to use by the school. In many schools, though, there is little involvement of SMS in knowledge about school policy or about what is happening in the school; training is sparse and SMS are rarely included in in-house activities for teachers. This role is poorly paid, and has no obvious career structure.

Other non-professional support staff

To date, this chapter has tried to mention all those support personnel who might commonly be a potential support to learning in a more or less direct way, at least for some of their employment time, as well as the key unpaid supporters of learning. But there are others, such as caretakers and maintenance workers, whose work in schools is not readily associated with learning support.

However, though their roles may be only very peripherally involved in learning, that does not mean that they have no role at all, or that – if properly managed – their roles might not be enhanced to include learning, however marginally.

Just as the lunchtime supervisors were found to have a significant role in socialisation and learning, so relations with caretaking and maintenance staff might have similar features, especially in the primary sector.

Occasionally, in the right circumstances, and for the right personnel, a more direct involvement may be appropriate. During one Ofsted inspection it was interesting to witness a lesson being conducted – under the overall control of the teacher – by the school caretaker. The pupils were thinking about time and planning, and the teacher had had the bright idea that the caretaker had to have an eye to both in his role. So she asked him to give a short talk about his job, followed by a question-and-answer session with the pupils. The result was that they found out how he timed his day: using a routine and regular times to switch on the heating, check for safety of the plant, rota the cleaning staff and so on. They learned about planning: how he had to order goods and services, check their arrival, supervise their use, account for their cost, and so on. There was social learning: about his relations with people who came onto the site, about his relations with staff and pupils, and about his management of his staff. All of this was learning, and though not a daily occurrence, was none the less important for all that.

To complete the picture of support staff in schools one must also mention those professionals who work part-time to support learning in various capacities. We review their roles below, looking first at the role of counsellors, and then at a collection of other roles.

Professional staff: counsellors

It is widely recognised that many children attending (or in some cases not attending) school need some level of guidance, support or counselling. This may be of an immediate nature (for example, when a friend is involved in a car accident) or rather longer term (a death in the family, or where a parent is alcohol dependent).

Traditionally, teachers – especially form teachers – have seen part of their duties as being the support of pupils in these kinds of circumstance. From the 1960s onwards, however, counselling courses have created a breed of specialists with particular skills. So there is a live debate about the extent to which the classroom teacher is now a counsellor to his or her pupils. On the one side the discussion may suggest that 'teachers are not social workers', and this argument has been strengthened by stealth, as it were, as the Government has reinforced the message that teachers are definitely about standards of achievement. On the other side, there are those that argue that education can only function effectively when it is the education of the whole person, that learning can work only when it is accompanied by psychological and emotional security and sound mental health. Attitudinal problems occur between teachers and counsellors, when teachers see counsellors as undermining their authority with difficult pupils through 'understanding' rather than sanction.

The result of this is that schools respond differently to the legislation (Education Act, 1997) about supporting students through counselling. Some make little provision other than relying on form tutors; a few have learning support assistants who have some counselling training; schools with a religious foundation may make use of local clergy; some schools have a leaven of staff who have received specialist training in counselling; some employ full-time professional counsellors or contract for them from the LEA. Some of the teaching personnel providing counselling have had formal training, but others have not – this is an issue that will not be pursued here as we are concerned with specialist counsellors.

One thorough review of the counselling practice of an LEA was reported by Chesterman, Helps and McNulty (1999). This turned up some interesting information.

Chesterman *et al.* trawled schools in Kent to discover the range of counselling practice. Of the 286 schools which responded to their questionnaire, 90 per cent provided informal counselling (and an average of 13 pupils were accessing this in each school) and 30 per cent formal counselling (with an average of 11 pupils per school making use of the facility). Informal counselling was provided by teachers, support staff, health visitors, education welfare officers, behavioural support staff, educational psychologists, the head teacher and by specially appointed mentors. Formal counselling was provided by counselling professionals.

Though schools were not fully conversant with the kinds of training that specialist counsellors had undergone, the research suggested that most had either been through the British Association of Counselling training or that of the UK Council of Psychotherapies. Chesterman *et al.* suggested that pupils receiving counselling as part of a statement of special need should have access to a specialist counsellor by the time they reached level 3 of the process. There was also a view that, where counselling was provided, many pupils did not then need further statementing for learning difficulties. The most success for counsellors appeared to be in the area of pupils with emotional and behavioural difficulties.

Counsellors (i.e. those with training, who give formal support) may work in one school or many. Their work facilitates the education of pupils with problems and of vulnerable children. For their work to be effective strong communication networks must be in place between them and the school staff. Schools have to both understand and value the work that they do – recognising the potential for deflecting learning problems, for example. It is essential that those in the school who have responsibility for counselling services understand the basic information about counselling qualifications, and who is and is not qualified to act.

Counsellors have to have strong inter-agency connections. They must not only deal with class teachers, but with heads and SENCOs, health professionals, psychologists and education welfare officers.

Counsellors have to work with great discretion and within important boundaries of confidentiality. Location and facilities are important, since matters of a personal and disturbing nature cannot be discussed except in a secure environment. While counsellors cannot discuss the detail of cases with school staff, it is important that opportunities are provided for staff and counsellors to share perceptions about the generalities of the role: what counsellors do, what constitutes success and so on.

Other professional staff

Many support staff in schools are people who are themselves professionals in their fields, and who come into the school on a part-time or casual basis to provide an element of expertise not otherwise available. Typically, this would include:

- health personnel, such as nurses;
- psychologists;
- peripatetic support teachers;
- social services' staff; and
- education welfare officers.

The integration of such staff into the normal running of the school can both maximise their benefit to the school and increase their ability to support learning, directly or indirectly. Too often, in practice, they are merely 'visitors' who come, carry out a function, and leave – sometimes with minimal impact.

Nurses may function in schools to carry out health checks, or to provide specific education (for example, sex education or drugs' awareness). Both functions support learning. In the first, face-to-face dealings with pupils and/or parents will provide information and advice; in the second, direct teaching is involved, with groups or whole classes. Yet none of these functions seem to be particularly systematic or well organised in the UK. Often the impact and effectiveness of services provided to schools by nursing and other medical staff depends on the initiative of an individual staff member, and his or her diligence in sustaining dialogue and coherence with the visiting health professional. This is well illustrated in the chapter by Dunkley in Mills and Mills (1995), which describes a school nurse's involvement in one school both in direct instruction on health matters to pupils and on related issues to parents. By contrast, in America, the National Association of School Nurses (2000) boasts an excellent website, and provides position statements for its members on some 60 topics at a time. These include medical areas such as:

- use of asthma inhalers;
- healthy school environment;
- indoor air quality;
- infectious diseases;
- nit free policies;
- postural screening;
- substance use and abuse;
- sun protection;
- mental health.

In addition, there are guidance notes on:

- case management;
- child abuse;
- corporal punishment;
- school trips;
- school meals, and many other topics.

It is worth adding that one of the insights that emerges when one looks analytically at support services for schools, is that the UK scene is often characterised by haphazard provision. This is illustrated in the case of drugs' education. While school nurses look after this responsibility in some areas, in others there are specialist drug awareness teams, members of which may or may not be qualified teachers and may not be medical personnel. The haphazard nature of the provision militates against a major theme of this book, notably the effective management of support staff. While the book tries to present as clean-cut a picture as possible of in-school support, the fact is acknowledged that this picture is subject to many exceptions and provisos, of which the various contributing authors are aware.

In Britain, the Schools' Psychological Service has what can fairly be described as a mixed reputation. Overall, the role of the school psychologist is valued: this is the professional who can diagnose the needs of and provide support

for, pupils with serious learning problems or who suffer from behavioural dis-
turbance. Since schools' psychologists deal with cognitive functions,
communication skills, perceptual skills, adaptive and personal and social
skills, the child's self-image, as well as behaviour, it is not surprising that the
range of their expertise is needed and valued. Teachers may feel de-skilled
when dealing with pupils who have a range of special needs in these areas,
and professional back-up is warmly appreciated.

However, since the advent of the special needs Codes of Practice referred to at
page 10, much of the time of the schools' psychologists is taken up with state-
ment-related activity. The workload is high, and progress often painfully slow.
This means that the psychologist is not readily available for other kinds of
work and may not always be seen as carrying out the most useful functions
that teachers associate with the role.

Schools' psychologists take a very immediate role in supporting learning.
They are the professionals who can advise how best to cater for pupils with
learning difficulties such as dyslexia; they may be able to suggest learning
approaches that may directly help a pupil and may sustain a pupil's social
integration into mainstream schooling.

In an American study, Long (1998) noted a phenomenon common also to the
situation in the UK: 'only a fraction of a school psychologist's day is spent in
the presence of teachers'. Other research (Fish and Massey, 1991) suggested
that this time amounted to less than an hour and a half per day. Yet Long
(op cit.) argues that the willingness of the teacher to carry out the recommendations of the schools' psychologist depends on good quality face-to-face
relations with the teacher. In asking teachers about the 'ideal' time allocations
that schools' psychologists should give to their various tasks, as opposed to
their actual time allocations based on measurements of time on the job, the
mis-matches became important. Teachers felt that psychologists should spend
just over half the time they actually did on administering tests, and half the
actual time on writing reports; but that they ought to spend two-and-a-half
times as much time on counselling students as the actual amounts.

Schools' psychologists, then, are genuine 'support staff', not directly involved
in the teaching of pupils but providing important under-pinning for teachers
and students. Professionals in their own right, they make an important contribution to the work of schools, even if this is limited by the burden of
statementing under current legislation.

The visible arms of the schools' psychological service for many teachers are
the peripatetic support teachers: those qualified staff who specialise in special
educational needs and who tour a cluster of schools withdrawing pupils for
remedial help. In a few cases these support staff include teachers with specific
responsibilities for able pupils or for individual disabilities such as dyslexia.
Increasingly, the squeeze on education budgets in LEAs, brought about by a
determination of government to remove the influence of LEAs by insisting on

devolving money to schools, has meant that support services have diminished. In one sense they fall outside the scope of this book – while they provide support for learning (and even some direct teaching) the personnel are trained teachers as opposed to paraprofessionals. Nevertheless, the key principle remains: the effectiveness of their work in supporting pupils' learning is dependent upon the effectiveness of their deployment by the management of the school. This is precisely the same issue that affects the non-qualified support staff in schools.

While most teachers will work alongside peripatetic teachers from the LEA, for some schools and teachers contact with social service personnel is a rare occurrence; for others it is a daily one. In the statementing process for special educational needs, the social services department (SSD) is required to provide information about the potentially statemented child and his/her circumstances. Though this is a formal process (and may be irrelevant in cases where the family is not known to the SSD), in some schools the nature of the pupils and of the catchment area is such that one or more members of staff may have a regular liaison role with SSD staff. Some pupils are, of course, under the care of the SSD because of the break-up of the family, others because of the need for the SSD to provide formal protection. SSD staff and teachers have a need, as well as an obligation, to work together in these cases. Contacts are usually maintained through teachers or senior managers with designated pastoral responsibilities. It is clear that the Code of Practice expects close co-operation between schools and SSDs; whether each side sees the other as easy to deal with is open to some doubt (Bowers, Dee and West, 1998).

The role of the Education Welfare Officer is to ensure that children attend school. They may operate from a base outside the school and may join police officers on 'truancy patrols' in areas where this is a regular problem. Some are employed within schools and play both an EWO and a counselling role as part of the school's holistic approach to child welfare.

Summary

Support staff of every kind can benefit a school directly through the service they render and the learning-related activities they undertake. But in some cases their benefit may go beyond this, freeing up teachers to do vital jobs in a profession dominated by administration and paperwork. Their value is real, and cost effective (Mortimore *et al.*, 1994 attempt to quantify the cost effectiveness, though their figures are too dated to be useful).

If there is a message here it is this: potentially everyone in the school community is a learning resource, even if they are not teachers and their role is not to teach. The issue is how to manage that learning potential for greatest effect.

References

Abbott, J. and Faris, S. (2000) 'Integrating technology into pre-service literacy instruction: a survey of elementary school students' attitudes towards computers', *Journal of Research on Computing in Education*, 33 (2).

Adams, J. (2001) 'School governors – non-executive directors', *Education Today*, 51 (1), 31–35.

Ballen, J. and Moles, O. (2000) 'Strong families, strong schools' www.eric-web.tc.columbia.edu/families/strong

Barnard, N. (1998) 'England to wait for classroom assistants', *Times Educational Supplement*, 28 August, 5.

BBC News (2001a) 'Teachers' anger over classroom assistants', BBC News Online, 15 January.

BBC News (2001b) 'Classroom assistants to relieve pressure', BBC News Online, 19 March.

Bowers, T., Dee, L. and West, M. (1998) 'The Code in action: some school perceptions of its user-friendliness', *Support for Learning*, 13 (3), 99–104.

Bradbury, P. (2000) 'What do governors want?' *Education Today*, 50 (1), 35–43.

Brighouse, T. (2000) *College of Teachers' Annual Lecture*. London: Royal Society of Arts 18 October.

Budge, D. (2000) 'Doubt over the value of volunteers', *Times Educational Supplement*, 21 January.

Chesterman, K., Helps, A. and McNulty, L. (1999) 'Counselling practices in Kent schools', *Education Today*, 49 (2), 35–42.

Crozier, G. (2000) *Parents and Schools: Partners or Protagonists?* Stoke-on-Trent: Trentham Books.

Davies, B. and Ellison, L. (1997) *Strategic Marketing for Schools*. London: Pitman.

Deem, R., Breheny, K. and Heath, S. (1995) *The Active Citizen and the Governing of Schools*. Buckingham: Open University Press.

Dettman, P. (1997) 'The Laptop Revolution' in Davies, B. and Ellison, L. (eds) *Reengineering and Total Quality in Schools*. London: Pitman.

DFE (1994) *Code of Practice on the Identification and Assessment of Special Educational Needs*. London: Department for Education.

DfEE (2000) *Governors' Guidance*. London: Department for Education and Employment.

Donovan, M. (1999) 'Rethinking faculty support' Technology source http://horizon.unc.edu/75/development/1999-09.asp

Dunkley, J. (1995) 'Good health to the school nurse' in Mills, J. and Mills, R. (eds) *Primary School People*. London: Routledge.

Education Act (1997). London: HMSO.

ERIC Digest 135 (2000) 'Becoming a technologically savvy administrator' http://eric.uoregon.edu/publications/digests/digest 135.

Ferguson, N., Earley, P., Fidler, B. and Ouston, J. (2000) *Improving schools and inspection: the self-inspecting school*. London: Paul Chapman.

Fish, M. and Massey, R. (1991) 'Systems in school psychology practice: a preliminary investigation', *Journal of School Psychology*, 29, 361–366.

Florian, L. (1998) 'An examination of the practical problems associated with the implementation of inclusive education policies', *Support for Learning*, 13 (3), 105–108.

Gillmon, E. (1998) *Building Teachers' ICT Skills: the problem and a framework for a solution.* London: Technology Colleges' Trust.

Goals (2000) *Educate America Act.* Washington: Congress of the USA.

Gold, K. (2001) 'New wave of support', *Times Educational Supplement*, 6 April, 6–7.

Hall, S. and Powney, J. (1995) *Education for pre-fives in the Lothian region: a summary of views of parents and staff.* Edinburgh: Scottish Council for Research in Education.

Hallett, T. (2000) 'Microsoft put a laptop on every child's desk', *The Source Journal*, 2 February.

Hancock, R, Marr, A. and Swann, W. (2000), *Times Educational Supplement*, 8 September, 20.

Hardcastle, L. (2000) 'Lift the heart of heads', *Times Educational Supplement*, 12 May, 33.

Hornby, G. (1992) 'Integration of children with special educational needs: is it time for a policy review?' *Support for Learning*, 7 (3), 130–134.

Johnston, A. and Pritchard, T. (1999) *Primary and early years education and care.* Derby: Professional Association of Teachers.

Kelly, A. (2000) 'Undergraduates fill in as teacher "associates"', *Times Educational Supplement*, 27 October, 8.

Kerry, T. (1981) 'Providing for slow learners', *Special Education: Forward Trends*, 8 (4), 9–11.

Kerry, T. (1993) 'Acquiring practical skills in nursery nurse courses', *Education Today*, 43 (4), 57–62.

Lauman, D. (2000) 'Student home computer use: a review of the literature', *Journal of Research on Computer Education*, 33 (2).

Lee, B. and Mawson, C. (1998) *Survey of classroom assistants.* Slough: NFER/Unison.

Lipson, L. (2000) 'Senior citizens as school volunteers: new resources for the future', ERIC Digest 93–4.

Long, K. (1998) School psychologist time allocation to professional activities: a comparison of teachers' and school psychologists' perceptions. Thesis – Specialist of Education degree. Ohio: Miami University.

Maynard, T. and Furlong, J. (1993) 'Learning to teach and models of mentoring' in McIntyre, D., Haggar, H. and Wilkin, N. (eds) *Mentoring: Perspectives on school-based teacher education.* London: Kogan Page.

Mercer, A. (2000) 'Class struggle', *Nursery World*, 2 March.

Mortimore, P., Mortimore, J. and Thomas, H. (1994) *Managing Associate Staff: innovation in primary and secondary schools.* London: Paul Chapman.

National Association of School Nurses (2000) web-site data on www.nasn.org/issues

Naylor, D. (1999) 'The professional development needs of midday assistants', *Professional Development Today*, 3 (1), 51–60.

New, S. (1993) 'Governing bodies and the teacher voice' *Journal of Teacher Development*, 2 (2), 70–80.

Newman, G. (2000) 'An assessment tool for 2000 plus', *Education Today*, 50 (3), 29–34.

Ofsted (1997a) *Update 24.* London: Office for Standards in Education.

Ofsted (1997b) *Training specialist teacher assistants: a guide to good practice.* London: DfEE.

Osborn, A. and Millbank, J. (1987) *The effects of early education.* Oxford: Clarendon.

O'Sullivan, F., Thody, A. and Wood, E. (2000a) *From bursar to educational resource manager: reengineering a key role in schools for the 21st century*, Working Paper 37, Lincoln: University of Lincolnshire and Humberside.

O'Sullivan, F., Thody, A. and Wood, E. (2000b) *From bursar to educational resource manager: methodological issues and literature review*, Working Paper 38, Lincoln: University of Lincolnshire and Humberside.

O'Sullivan, F., Thody, A. and Wood, E. (2000c) *From bursar to school business manager.* London: FT/Prentice Hall.

Phillips, J. (1999) 'Research Group Report', *Governors' News: Journal of the National Association of Governors and Managers*, October 1999.

Plowden, Lady B. (1967) *The Plowden Report*, v (1) (2). London: HMSO.

Rayner, S. and Ribbins, P. (1999) *Headteachers and leadership in special education.* London: Cassell.

Russell, S. (1995) 'Continuity in the midst of change', *Primary School Manager*, 6, 14–15.

Shepherd, G. (1992) 'On being a teacher governor', *Networks: Norfolk INSET journal*, 2 (3), 35–36.

Shifflett, D. (1994) 'What effect do volunteers have on a rural primary school?' ERIC document ED 373945.

Shuttleworth, V. (2000) *The special educational needs co-ordinator.* London: Pearson.

Swann, W. (1995) *Learning for All.* Course material E 242. Milton Keynes: Open University.

Taylor, F. (1997) 'Governors, parents and primary schools' in Cullingford, C. (ed.) *The politics of primary education.* Buckingham: Open University Press.

Taylor, G. (2000) Does ICT really improve learning?', *Education Today*, 50 (4), 23–30.

TES (1998) 'Boys dominate the keyboards' Uncredited article, *Times Educational Supplement*, 18 December.

Thody, A. (1999) 'From political servant to community democrat', *Education Today*, 49 (1), 37–44.

Thornton, K. (2000) 'Governors say pay up or ease off', *Times Educational Supplement*, 22 September, 1.

Visser, J. (2000) 'A feeling of belonging' *Times Educational Supplement*, Special Needs Supplement Autumn, 4.

Webster, G. (1999) 'The inclusion of children with complex learning needs into mainstream primary schools', *Forum 3–19*, 41 (1), 31–34.

Wedell, K. (1994) 'Special needs education: the next 25 years', *PGCE Training Materials*. Milton Keynes: Open University.

Young, B. (2000) 'Gender differences in student attitudes towards computers', *Journal of Research on Computing in Education*, 33 (2).

2

■ ■ ■

Support staff – some international perspectives

Introduction

Educational paraprofessionals can provide strong, multidimensional support for students' academic success (ed.gov., 1997a).

The previous chapter looked at the roles played by support staff in the United Kingdom (UK). Here we examine what may be learned from the use of support staff (often called paraprofessionals) in other countries.

As suggested earlier, the philosophical basis for the use of support staff in education is that they provide teachers with more time to teach, augmenting, but not replacing, the work of the trained professional educator. Support staff in the classroom are assistants to the teacher, assisting students in their learning. Other non-classroom based support staff also assist in this learning, but in a variety of ways, some direct, others indirect – these are some of the issues addressed in this chapter.

An American perspective

Support staff apparently have a higher profile in the USA than in the UK, and there is a move afoot to view paraprofessionals more as 'partners' in the process of educating the nation's young people (Special Education Resource Center (SERC), 2000). This move has been motivated in part by the advent of new forms of learning (information and communications technology (ICT)), and the increasing diversity of learners in schools. SERC notes that 'the roles and responsibilities of both paraprofessionals and education professionals are constantly changing', and that they provide 'support for students and professionals in a variety of programmes'.

It is fascinating to learn that, as long ago as 1977 in the USA, an attempt was made to distinguish between the roles of teachers and of paraprofessionals in learning. Thus the Kansas State Department of Education noted that 'the teacher and the paraeducator represent a differentiated team' (Kansas State Department of Education, 1977). The document then went on to delineate the roles as in Table 2.1.

The paraprofessional

The role of the paraprofessional within the classroom is primarily the same across continents. He/she provides support for staff and students, and this support, for the most part, may be defined as generic. Pupils who benefit from the work and role of the paraprofessional include:

- early years pupils;
- those with special needs;
- youngsters for whom the school language differs from the home language;
- students with disabilities who, because of the attachment of a paraprofessional, can be educated in mainstream schooling.

Pickett (1995: 5) emphasises from the outset that 'paraprofessionals are not 'mini-professionals'. ... They work alongside, support and expand the programmatic and administrative duties of teachers ...'. Pickett accepts that in America as elsewhere there is 'no universally accepted definition for the term paraprofessional' and suggests that job titles may provide the definition. She also notes that there may be different levels of paraprofessional positions, with entry level at, say, supervision duties in the playground or dining hall; through level two where the paraprofessional may assist with supervising independent study, reaching level three with the title of 'transition trainer/job coach' where s/he may 'supervise students in community learning environments' (p. 7). (This last may be most relevant in the USA, but provides an illustration of the extent and breadth of work undertaken by paraprofessionals supporting learning.)

In the USA, the role of paraprofessional, as elsewhere, is ambiguous. Analyses of tasks performed by paraprofessionals reveal that they *are* likely to tutor individual or small groups of children, observe and gather data about student performance – in short, their duties, and those of the classroom teacher, are likely to overlap in the learning context. But Pickett reminds us (p. 5) that it is 'teachers or other professional staff members who are responsible for evaluat-

Table 2.1 The role of the paraeducator

The paraeducator may perform these instructional duties:

1. Assist in organising field trips.
2. Read aloud or listen to children read.
3. Assist students in performing activities that have been initiated by the teacher.
4. Hand out papers and collect work.
5. Assist with supplementary work for advanced pupils.
6. Provide special help such as drilling with flash cards, spelling and play activities.
7. Assist in preparing instructional materials.
8. Reinforce learning with small groups.
9. Assist children in learning their names, addresses, telephone numbers, birthdays and parents' names.
10. Supervise free play activities.
11. Prepare flash cards and charts.
12. Prepare art supplies and other materials.
13. Hear requests for help, observe learning difficulties of pupils, and report such matters to teachers.
14. Score objective tests and papers and keep appropriate records for teachers.

Instructional duties the paraeducator may not perform:

1. Be solely responsible for a classroom or for a professional service.
2. Be responsible for the diagnostic functions of the classroom.
3. Be responsible for preparing lesson plans and initiating instruction.
4. Be responsible for assigning grades to students.
5. Be used as a substitute for certified teachers unless he or she possesses the appropriate substitute teacher certificate and is hired as a substitute.
6. Assume full responsibility for supervising assemblies or field trips.
7. Perform a duty that is primarily instructional in nature.
8. Be assigned to work with the most 'difficult' students the majority of the day.

Non-instructional duties the paraeducator may not perform:

1. Shall not assume full responsibility for supervising and planning activities.
2. Shall not take children to clinic, dental or medical appointments unless permission is granted by authorised personnel.
3. Shall not prescribe educational activities and materials for children.
4. Shall not grade subjective or essay tests.
5. Shall not regulate pupil behaviour by corporal punishment or similar means.

ing data, diagnosing needs of individual and groups of students and prescribing the programs to meet identified needs', thus confirming her original assertion that the paraprofessional workforce 'assists teachers and other professional educators' (p. 2).

Given the apparent overlap of duty between paraprofessionals and teachers, as part of this international perspective it is worth considering the career development of support staff and their further professional development. In a country as seemingly wealthy as the USA, it might be expected that their paraprofessional workforce is able to access worthwhile and meaningful training, but this does not always appear to be the case. Pickett discovered that:

1. *while paraprofessionals spend most of their time providing instruction and other direct services to students and/or their families, anywhere from 70 to 90 per cent are hired without training;*
2. *few states have established criteria or guidelines for training paraprofessionals';*
3. *most state and local education agencies have not developed systematic ongoing pre- and/or in-service programs for the paraprofessional workforce* (p. 8).

The contribution that a paraprofessional may make to students' learning is wide and varied and not necessarily located within the academic sphere. Paraprofessionals are to be found in increasing numbers among America's ethnic minority groups and provide an excellent resource for meeting the needs of racial, ethnic and language minority groups. Involvement of paraprofessionals with students for whom the school language is not the home language and who may have limited proficiency in English (Limited English Proficient special needs students), is, in part, a response to the shortage of qualified special education personnel to work with language deficient students. This is not to diminish the role of the trained paraprofessional. Indeed, much valuable work has been done with, for example, students from the Spanish speaking districts in California – such success enhances the part played by the paraprofessional from the community's (usually female) ethnic minority.

Home-school liaison officers

But not all paraprofessionals in the USA work face-to-face with young people in school. Increasingly they are used as 'home-school' liaison – 'paraprofessionals facilitate communication among teachers, parents and other community partners. Educating parents and stimulating community involvement may be important parts of their work' (ed.gov, 1997: 1, 2). This resembles the role of the Education Welfare Officer in the UK, but there is no universally accepted definition for paraprofessional.

Parents

The role of the parent within the American public education system bears a great resemblance to the role of the parent helper (volunteer) in the UK system in that they work unpaid, in the classroom under the guidance of the qualified professional. Research done in a rural primary school (Shifflett, 1994) bears striking similarities to parent helper experience in the UK (*see* Chapter 16). Parent volunteers:

- chaperoned trips;
- helped with non-routine events such as career days;
- worked with individual students;
- worked with small groups of children;
- helped children in the lunchroom;
- provided clerical or library support.

Despite Pickett's assertion that the training of paraprofessionals was minimal, evidence of training of volunteers was earlier outlined by Powell (1988) who describes an initiative in a non-denominational pre-school in the American Northeast thus:

> *A four session training programme for classroom volunteers covered school policies and procedures, classroom procedures and management, child development and curriculum, positive reinforcement and behavior management, and work attitudes and confidentiality. This program was followed by hands-on training in the classroom.*

Although this evidence is dated now, as a management strategy, training parent volunteers is vital if the ethos of the school is to be understood by all who support student learning. It is, however, an area which is all too often neglected – not least through lack of available resources.

Parent technicians

In some states, parent paraprofessionals (known as 'parent technicians') receive a wage and reach *out* to involve, not the children, but other parents, in their children's education. These parent technicians 'serve as community liaisons to the parents of at-risk students' (ed.gov, 1997a: 1), and work with teachers funded under a programme known as Title 1 of the Elementary and Secondary Education Act. This is the largest federal education programme, which encourages involvement of parents in school activities and in their children's schoolwork and 'requires districts and states to seek parents' input in the planning, design and implementation of local programs' (eric-web, undated: 2). Work is done predominantly with the families of ethnic minority students. The programme supporting the parent technicians, and thus students' parents, uses creative strategies to link home and school – conducting home visits; organising parent workshops in the school's Parent Centre;

working with community agencies; liaising with staff or attending staff conferences – and funds professional development programmes and in-service training. For students to gain maximum benefit from their years of compulsory schooling it is recognised that school alone cannot hold sole responsibility. 'Schools must become places where families feel wanted and recognized for their strengths and potential' (eric-web, undated a: 1).

The role of the family in the education of the child is very strong in America. Some may argue that school-family partnerships are somewhat peripheral to the main thrust of both this chapter and the book. But, if we, as managers of the paraprofessionals within our schools, do not look at the experience of other countries, then perhaps we do our own children a grave disservice.

The seniors' programmes

The USA extends the term 'school volunteer' beyond the previously accepted norm of 'parent volunteer'. As part of its cultural heritage, America respects its older citizens and it is to these persons, in an age when the supply of mother volunteers has dwindled because of their need to seek employment, that many states have now turned. 'Senior citizens have discovered that volunteering offers an avenue for exercising skills and talents gained through a lifetime of experience' (American Association of Retired Persons, 1992), and figures quoted by Gallup (1992) showed that over 41 per cent of Americans over 60 years of age performed some form of volunteer work (though these figures do not relate solely to educational establishments).

At first glance there appears to be little difference between the senior citizen volunteers in the USA and the parent volunteers in the UK. Common activities include:

- story reading;
- taking part in field trips;
- tutoring small groups or individual students;
- using specialist personal skills (first aid, art, craft or sports activities) to enhance the curriculum of the students.

In Salt Lake City, the Senior Motivators in Learning and Educational Services (SMILES) volunteers work with special education students, while in North Carolina, after-school services link children with volunteer older adults (Lipson, 2000).

This brief consideration of the role of senior citizen volunteers should perhaps be concluded by considering what the benefit to student learning might be. Lipson (p. 2) suggests that senior citizens can:

- enliven a classroom by offering new and unique perspectives to traditional topics;

- share their expertise;
- share their skills and experiences;
- fill a personal gap in the experience of the students through the global decline of the extended family;
- help to dispel the negative stereotypes that youth and older adults may have about each other.

It is clear from this brief review that benefits, both educational and social, are to be obtained through taking a broader perspective of the term 'volunteer'.

School governance

New patterns of school governance have resulted in public school governance becoming 'the subject of increasing scrutiny. ... Proponents of change have recently recommended a number of new approaches – and variations on old ones – to meet the complex challenge of improving public education through different forms of school governance' (Renchler, 2000).

According to Renchler, experience in the USA is similar to that in the UK following the Education (No. 2) Act 1986: there has been resistance to proposed change and the public debate continues on whether or not the new models for school governance are appropriate.

Why is there a need to change the methods of school governance in the USA?

Problems such as 'lagging performance among minority students and students in urban areas' (Renchler, 2000: 2) are common across both the USA and the UK. In the UK, it is the governors who are charged with having 'a key role to play in helping [the] school provide the best possible education for all its pupils' (DfEE, 2000), and while Renchler suggests 'there is little quantitative evidence that governance structures affect student academic achievement' he suggests that such experimentation may 'stimulate educators and students to perform at a higher level'.

In the USA, much of the current debate focuses on the (sometimes fraught) relationships between teachers, principals, superintendents and school boards. In *A Guide to the Law for School Governors* (DfEE, 2000: Ch. 5, p. 2), mention is made of the head and governing body working together in 'close and balanced partnership' to produce a 'well managed school'. Renschler (2000: 2) cautions that 'poor school performance won't be adequately addressed' until those groups 'work together as a team'.

Accountability in the governance system

At present there is no unifying system of governance across states. School boards as well as school superintendents have become targets within the culture of blame. A recent report by the Educational Research Service and the New England School Development Council (Goodman and Zimmerman, 2000) suggests that 'state laws should limit the board's role to policy making, assign day-to-day operations to the superintendent and most important, empower the board and superintendent to function as a unified leadership team'. In this aspect of school management, the USA could learn from the UK.

Conclusion

Increasingly, schools in the USA are turning to the recruitment and retention of support staff to increase the number of adults able to work within the classroom, along with the professional teaching staff. The introduction of the paraprofessional into the classroom has meant that, in turn, the role of the teacher is evolving to embrace the role of human resources manager as well as facilitator of students' learning. To minimise confusion about the role of the paraprofessional, systematic training, well constructed job descriptions and a career structure are imperative. Increasingly, in the USA the paraprofessional is viewed as a viable means of enriching services to students. A similar perspective has been observed in Europe, and this follows as the case study below.

The European perspective

Case Study 2.1
A Portuguese approach to integrated school and social care using a range of teachers and other support staff

An opportunity to compare and contrast social care and education, and the use of support staff in the education systems in Portugal and the UK arose during a study visit to a seaside town some 30km south of Lisbon. The purpose for the visit was to experience at first-hand some of the issues that Portuguese special needs support staff and educators faced on a daily basis, to make comparisons between the two education systems, and to discover the similarities and differences in each. What emerged was somewhat surprising, in that we discovered a cradle-to-the-grave system of support that paid particular attention to those with special needs and to equality of opportunity.

Context

Sesimbra might fairly be described as a large village. The sea is the epicentre of all that constitutes daily life. Families make their daily living from the sea, young men still aspire to follow their fathers into the fishing way of life, and significantly, the most up-to-date educational establishment is the vocational school catering for the training and re-training of the area's fishermen.

A primary school visit

The initial focus of attention was to be the integration of students with disabilities into Sesimbra's mainstream schooling system and how teachers and support staff cope with this. We visited a small primary school and immediately became aware of a huge contrast with the UK – class sizes were much smaller overall and for those classes that included a child with special needs, class size was renegotiated. Generally, one child with special needs reduced the total class size by one, two pupils by two. Thus the class we visited contained 19 children instead of the usual 20, one of whom had mild Down's Syndrome.

Following the English pattern, the pupil, Elaine, had a classroom helper, Isabel, who worked with her on a one-to-one basis every morning. The class teacher had worked out a very personalised individual educational plan for Elaine, akin to an Individual Education Plan (IEP) in the UK. But the work provided was apparently more specifically tailored to the immediate needs of the student than in many UK settings. For example, because Elaine's understanding was limited to those words that had a special meaning for her, the books personally prepared for her contained words that, seemingly, might have been beyond her comprehension, e.g. scooter (her brother's mode of transport was the scooter). Word recognition, too, related to her experience: 'Elaine's bed' she could understand and recognise, but not 'Helen's bed'.

In Portugal, progress for all children with special needs is closely monitored. For Elaine this meant that her education was taking place in a class two years younger than her chronological age, a significant contrast with much of the UK system. At eight, she was being educated with six-year-olds, with the aid of her care assistant who like most classroom assistants in Portugal, was unqualified. Such care assistants receive on-the-job training both from the staff with whom they work as well as from the specialist peripatetic teacher during her twice weekly visits to monitor Elaine's progress.

In conversation with us, the teacher emphasised the need for good personal relationships between herself and Isabel – and it was clear that there was a good rapport between them. She noted, however, that not all classroom assistants were 'as good with children as Isabel is', and that this was sometimes a cause for concern within the Portuguese teaching profession. As in the UK, issues of variable training and competence intrude.

Secondary issues

Subsequently, a visit to a lower secondary school (roughly equivalent to a middle school in the UK) confirmed the findings of the primary class in relation to children with special educational needs. Students had work specially prepared for them (in Portugal, all classes are mixed ability in schools of under secondary age range). For less able students a study plan is compiled, progress is carefully monitored, and only when the student is deemed capable of making progress in the next class is he or she allowed to go 'up'.

Visit to a specialist unit

A large airy building housed the Special Educational Needs integrated unit (for comparison, most closely akin to a Family Centre in the UK). Purpose built, the unit catered for the *needs* of its children rather than for the children themselves. Children rarely visit the centre unless accompanied by their parents during diagnostic or follow-up sessions – rather, the area's specialist professional support team such as psychologists, speech therapists, and those qualified in rehabilitation techniques go into the community and work from the unit. These teams respond to family needs, and again, intervention is generally outside the centre, i.e. in homes or in schools.

The building that houses the team is well designed – there are special rooms for those working with the children or with families on a one-to-one diagnostic or follow-up basis. Unlike the UK Family Centre, in Sesimbra the emphasis is on an educational model rather than a social services model. Special observation suites of rooms allow for observation of the child and/or family when necessary.

There appears to be no equivalent of this country's statementing procedures; a request for assessment at the Centre may be made by a parent, by teacher referral or in the case of pre-school referral, via social services' evaluation.

But the unit is not concerned solely with youngsters of school age or pre-school. It is integrated within the community, and at the same time the community integrates within it.

- There is a room equipped with specialist equipment to encourage stimulating play – the equipment is borrowed by team members and loaned to families for use by children in their home environment.
- Young mothers with special needs use the Centre's facilities; they receive training in child-care, home management, parent-craft, and communication skills. This facility is available whether or not the child has special needs – neither age nor ability becomes a barrier.

As well as providing support for the community, there are also smaller units within the centre catering for group activities and providing a service to the community. These are staffed by professional and support staff. The facility includes:

- A spacious, well-designed, user-friendly environment, most resembling a village hall, is available for community use. Parents can leave their children under the watchful eye of centre staff while they shop.
- Carpeted areas encourage reading and quiet games, e.g. chess.
- The library area stimulates cognitive skills, while motor skills are encouraged through the use of art, craft and painting activities. There is a wealth of equipment – from face painting and collage design to scientific experiments. During the summer vacation, activity weeks are designed and the resulting work is exhibited to the public. Visiting specialist staff may support this work.
- The computer room, although small, is available throughout the day and school aged children are actively encouraged to use the 'library-cum-computer' area during school hours when they are not required to be in attendance, after school and during school holidays. (Sesimbra schools work an extended school day of 8 a.m. to 6 p.m., and pupils are not required to be at lessons the whole time.) Access to the Internet is available at no cost to the young people, though this has to be monitored, such is its popularity. No one is allowed to spend more than half an hour a day using this facility, so that each individual is encouraged to engage in other learning activities.

Three further specialist units are located within the Centre: a nursery, a kindergarten and a unit for those with learning difficulties – again with appropriately trained staff.

The nursery unit caters for 12 children, there is a long waiting list for places, and as with many English public schools, requests for places are entered before the child is born. Children with special needs are admitted and as with mainstream and kindergarten provision, the admission of a special needs child reduces the overall class numbers.

Entering the kindergarten classes, one had the feeling of being transported into the young person's world. The room sang with colour, the youngsters were identically dressed in 'kindergarten' smocks (identical hats on pegs for outdoor activities); carpeted areas for quiet time, water areas for organised play. The staffing ratio was three to four children to one adult; a qualified nursery teacher had overall charge with the remainder unqualified auxiliary staff, all of whom must hold the basic school qualification and attend 'on the job training' in child management and child care. The kindergarten day starts at 8.30 a.m. and finishes at 6.00 p.m.

The kindergarten was a hive of activity – the children had regular swimming lessons; they were able to use the outdoor facilities on a daily basis (but then Portugal is blessed with that rare English commodity – sun); indoor activity stretched the able and increased the confidence of the less able; the handicapped youngsters were well integrated, each having the benefit of a full-time assistant. Again, the class size was reduced to accommodate their needs without detriment to other youngsters. The social composition of the groups ranged from children from families from the highest socio-economic status to a child from a home in a government slum clearance area.

Provision for children/adults with disabilities

Children born with learning difficulties may be catered for at the Unit, but only while of pre-school or kindergarten age. During normal school years (aged 6–16) they will be integrated into mainstream education (*see* Elaine's case at p. 43).

For those youngsters whose handicaps are more severe, special provision is made during the period of youth and young adulthood. Severely handicapped youngsters are educated through special school provision until the age of 18.

The Unit caters for 60 young people who remain unemployed because of their disability. Some of these receive support initially within the unit, for the first two or three months; others may be supported in the workplace if, and when, they find employment. Disabled youngsters are taught social skills that may eventually help them to obtain sheltered employment in the immediate area. There is a well-equipped home economics area where both young men and women are taught basic hygiene as it relates to the home and food environment; they prepare simple meals and, on a rota basis, invite a friend (often a member of staff) to a mid-day meal.

Other areas of social skills acquisition include basic laundry and garment repair services; car washing, gardening and secretarial skills. The students offer their skills to the local population – 1,000 escudos (£3.50) for a car wash and 'valeting' service; individual rates are negotiated for gardening skills. This latter venture is especially popular with the local schools – Unit rates undercut the market-orientated gardening services quite considerably.

As well as acquiring practical skills, the young people are taught how to work in the outside world. Group sessions deal with thorny issues such as rights, duties and conditions of employment, how to negotiate with employers, how to access banking facilities. Training for the 'real world' is a continuing goal – young people with mild to moderate disabilities expect their new found skills to equip them to lead a life similar to their peer group.

Most of the young people we encountered expected to leave eventually, the combination of life and work skills with basic remedial education equipping them to undertake light work. For the one or two young people for whom this was impossible, employment was found within the Unit. But this was no *sine cura*. The ex-student we encountered (who was profoundly deaf) worked within the laundry. She was self-employed; she negotiated her own workload; she managed her own time; she worked on a basis whereby customer satisfaction was paramount because if she failed in her tasks, then her income ceased.

Conclusion

There is a tendency among the British to think of foreign nations (other than the USA or Australia) as somewhat backward in the fields of care and education. This study visit proved to be a humbling experience in that it showed some UK ideals operationalised in a country which does not have the advantages of a long history of democracy and universal education. What we saw proved to be an excellent model, and one to emulate.

Some management issues arising from the case study

This case study illustrates some of the complexities that face managers when dealing with the differing educational and social needs of students in their care. Managers need to:

- ensure (as in the case described) that the assistant assigned to the student keeps him/her on task;
- take account of the student's probable limited concentration span;
- vary the material for the student;
- prepare work on a daily basis;
- involve the assistant in the preparation of the student's work;
- familiarise themselves with the student's progress by consulting with his/her assistant at the end of each session – morning, afternoon, day, week;
- acknowledge and praise the assistant's work and his/her commitment to the student.

Data giving other European perspectives was obtained via embassies and where appropriate from their respective local authorities. Short descriptions of some aspects of the roles of support staff in mainland Europe follow.

The Netherlands

Information from the Netherlands suggests that the role of the classroom assistant is a new phenomenon: 'classroom assistants are new, (they) are paid less than teachers and have no teaching permit. In secondary schools we have Teaching Educational Assistants who assist teachers and prepare for labs (chemistry/physics etc.)'. When asked what kind of roles support staff occupied and whether such staff were involved in pupils' learning, the response re-iterated that assistants did not teach, but interestingly, it was noted that 'sometimes janitors assume the function of ICT co-ordinator; they are public servants and get wages according to their rank'. Dutch schools make use of parents, on a voluntary basis, with most of their time being given to helping with reading and sometimes IT. There is no indication in the response that voluntary helpers had any impact upon the learning of students – but given that, as in almost all other countries discussed here, their use was directed to supporting children's reading development, it is difficult to see in this respect at least how 'teaching and learning' could fail to take place.

Belgium

General information on the educational system in Belgium proved difficult to obtain. However, a response from the *Ministerie van de Vlaamse Gemeenschap* indicated that in Flanders, in secondary education at least, the category 'educational assistance staff' applied.

> The educational assistance staff is responsible for the counselling of pupils. This contains taking care of pupils with problems, mediating between pupils, parents and personnel, helping pupils with their study choice, teaching values and social skills....
>
> Paramedics in special secondary education are encharged with caring and medical tasks and take, together with teachers and educational staff, care of the teaching of social skills, in order to...guarantee its integration in society. ...In secondary education in Flanders, we do not work with 'parent helpers', 'classroom assistants'.

Private letter 15 March 2001 (emphasis not in original)

Germany

The role of support staff in student learning in Germany does not appear to be widespread.

> German schools do not make intensive use of support staff...Students in primary schools and secondary schools are being taught by full-time teachers, most of them

having the status of civil servant. The use of support staff depends upon the various structures of the various schools. Most schools nowadays have computer classrooms and therefore hire IT service personnel. These IT experts are, however, not allowed to teach classes, unless they have a teacher's licence.

Letter: 4 January 2001 (Embassy of the Federal Republic of Germany)

Central and Eastern Europe

Obtaining information from public sources (local authorities, embassies etc) proved difficult in relation to mainland European countries. Limited information became available when personal representation to contacts in other European countries was established, but it tended to be 'of a kind', i.e. we made contact with The English Schools in Europe. This gave us some detail about what happened in English speaking schools in the Central and East European Schools' Association (CEESA), but did not enhance our knowledge of what happened in state schools in Central and Eastern Europe, except in the instance below – the education of Romany children in the Czech Republic.

Colleagues in CEESA schools were invited to describe the use to which paid and voluntary support staff were used in their schools. Responses were, however, individual because there is not one 'standard "CEESA school" policy on anything. All CEESA schools are independent and do different things' (e-mail (David Cobb) dated 16 February 2001). Information was gathered using a quick and easy questionnaire (*see* Table 2.2).

Because the questionnaire was despatched to CEESA schools by a third party, we cannot measure how many schools were invited to respond. We were told, in passing, that 'most of the larger schools have many support staff members of the staff'. Despite this assertion, response to the questionnaire was limited.

One response, from Bulgaria, indicates that in English speaking schools, at least, the pattern relating to the role of support staff is not much different from that observed in the UK. Paid support staff are employed as classroom assistants, ICT technicians and as assistants to students who needed English as a second language support. These support staff *are* involved in student learning, 'both directly and indirectly: all have been/are involved in programmes of professional training, largely administered by ourselves, but we have also significantly funded them on external courses in Sofia and in the UK'. When we probed conditions of service for paid support staff, our respondent noted: 'As we are a unique institution in Bulgaria, we have our own salary scale for them and our own recruitment criteria'.

Volunteers in CEESA schools play a role as helpers within the school's classroom and as members of the school's 'Board'. The former work directly with students: 'they are always parents and work in a classroom situation at the invitation of, and under the supervision of, our qualified teaching

Table 2.2 Questionnaire to CEESA schools

UNIVERSITY OF LINCOLNSHIRE AND HUMBERSIDE
Research into the Role of Support Staff
B) International Dimensions (CEESA schools)

PAID SUPPORT STAFF

1. Do CEESA schools make use of paid support staff?

Yes _____   No _____

2. If yes, what roles do they occupy? (e.g. Information & communications technology (ICT) technician; laboratory assistant; special needs support?)

3. To what extent are paid support staff involved in students' learning?
directly ....
(e.g. face-to-face instruction; do special needs assistants teach their assigned pupils?)
indirectly ....
(e.g. making resources available)

4. Under what conditions of service do paid support staff operate? (e.g. are there recognised pay scales/national qualifications/training requirements?)

VOLUNTARY SUPPORT STAFF

5. Do CEESA schools have the equivalent of the UK governor?

Yes _____   No _____

6. If so, please describe the governors' roles *with special reference to their roles in pupils' learning.*

7. Do CEESA schools make use of unpaid helpers?

Yes _____   No _____

8. If so, please describe the unpaid helpers' roles *with special reference to their role in pupils' learning.*

---

staff'. The Board members bear resemblance to governors in the UK, and effectively set policy, hire/fire the directors and sometimes control the hiring/firing of teachers as well.

Another response from Central Europe paints a similar picture: paid support staff assist in the computer laboratory, the library, the kindergarten and first grade. All support staff are involved directly with students under the direction and supervision of a qualified teacher. Support staff also supervise the lunch room and the playground. This respondent noted that 'aides have a salary schedule and benefits package. There are no national qualifications or training requirements.'

The role of support staff in the education of Romany children in the Czech Republic

A unique project in the Czech Republic has recently been designed to facilitate the absorption of Romany (Roma) children into mainstream school. Unofficial statistics suggest that there are approximately 70,000 children of Romany ethnic origin who are of school or pre-school age and special attention is given to the education of members of the Romany ethnic minority. In Czech (state) schools, the only use of assistants (Romany pedagogical assistants) is with Romany children in 'experimental preparative classes within primary and special schools'. The rationale for the use of assistants is that they 'participate in socialisation and language preparation of [these] children…The activities within the preparative classroom concern, above all, the elimination of language handicap of Romany pupils and are adapted to their individual needs.' Romany pedagogical assistants are paid according to their 'achieved educational level' and have to have completed a ten-day pedagogical minimum training (Roma Assistants Document, undated).

Impressive changes in attitude towards the rights of Romany children have been made, and it is no longer accepted that these students should, of necessity, be educated in special schools. Similar practices occur in the UK, with good practices established by the Traveller Education Services (TESs) of local authorities. Bhopal (2000, Research Brief No. 238) notes that 'it is essential that schools employ special support measures for Gypsy Traveller children. This may include pastoral care systems…Other support measures which help Gypsy Traveller children may include, study support, mentoring programmes, homework clubs and sanctuary areas.'

Outside the Romany initiative in the Czech Republic, use is sometimes made of non-qualified staff in state schools. University students, for example, may teach outside the regular syllabus in subjects such as foreign languages, while parents may help school personnel in organising extra-curricular activities. Generally, though, state schools in the Czech Republic do not recruit assistance personnel without qualifications.

Parental involvement in the education systems within the European Union

Across much of the European Union, the education reforms of the 1980s and 1990s reinforced the role of parents within the education system. They gave a statutory basis to parental participation, with the level varying from one country to another. This statutory legislation did not involve parents in the face-to-face learning/teaching role of the school, what it did ensure (in most instances) was an indirect *control* by parents of the learning that takes place in school. However, parent representation on governing bodies/ boards of managers effectively ensures a degree of participation in the appointment of teaching staff, thus ultimately affecting the student learning that takes place.

The role of support staff in Australia

Surprisingly, it was difficult to ascertain the support systems operating in Australia. Personal conversations with Australian nationals indicates that there is no coherent policy across the country. Individual states have different rules regarding the hiring of educational, non-teaching, personnel for the state sector. Within the independent sector, schools have a high degree of autonomy over their employees, the only constraint being a need to conform to the requirements of state law, e.g. an unqualified assistant cannot be left in charge of a class of students.

There are indications that parental involvement, in the form of voluntary helpers, takes place both within the learning and social environment. At Eastwood Heights Public School (2000), for example, 'the school always welcomes the assistance of parents in such programs as Gross Motor and Reading', while the head of a school in the independent sector noted: 'I paid a couple of parents who came in to help the teachers. I didn't like putting them in the same class as their children...for the most part, they acted as helpers going on outdoor activities, such as going to the park.'

Conclusion

What lessons can UK schools learn from the rest of the world?

- Above all, it is disappointing to note that generally there is as much inconsistency and ambivalence in the thinking about and deployment of, support staff internationally as there is in the UK.
- The roles of governors in schools is perhaps better thought through in the UK than elsewhere.
- In the USA there is a more flexible and open approach to the use of support personnel in schools, as evidenced in the SMILES and similar initiatives described earlier.

- Material in the Portuguese Case Study (*see* page 42) suggests that, when there is careful integration between support staff and teachers, and between education and social provision, a more integrated and more intimate relationship can be forged for the benefit of the pupils, students and the community.

- Here and there, such as in the material from the Kansas Education Department, there is a better conceptualisation of the differentiated roles of teachers and support personnel than in most UK settings.

- There are strong hints, for example in the Roma project, of the potential of support staff to strengthen provision for minorities.

References

American Association of Retired Persons (AARP) (1992) *To serve, not to be served: A manual of opportunity and a challenge.* Washington, DC: AARP.

Bhopal, K. (2000) *Working towards inclusive education: aspects of good practice for gypsy traveller pupils.* Research Brief 238. London: Institute of Education.

Department for Education and Employment (2000) *A Guide to the Law for School Governors.* London: DfEE Publications.

Eastwood Heights Public School (2000) http://www.eastwoodht-p.schools.nsw.edu.au

ed.gov (1997a) 'Roles for Education Paraprofessional in Effective Schools' http://www.ed.gov/pubs/Paraprofessionals/roles1.html

ed.gov (1997b) 'Parent technicians' http://www.ed.gov/pubs/Paraprofessionals/norfolk/html

eric-web (Undated a) 'Making Federal Programs Supportive' http://eric-web.tc.columbia.edu/families/strong/federal.html

eric-web (Undated b) 'School-Family Partnerships' http://eric-web.tc.columbia.edu/families/strong/sfp.html

Gallup, A.M. (1992) *Giving and volunteering in the United States.* Washington, DC: Independent Sector.

Goodman, R. and Zimmerman, W. Jr. (2000) *Thinking differently: recommendations for 21st century school board/superintendent leadership, governance, and team work for high student achievement.* Arlington, VA: Educational Research Service; and New England School Development Council. 33 pages.

Kansas State Department of Education (1977) *Guidelines for Training, Utilization and Supervision of Paraeducators and Aides.* Topeka: KSDE.

Lipson, L. (2000) 'Senior citizens as school volunteers: new resources for the future', Digest 93–4.

Pickett, A.L. (1995) *Paraprofessionals in the education workforce.* Washington: National Education Association.

Powell, C. (1988) *Development of a volunteer parent participation program in the pre-school.* Master's thesis. USA: Nova University.

Renchler, R. (2000) 'New Patterns of School Governance' ERIC Digest 141
http://eric.uoregon.edu/publications/digests/digest141.html

Roma Assistants Document (Undated). Private e-mail attachment.

Shifflett, D. (1994) 'What effect do volunteers have on a rural primary school?'
http://ericae.net/ericdb/ED373945.htm

Special Education Resource Center (2000) 'Paraprofessionals as partners.' Connecticut:
SERC.

3
■ ■ ■

Support staff and management theory

The purpose of this chapter is to locate the work that is set out in Part Two of this book into the appropriate theories of leadership and management that are currently used to organise schools. The construction of this theoretical underpinning is both selective and personal, but is a logical view of how and why support staff should be deployed as suggested in this text.

Three main theories of management are blended into this underpinning. They are:

- Issues of quality management such as Total Quality Management and its successors.
- Issues centring around reengineering, change and school improvement.
- The view of the school as a learning organisation, and the business of school managers as learning leaders. This element includes issues of teamworking.

The boundaries between these theories are not always clear; nor should they be. In the life of the school, management is a 'messy' business rather than a clean-cut one.

Underpinning the quality issue is a belief that every member of a successful organisation will have a commitment to that organisation – loyalty, a set of shared values and behaviours (Bendell, undated). Market theories have stressed the role of the internal market in schools – the need for every member of staff, including support staff, to 'own' the school's aspirations (Davies and Ellison, 1997a: 77). This means that a school's mission and vision will be articulated, known and shared by the head, teachers, pupils, parents, governors – and of course by the support staff!

Tom Peters (Peters and Austin, 1985) makes clear that in a 'quality conscious' organisation the management will be seen to be committed to quality, that operations will be scrutinised for their quality, that barriers to delivering quality will be identified, and that quality awareness will lead to a commitment to quality – by everyone. Thus, the school secretary who can't find a copy of the school brochure to give to a parent who has called in on the off-chance of collecting one, the receptionist who growls down the phone at callers, the bursar who fails to appreciate the significance of effective use of a government grant to promote a curriculum innovation, or a school nurse who is unsympathetic with a nervous pupil will probably be selling the quality of the organisation and its intentions short.

Although there are those who resist the notion of marketing in schools and, above all, the thought of students or parents as clients or customers, the reality remains. Champy puts the imperative for marketing colourfully:

> In today's market places it is no longer a question of caveat emptor but of caveat factor. Customers today are characterised by their relentless demands in quality, service, and price; by their willingness to act on a default of contract; by the disloyalty. All this puts them as far away from the gentle, loyal customers of the 1950s and 1960s as a pirate crew is from a platoon of crew-cut Marines.
>
> Champy, J. (1995) New York: Harper Business, p. 17

Thus, support staff are both the market (part of the internal market of the school) and the means by which the school is marketed – to those within the structure (such as pupils and teachers) and those outside it (the wider community, parents of potential pupils etc.). This must be recognised by schools and their treatment of support staff has to be modified accordingly – to include them in the events, debates and activities of the whole of the life of the school. It also has to be recognised by support staff, including the unpaid support staff included in this book, so that they take on board the professional responsibility to market the school and its quality to the outside world. Schools that exclude support staff from in-service events, or support staff who bad-mouth the school to their friends, are failing to live up to their marketing and quality ideals.

Though there has been some backlash (Davies and Ellison, 1997b) against theories of total quality management (TQM) in schools, the principles of this philosophy remain valuable and the standards set by it remain high. Marsh defines TQM:

> Total quality is a philosophy with tools and processes for practical implementation aimed at achieving a culture of continuous improvement driven by all the employees of an organisation in order to satisfy and delight customers.
>
> Marsh, J. (1992) The Quality Toolkit. Reading: IFS International. p. 3

TQM means:

- For the receptionist, going out of one's way to be welcoming to visitors to the school, sitting them in a pleasant space, offering them coffee....

- For the head's PA, developing a helpful telephone manner and ensuring the caller is satisfied with the outcome of the call before signing off.

- For the classroom assistant, picking up that 10p book at a car boot sale because it will fit precisely into Darren's needs and interests.

- For the laboratory technician, double-checking delivery dates so that a critical science lesson can go ahead without a hitch.

- For the caretaker, looking beyond the jobsworth mentality ('more than my job's worth to get the heating up another degree') and so on.

So marketing and quality are essentially about attitudes – from the school to the employee and vice versa. Implicit in all of this, are attitudes towards and essentially about, change for the better. Morrison sounds a warning:

> *Change is inescapably and intensely personal, because it requires people to do something different, to think something different and to feel something different.*
> Morrison K. (1998) *Management Theories for Educational Change*, p. 121

Change is often threatening for many people. Yet so is the opposite: the feeling that they have no control, that things are not right, that they just drift on and yet have no power to change them.

Change, like evolution, is a natural – even an inevitable – phenomenon. The trick is to involve employees in the changes. Thus Wickens (1995) argues powerfully that management needs to make optimum use of the talents of people within the organisation. People are more likely to change when they feel trusted. The key to effective change is empowerment: giving employees some control over situations, and celebrating their successes and achievements. Change is more likely when it comes from participants rather than being imposed from above, especially when the participants are involved in goal-setting that relates to their jobs. Change should bring tangible benefits.

In the present climate the need for change is driven in part by government demands for school improvement – better results at SATs and GCSE, for example, and the need to perform well during Ofsted inspections. These processes involve not only the employees of the school, but also the unpaid volunteers and governors whose roles are covered by this text. Thus, the performance of the laboratory technician or of the technical officer for ICT may, indeed will, have a direct bearing on the quality of learning in the school. The work of classroom assistants and of special needs assistants will do the same. Their work will be scrutinised during inspections by Ofsted. So will the activities of volunteers and parent helpers. Governors have statutory duties, meet and discuss with inspectors and will be held accountable. There can be no escape from the fact: *all the post-holders whose roles, paid and unpaid, are covered by this text have a shared responsibility for the continuous improvement of the school – and they must be involved in change towards that end.*

These are the reasons that this text adopts the positions that it does. It insists that all of the roles discussed have a relationship to the sum total of learning that takes place in the school and each of the roles has a direct involvement in learning as the basis for its existence. Second, it pursues a line of thinking that tries to establish ways to manage those roles to make them integral to, and increasingly effective as part of, the learning process.

To be really valuable, change has to be more than tinkering at the edges. Radical change is sometimes known as reengineering. Champy's (1995) model is helpful. He argues that we have to get away from the fantasy that there is a perfect organisation, and one right way of doing things. We have to 'trade in the airy abstraction of *ex officio* authority for the messier reality of existential authority' (op. cit.: 27). We have to see people as multi-skilled; but we have to encourage them in individual accountability.

These insights work in two broad ways. First, in managing the roles that are dealt with here, those responsible for the leadership of schools have to trust support staff to work effectively. They have to abandon some control and hand it over to the support staff in return for their accountability. They must recognise the skills the support staff have rather than remain fixated on the 'otherness' of teachers bestowed through their professional qualifications. In the Strategies for Management suggested in Part Two (see page 61) we have tried to incorporate these principles. Research reported in this text shows that some support staff felt that they were well managed, while others were not. In this we were reminded of an uncredited quotation in Samuel (1997):

> *There is probably no greater waste…than that of willing employees prevented by insensitive leadership from applying their energies and ambitions in the interest of the [organisations] for which they work.*

Secondly, support staff themselves must shoulder the implications of this way of operating. They must play their part in the organisation by bringing to it a particular vision, or what Champy (1995: 31) calls 'living the question'. He encourages a mind:

- perpetually ready to revolt against its own conclusions;
- prepared not for disbelief…but for a constant, graceful scepticism;
- of democratic hospitality to other views;
- that is profoundly questioning.

We have tried to open the minds of the support staff who are its subjects, to the bigger picture of the educational world that they inhabit. They are well equipped to respond in many cases, since they often bring to it knowledge and experience of other worlds than schools and can apply that knowledge to the good of the school. This is well illustrated in the text.

So, support staff along with others bring attitudes of reengineering to their roles. The context of those roles is the school, but the school construed as a learning organisation. What, then, is a learning organisation? Southworth (in Burridge and Ribbins, 1994) maintains it has five characteristics:

- a focus on pupils and their learning;
- teachers who are continuing learners;
- teachers and other (i.e. support) staff who collaborate with and from each other;
- a school that 'learns its way forward';
- a head who is the learning leader.

This learning focus is the central concern of this book. Indeed, some will suggest that we have emphasised it too much, but that is not our view. Though we have talked for convenience about 'management strategies' in Part Two we are conscious that these are delivered by 'learning leaders'; there is no implication in them of applying mechanistic processes towards predetermined and closed goals. We have to be aware that to achieve the status of the school as a learning organisation, or to adopt the kind of thinking and acting that are implicit in reengineering approaches, brings us to the final piece in the jigsaw of management theory underlying this text: team working.

Implicit in much of what has been said and in the strategies suggested in Part Two for the effective management of support staff roles, is the view that successful school enterprises are run by teams. For most readers there will be little need to rehearse the invaluable work of Belbin (1981). The implications of this work are important for the deployment of support staff. Support staff usually have (and are employed for) their specific skills, which are often needed in team contexts in schools. Thus the laboratory technician is part of the science department team, the bursar may be part of the senior management team and so on. Support staff often have broader skills and experiences to contribute to the team. Some support staff may lead teams. Knowledge of teams, their characteristics, and how they operate effectively is critical for support staff and for their managers (a good summary can be found in Morrison, 1998: Chapter 7).

In conclusion, then, support staff and their leader/managers might do well to reflect on the characteristics of 'super-teams' (based on Morrison, op. cit.: 189).

Super-teams…

- constantly re-visit what they are trying to achieve;
- are persistent;
- set high expectations and standards;
- are highly committed to each other and to the task;
- communicate effectively with others;

- are proactive;
- bring in others to help the work of the team;
- prioritise and hit their targets;
- are never fully satisfied.

Perhaps 'creative dissatisfaction' should be a watch-word for us all.

References

Belbin, R.M. (1981) *Management teams: why they succeed or fail.* Oxford: Butterworth/Heinemann.

Bendell, T. (undated) *The quality gurus.* London: Department of Trade and Industry.

Burridge, E. and Ribbins, P. (1994) *Improving education: promoting quality in schools.* London: Cassell.

Davies, B. and Ellison, L. (1997a) *Strategic marketing for schools.* London: Pitman.

Davies, B. and Ellison, L. (1997b) *School leadership for the 21st century.* London: Routledge.

Morrison, K. (1998) *Management theories for educational change.* London: PCP.

Peters, T. and Austin, N. (1985) *A passion for excellence.*

Samuel, G. (1997) 'Introducing TQM at Heathland School' in Davies, B. and West-Burnham, J. (1997) *Reengineering and total quality in schools.* London: Pitman.

Wickens, P. (1995) *The ascendant organisation.* Basingstoke: MacMillan.

Part Two

■ ■ ■

Support staff roles and their management

4
■ ■ ■

The role of classroom assistants in supporting learning

(N.B. All references to teaching assistants use the female pronoun as this reflects the gender of the vast majority. Much of the chapter can be applied more or less directly to the roles of nursery nurses. We have used the term 'classroom assistants' to describe this group of post-holders, in contrast to the frequent use of 'learning assistants' by LEAs and schools, or the Government's preferred 'teaching assistants'. The nomenclature, and the reasons for it, are outlined in Chapter 1.)

Introduction

This chapter seeks to examine the impact of the support offered by classroom assistants on pupils' learning. Case study evidence is based on classroom observations carried out as part of Specialist Teacher Assistant training over a number of years. The focus of such training is mainly on work at Key Stage 1, but the examples of good practice identified and discussed apply to the learning support offered by classroom assistants across the primary age range.

Two main case studies illustrate the varied support role of these post-holders and reference will be made to a number of other examples of good practice in supporting learning. The role examined here is one of a general classroom assistant, not a learning support assistant employed specifically for support-ing a pupil/s with special educational or behavioural needs (*see* Chapters 6 and 7). The role of the classroom assistant may be to work with any class and with any teacher in the school, supporting such pupils as the class teacher decides. This may involve intensive one-to-one support for an indi-vidual pupil or support for a small group of pupils in any curriculum area. The assistant may be asked to work with pupils of any ability, perhaps on a rotating basis, so that both teacher and assistant work across the ability range in the class. The classroom assistant may stay in the same classroom with the pupil(s) she is working with or she may take them for work outside the classroom.

Case Study 4.1
Providing support for a small group outside the classroom: Sarah's story

(Points in brackets refer to following sections on support for learning)

Background

A small group of six lower ability pupils had experienced difficulties with the concept of repeated addition and the planned progression to work on division. These difficulties were identified by the assistant during the previ-ous small group activity and she had discussed them with the class teacher who decided that further work on repeated addition was necessary before moving on to division.

Activity

Sarah took the group to work outside the classroom in a separate area. The task was to revise the concept of repeated addition and to produce multipli-cation, array and addition sentences.

Sarah quickly checked that pupils had brought their pencils, rubbers etc. with them and she directed them to their seats. The tables were already laid out with counters and worksheets. During the transition from the classroom Sarah listened to several pupils telling her about how they had used the previous day's work in a related activity. (Behaviour management and self esteem)

She made a brisk start by questioning them to encourage recall of the previ-ous session on repeated addition. She used the white board to write an example and invited pupils to write their answer to the question, encourag-ing the other pupils to confirm if the answer was correct. Sarah used key vocabulary to remind the pupils of the concept of 'lots of' or 'groups of' and she revised the definition of 'array' and questioned pupils regarding 'rows' and 'columns'. A worksheet was introduced and Sarah worked through the first example with the whole group. Sarah read the instructions and directed questions at particular pupils to check understanding. Before asking them to proceed with the next question Sarah asked if anyone did not understand and responded positively to the pupil who had difficulties. She informed them all that she would come round in turn to check and help them individually. (Cognitive skills' development)

The pupils started the first question by working independently. Sarah had positioned herself near a pupil she had expected would need assistance and she focused initial support on this pupil. With each pupil Sarah moved closer and bent to their level. She smiled and spoke quietly. She prompted and gave further examples, particularly directing attention to the first worked example on the sheet. She encouraged the use of counters to provide a concrete visual aid for arrays and repeated the key terms for reinforcement.

Sarah checked work as she moved around the group. To do so she went through the question, counting aloud and commenting on exactly what was correct, before ticking the work. Where the answers were wrong she encouraged pupils to see the errors themselves by referring them back to the previous example. She then prompted by asking them to explain where they had got their answer from to work out the reasoning. (Metacognitive skills)

When all the pupils had completed the first question, Sarah went through it with the whole group to consolidate and then the pupils worked through the remaining questions at their own pace. She provided positive feedback through praise of work and effort. Sarah continued to circulate around the group, providing equal attention to all six pupils. She knew them all by name and was aware of their ability levels so her expectations were appropriate. (Self esteem)

Sarah maintained a brisk pace for the task, encouraging them to complete the worksheet and reminding them of the time available. When it was time to return to the classroom she praised their efforts, encouraged them to tidy up and move quietly back to the rest of the class.

At the end of the lesson Sarah gave a brief verbal report to the class teacher and made notes in her class logbook of the pupils' achievements. (Recording and reporting back)

Case Study 4.2
Providing individual learning support within the classroom: Marilyn's story

Background

The teaching assistant, Marilyn, was asked to provide focused support for one pupil, Adam, who needed some extra help with number work and who was having difficulty remaining on task. His attention-seeking behaviour was also a cause of concern and was causing some distraction to the rest of the class.

Activity

Marilyn invited Adam to work with her within the classroom on an individual basis. She explained that the teacher wanted him to carry out a special task which was similar to the work the rest of the class was doing, but required Adam to demonstrate how well he could recognise and form his numbers. She emphasised how well he had worked with her on the previous occasion and said she wanted him to show the teacher that he could produce really good work. (Self esteem)

The task was to recognise numbers one to ten, to form the number five correctly and to identify the number five from a set of numbers. Marilyn had organised a range of resources to support this task: a set of numbers on coloured backgrounds, join-the-dots worksheets for number five, Adam's exercise book, a sand tray and a number game. Marilyn maintained a brisk pace in using a range of learning support strategies. She introduced the set of numbers and they counted to ten together, then Adam counted independently. She checked Adam's ability to select the number five, moving the cards around for further checking. She used multi-sensory approaches, asking Adam to trace the number five in the sand, then she traced a five on his back and on his hand and he did the same on her hand. They played a checking game tracing different numbers in the sand and on each other's hands. Adam was then asked to form the number five, first joining the dots and then copying this in his exercise book. They then played some number games to reinforce number recognition and finally Adam coloured in some large pre-formed numbers. (Cognitive skills development)

Marilyn carefully encouraged Adam's independence, prompting and assisting, but refusing to do the work for him. She was firm in insisting that he remained on task, but offered ample praise and encouragement, including appropriate incentives. She moved away to help other pupils, saying 'You do it while I'm not looking and then I'll see how well you've done'. While working with other pupils, she kept an eye on Adam and returned to him when she felt he was becoming distracted. On her return she demonstrated her satisfaction with what he had achieved, stating that she knew he could do it on his own and so confirming her high expectations of his attainment and behaviour. (Autonomous learning)

Marilyn demonstrated a very patient approach throughout the task and she remained calm and very positive. She unobtrusively removed distractions and spoke quietly to avoid disrupting the class. Her body language was supportive: she sat close to Adam, almost 'blocking out' the distraction of the rest of the class who were working with the teacher; she smiled, shared touches of humour. Marilyn gave carefully focused feedback, highlighting what he had done well and what he needed to improve. She also encouraged him to self-assess his work to identify which numbers he thought he had written correctly and to compare these with earlier work. Marilyn knew Adam's preferred rewards and was aware that he enjoyed and was proud of his colouring skills. She used incentives for remaining on task very effectively, particularly in giving Adam some choice of reward: depending on the level of his achievement, he was allowed to pick the design and the colour of the reward stamp and he could use the stamp himself, choose which numbers to colour and use his preferred colouring pens. (Behaviour management)

Marilyn made very productive use of the time available and Adam achieved all the objectives very successfully. Pacing was particularly brisk with quick changes between activities and approaches to maintain interest. Marilyn took care to show him that he was engaged in similar work to the other pupils. She took the opportunity to point out Adam's achievements to other pupils and to the teacher at the end of the lesson so that he could receive public recognition of his work. (Self esteem)

Marilyn took the opportunity at the end of the lesson to report back to the teacher on specific points of Adam's progress. She showed the teacher the improvement in his formation of the number five as demonstrated in his workbook and gave details of his attainments in number recognition on the basis of observations through the number game. She made suggestions for further work on number formation, including a brief revision of numbers covered to date. (Feedback to the teacher)

The role of the classroom assistant

In Janet Moyles's particularly useful research project (1997) into the role of assistants, she notes that the role of the class teacher generally requires her to be constantly moving around the classroom, monitoring all the pupils, whereas the assistants tend to be stationary, working with small groups around one table. Assistants are thus able to provide 'more sustained and concentrated activity support on an individual basis'. This difference in focused support can allow the assistant to respond more easily and immediately to an individual pupil's needs and can have a very beneficial effect on pupils' learning.

Support for cognitive skills development

The learning support offered on an individual or small group basis by a classroom assistant may be particularly effective because it is directly focused on the individual's needs, and pacing and level of instruction can be quickly adjusted to match those needs. The interaction between the pupil and a supportive, informed adult can considerably advance the pupil's understanding, raising the cognitive level of the task by appropriate intervention. Instruction can be focused within the pupil's 'zone of proximal development (ZPD)' seen by Vygotsky as the difference between the learning a pupil can achieve alone and unaided and what s/he can achieve with the help of others. Faulkner (1995) highlights Vygotsky's distinction between the child's *actual* developmental level and his/her *potential* developmental level as the difference between (a) the demonstration of understanding and the ability to use ideas and concepts without help from another person (*actual* level) and (b) 'when children are operating within their ZPD (their *potential* developmental level) [when] they can work with more advanced ideas and concepts, provided they are receiving the support of someone who already has a more sophisticated grasp of the relevant concepts'.

The concept of 'scaffolding' recognises that the adult can provide the framework and support for building up learning, but it is the pupil who constructs the edifice. Scaffolding 'occurs when a teacher recognizes that a learner is in need of assistance and offers prompts, suggestions and hints to help the learner solve the problem. As soon as the teacher sees that the "scaffold" is working, she gradually begins to remove the prompts and cues used to construct it' (Borich and Tombari, 1997).

A classroom assistant's work with pupils on the concept of division is a relevant example of scaffolding with the repeated practical work of sharing counters between hoops until the pupils grasped the concept of remainders, then the hoops were removed as the practical reinforcement was no longer needed.

It is of course possible to enrich the learning capacity of a task or to inhibit it: 'the key to good scaffolding is to achieve the right balance between too much support and too little' (Borich and Tombari, 1997). There is a danger, especially with an inexperienced classroom assistant, of unwanted interruption rather than supportive intervention. The assistant may feel the need to be seen to be constantly involved with the group of pupils and the fear of appearing redundant can lead to unnecessary interruptions or distractions.

An assistant, leaning over suddenly to check on work, disturbed the pupil who was in the process of counting and the assistant had to apologise for stopping her and withdraw to allow the pupil to continue.

The effective assistant seizes the 'teachable moment' perhaps more easily than a class teacher, since the assistant is working with small numbers of pupils and may be in a position to respond more directly to the opportunity of reinforcing a concept or discussing a query raised by a pupil as part of a task.

In playing a general number game, the assistant took the opportunity of revising the definition of an odd /even number, almost as an aside and without losing any of the fun generated by the game.

Differentiation is obviously easier to plan and manage when working with a small group of pupils of relatively similar ability. The assistant does, however, need to be sensitive to pupils' awareness of being different to the rest of the class when they are given differentiated tasks or if they work outside the classroom with the assistant. Some pupils like to feel they are a 'special' group working with their own 'helper' but others feel the stigma of difference and the assistant needs to minimise those differences (*see* Marilyn and Adam in Case Study 4.2 at page 66) and share her support with a range of pupils, where possible.

As part of her support for learning, the assistant reinforces key concepts and vocabulary introduced by the class teacher. The repeated use of subject-specific vocabulary and the revision of key concepts is very valuable for a pupil who is struggling to understand material just beyond his/her intellectual grasp. However, the assistant must beware of merely repeating the teacher's instructions at the start of the task since pupils quickly realise that this facility will be available to them and so they do not concentrate during the teacher's exposition.

The effective assistant will personalise the resources used in a learning activity to meet, more directly, the needs of an individual or small group. An assistant who has developed a close relationship with a pupil will be aware of that pupil's personal interests outside school and will make use of that to increase the pupil's motivation and sense of satisfaction.

A pupil who appears uninterested in reading and is reluctant to select books to take home or to read in quiet reading time may be more motivated if the assistant can locate a number of books relevant to that pupil's personal interest in, for example, dinosaurs or cars and if she can take the opportunity to discuss key points from the books. The assistant can also refer to this interest in other learning tasks by counting cars or measuring dinosaurs in numeracy, or using these examples as the basis for number games or worksheets.

The assistant is able to move quickly and seemlessly between resources, personalise them to ensure pupil motivation and use a wider range of resources on a one-to-one or small group basis than is possible with a whole class.

Support for problem solving skills

The effective classroom assistant encourages pupils to feel that it is acceptable to take risks and to get the answer wrong, especially if working on a one-to-one basis or with a small group of similar ability. She gives praise for trying and uses errors positively as an opportunity for learning. She admits to her own uncertainties and models ways of dealing with them, e.g. looking up the spelling of a word in the dictionary. She will use questioning to probe the reasons for error and to encourage pupils to see where they have gone wrong. The assistant encourages perseverance in a difficult task by recognising difficulty and providing support, or she can anticipate potential problems and be prepared to provide assistance before frustration sets in (Redl and Wineman's 'hurdle help' as discussed in Smith and Laslett, 1993). She provides opportunities for developing investigative skills in some tasks and for seeking a range of solutions to problems. She reminds the pupils of the need to use reference material, word books, display material, classroom resources etc. as sources of information, rather than relying on the teacher to provide the information. When marking work she will check it aloud against the set criteria, e.g. saying 'Yes you have remembered the capital letter at the start of the sentence' or 'I'm glad to see that you have measured from 0 on your ruler' to reinforce an understanding.

Support for developing metacognitive skills

Pupils need to reflect on how they learn in order to develop their ability to transfer learning to a range of contexts. They need to become more aware of their own thinking as an active process. The insightful classroom assistant will look for opportunities to discuss preferred learning modes with the pupils and encourage them to identify their most effective learning approach for themselves. Based on her knowledge of the pupils, the assistant will ensure that pupils for whom visual aids are most effective have access to such resources, or she may plan to incorporate active practical involvement in the task to cater for pupils with a preferred learning mode of physical involvement. She discusses the effectiveness of the different approaches with the pupils to raise their awareness of different modes of learning.

An effective assistant will make the opportunity to ask pupils to explain how they arrived at a solution to a problem (the stage in cognitive apprenticeship termed 'articulation' by Borich and Tombari (1997): 'the way of determining if the learner understands the process'). The assistant may then encourage pupils to compare different strategies for achieving the same answer to enable them to judge which is most effective. She can subsequently remind pupils of the effective strategies used and relate these to new tasks. Crozier (1997) suggests that lower achievers in particular have an 'under-use of learning strategies that, in turn, makes success less likely' and the classroom assistant may help such pupils by the explicit direction to identifying such strategies. She encourages pupils to ask questions and to check their own understanding. She helps them to make connections between previous and new learning and discusses ways of transferring learning to a range of contexts. The classroom assistant can demonstrate a real interest in the subject and show enthusiasm for learning. Above all, she will show pupils that they are learning all the time and will model effective strategies for learning.

Support for increased self-esteem and self-confidence/emotional skills development

The classroom assistant is particularly well placed to support the emotional development of pupils. To make optimum use of this support, the impact of emotional factors on learning must be recognised. With too heavy a focus on developing cognitive abilities the importance of pupils' attitudes and anxieties can be ignored. Park (2000) emphasises the inter-reliance of thinking and feeling (describing them as 'engaged in a continuous dance'). He argues that the 'quality of feeling shapes the depth and meaningfulness of thinking' and advocates dialogue as the process which best supports the thinking-feeling link. But opportunities for true dialogue in a busy classroom tend to be very limited. The assistant may, however, be able to build on existing effective relationships in order to share ideas and opinions with pupils, encouraging real interaction within a small group. The assistant can sometimes be more in tune with a pupil's emotional state and well-being than the teacher.

The individual attention of an adult focused on a child who is lacking in self-esteem can be very rewarding. Instead of needing to resort to attention-seeking strategies, the child is assured of individual attention. The classroom assistant can offer a 'listening ear' for pupils who may not wish to talk to the teacher or may not feel it is appropriate to tell the teacher if she appears busy. A study of early years classrooms by Hughes (1997) (discussed in Dowling, 2000) refers to the 'custodial role' of the teacher contrasted with the perception by children that other adults in the classroom were 'more approachable and therefore able to be questioned and sometimes interrupted'. The importance of the adult in 'nurturing talk' is vital in working with younger children, but is also important in helping older pupils develop oral skills and the ability to verbalise. The assistant may be considered by some pupils to have more time available to share news, or the walk to another classroom or the library may provide an opportunity for a quick discussion between pupils and the assistant.

Hayes (1998) describes the danger of the teacher being 'unaware of the real purpose of the comment or simply being too busy to give it adequate attention […] hearing what is said but failing to listen to the thinking behind the words'. The assistant may provide emotional security for a pupil and can listen to their concerns or share news with them. The active listening skills demonstrated by the assistant and the shared knowledge of the pupil as an individual form an important foundation for an effective working relationship as the pupil feels valued and respected with a significant adult making time to listen to him/her.

If a pupil experiences some difficulty in learning an aspect of school work, he/she can quickly come to believe that they are unlikely to be successful in a range of learning tasks. Rather than risk facing continual failure, they will avoid doing the tasks. 'A lack of self-confidence and little expectation of success accompany failure and lead to the adoption of strategies that attempt to protect the self-image from the psychological consequences of failure' (Crozier, 1997). Pupils may therefore opt to do simple tasks which they know they can achieve and demonstrate learned helplessness when asked to tackle a more demanding task. The role of the classroom assistant is to engineer a series of small successes, putting satisfactory progress within the reach of the pupil who begins to experience the pleasure of success and his/her self confidence is improved. The assistant cannot accept the pupil's helplessness, but can offer support to tackle the task and show her confidence in the pupil's ability to achieve.

An effective classroom assistant will herself model success at difficult tasks which require effort rather than mastery of simple things. She must take care to avoid a 'perfect' performance and perhaps show her own mistakes (deliberate or otherwise) or discuss her own areas of difficulty in some tasks which the pupil finds achievable, for example, a lack of drawing skills. Confidence in their own ability to tackle a task can also be enhanced by the teaching assistant who can:

- 'translate' the task at the pupils' level;
- scaffold learning;
- restructure the task into graded, achievable steps; and
- provide appropriate resources to enable the pupil to turn potential failure into success.

During work, the assistant provides encouragement and checks unobtrusively on progress to avoid frustration.

> During whole class work, on the carpet, in numeracy the teaching assistant may sometimes act as a sounding board for the pupil to rehearse answers before risking a public response to the teacher's question, providing an opportunity to avoid failure if the answer is incorrect.

Well-focused and abundant praise from the classroom assistant will foster a sense of achievement. The assistant's higher expectations will often be realised by a previously underachieving pupil, because the adult has shown confidence in the ability to learn. Equally the assistant's obvious disappointment when pupils produce work which falls short of their personal best can demonstrate that their work is noticed and that it matters to someone when they do not try.

Extrinsic motivation may sometimes be very effective in encouraging pupils to persevere with a difficult task. The assistant, who knows the pupil well, will know what incentives (stickers, stamps, merit points etc.) are most appropriate to motivate the individual pupil and the kind of praise the pupil will best respond to. Some pupils find effusive public praise an embarrassment and prefer a whispered comment or even a smile and a 'thumbs up'.

Support for collaborative skills

Many pupils have difficulty in learning to work with others and need help in learning collaborative skills. In managing small group activities, the classroom assistant may reinforce group rules at the start of an activity and remind pupils of those rules throughout the task. She will teach the value of listening to others and respecting their opinions by her interventions and reminders. She will explain that her support must be shared equally among the group and she will teach pupils that they must wait their turn as every child has an equal right to her support. She will encourage co-operative peer support with pupils taking responsibility for helping another child who is facing difficulties, recognising that by explaining, the pupil is reinforcing their own knowledge of the task.

The assistant will be a role model in demonstrating interest and valuing opinions equally among the group. She will show courtesy to all pupils and reinforce the value of sharing resources and collaboration by highlighting opportunities and praising pupils who co-operate. The assistant may help pupils manage their group skills by controlling dominant pupils and encouraging those who are reluctant to participate. She can allocate roles to ensure full involvement and directly explain the value of sharing the task and using all the pupils' skills.

Support for behaviour management

The classroom assistant will actively support the class teacher's approach to behaviour management and reinforce agreed rules in working with pupils, for example, reminding pupils about the need to raise their hand to answer a question. She must maintain the same standards as the teacher and agree with the teacher appropriate rewards or sanctions for behaviour.

In the classroom, the assistant can position herself at the edge of the class for 'troubleshooting'. Proximity to pupils will help her to monitor or control behaviour, or provide extra help with a topic. The DfEE guide (2000), in reviewing good practice in working with classroom assistants, notes that 'often the input of an attentive adult will prevent pupils' minds wandering off their work, which can happen in a large group with only one adult'. The assistant will quietly remind pupils of the class rules and remove distractions. Her own behaviour will be a role model in listening to the teacher, demonstrating interest and joining in as appropriate.

> Pre-emptive measures for behaviour management of a small group outside the classroom can include ensuring that:
>
> - there is an orderly transition to another room;
> - all resources are readily available from the start of the activity (but that they are not accessible as a distraction);
> - pupils are seated by the classroom assistant so that there is plenty of space and individuals are not sitting next to a pupil who will distract them;
> - the classroom assistant selects her own seating position near to a pupil who may be disruptive.

During the activity the assistant may adopt a range of appropriate techniques in managing behaviour from planned ignoring to naming a pupil and proximity control. She can ensure the task is achievable or provide more focused assistance and praise the pupil's efforts. She can emphasise her high expectations and offer the possibility of a reward as an incentive or refer to agreed sanctions if rules are not followed.

An effective classroom assistant will maintain interest in the task by demonstrating her own enthusiasm and by ensuring examples are relevant and appropriate to the pupils' interest. She will seek opportunities for active involvement, for example, asking pupils to write the answer on the whiteboard. She monitors the time and ensures that the pace is brisk through repeating her expectations of progress and perhaps encouraging some competitive element if appropriate or some reference to the pupil's previous achievements. The assistant ensures that adequate time warnings are given to allow pupils to develop their own time management skills and to complete the task.

Support for autonomous learning

There is a danger that pupils can become over-dependent on support from a classroom assistant. The assistant must encourage them to develop as more independent learners. HMI (1992) noted that the most effective assistants were 'those who understood that they should not, generally, do for pupils what they should do for themselves'. It is possible to build the pupils' confidence in their own ability to cope with the level of the task by ensuring that the activity is planned in small, achievable steps, so that success is ensured and progress is obvious. This scaffolded support needs to be removed gradually as the pupil gains in confidence and ongoing praise recognising achievement provides the foundation for further confidence and increased self-esteem.

The assistant will become vigilant in observing at a distance to monitor the pupils' levels of progress and avoid potential frustration. She can intervene when necessary, but not when this would be an unwanted interruption. She may provide suggestions and hints, but must avoid doing the work for the pupil. This can be a challenge when the teaching assistant may perceive that she, herself, will be judged on the pupil's performance in completing the task correctly. Moyles (1997) quotes a classroom assistant's comment 'If you leave them alone they will colour cabbages red'. Equally it requires self-discipline to avoid stepping in to complete a task for a pupil who is clearly struggling, but autonomous learning is a key life skill and needs to be nurtured.

The classroom assistant will seek opportunities to offer pupils an element of choice. These may be quite small – e.g., the choice of a particular sticker as a reward, which way to help in tidying up, selecting a reading book, which of two worksheets to complete first or which activity to do first in a particular lesson. In group work, the creation of choices may involve an awareness of majority voting and the need for compromise. The assistant will encourage pupils to take responsibility for their own learning, she will remind them of the need to check their work for errors and, by valuing their efforts, will encourage them to take pride in their work.

Support for the teacher

In the classroom, an assistant provides not just another pair of hands, but another pair of eyes, ears and an informed brain. She will observe from a different physical location from the teacher and see behaviour or levels of concentration which are less visible from the teacher's perspective; she can then follow a planned strategy to remedy immediate problems or report back general comments to the teacher.

An assistant will provide informed feedback to the teacher about the progress of individuals or small groups who have worked with her away from the main class. She can highlight specific areas which caused difficulty or in which pupils performed well. Brief written notes made by the classroom assistant may be used by the teacher when planning the next lesson, enabling the teacher to decide if that group needs to spend some time with the teacher while the classroom assistant works with another group. If the teacher gives the classroom assistant precise instructions about the aspects of pupil progress on which feedback is required then a very brief response noted against those points is all that is required. The classroom assistant may devise a system for indicating the amount of support given to pupils, perhaps brief notes on the worksheet or the use of different coloured pens, to show exactly how much help was needed to complete the worksheet. The teacher is more aware of details relating to particular pupils' progress and can plan future learning support accordingly.

If a classroom assistant is viewed as part of a professional team then collaboration between two colleagues working together to support learning can significantly enhance the learning experience for all pupils in the class. The work of the assistant can only directly underpin the teacher's planned instruction if the teacher manages the learning environment effectively. The teacher needs to provide the assistant with a clear plan for the week/lesson which highlights points of focus for the assistant to work on with the children, key concepts/vocabulary for emphasis and/or particular pupils' needs for attention. Strategies for effective support need to be discussed and the opportunities for feedback and review need to be planned. A study carried out by Mortimore *et al.* (1994) into the employment of additional support staff in school highlights a number of key benefits, principally for teachers and pupils, but sounds a note of caution: 'it does, however, also require teachers to exercise supervisory skills if the benefits of support are to be maximised'.

Strategies for the management of assistants within the classroom in order to ensure more effective deployment of such valuable support merit a closer discussion, which follows in Chapter 5. However, what this chapter has established are the actions a classroom assistant should take to become an effective part of the 'learning' team, and the central role – for many pupils – of the assistant in the learning process.

References

Borich, G. and Tombari, M. (1997) *Educational psychology: a contemporary approach.* 2nd. edn. New York: Addison Wesley Longman.

Crozier, W. (1997) *Individual learners: personality differences in education.* London: Routledge.

Department for Education and Employment (2000) *Supporting the teaching assistant – a good practice guide.* London: DfEE.

Dowling, M. (2000) *Young children's personal, social and emotional development.* London: Paul Chapman.

Faulkner, D. (1995) 'Play, self and the social world' in Barnes, P. (ed.) *Personal, Social and Emotional Development of Children.* Buckingham: Open University.

Hayes, D. (1998) *Effective Verbal Communication.* London: Hodder & Stoughton.

Her Majesty's Inspectorate (1992) *Non-teaching staff in schools.* London: HMSO.

Mortimore, P., Mortimore, J. and Thomas, H. (1994) *Managing associate staff.* London: Paul Chapman.

Moyles, J. (1997) *Jills of All Trades.* London: ATL.

Park, J. (2000) 'The dance of dialogue: thinking and feeling in education', *Pastoral Care in Education,* 118, 3.

Smith, C. and Laslett, R. (1993) *Effective Classroom Management.* 2nd edn. London: Routledge.

5

■ ■ ■

Managing the role of the classroom assistant

Professional teamwork

If the professional teamwork between teacher and assistant is to be effective, both colleagues need to demonstrate respect for each other's roles and responsibilities within the classroom. 'In the cause of harmony and professional effectiveness, each classroom partner clearly needs to respect the integrity of the other' (Mills and Mills, 1995). The teacher must show respect for the role of the assistant and for the individual fulfilling that role, since the teacher will be a model for pupils in the class. Pupils quickly pick up any nuances reflecting potential, or actual, negative attitudes and if they feel the assistant does not have the teacher's confidence or respect, they may refuse to recognise her authority and misbehave when working with her. Quite minor comments about 'Mrs X not understanding what I wanted her to do' when addressed to a group of pupils can quickly undermine the pupils' confidence in the assistant. If the assistant is seen as 'unqualified' to mark work or unable to award reward points without first seeking the teacher's permission, pupils will avoid seeking her assistance and form potentially disruptive queues for the teacher to mark work which could equally well be marked by an informed assistant.

The teacher must be sensitive in addressing the assistant within earshot of the class and should seek to support the assistant in public even if private discussion/disagreement takes place later. The status of a classroom assistant can be perceived as a lowly one by some pupils and the sneering comment 'You're not the teacher, you're only a helper' should never arise in a classroom where all adults are treated with respect. Equally, the assistant needs to demonstrate respect for the class teacher and must never try to undermine his/her authority in front of the pupils, by seeking to criticise a punishment as unduly harsh or siding with a pupil.

Only a true working partnership in the classroom can help pupils to achieve their full potential. Rita Headington remarks on the variety of roles adopted by assistants but emphasises that 'partnerships are formed whose aim is to move the children forward and within which the roles of teachers and assistants are different but complementary' (Headington, 1997). Suzi Clipson-Boyles argues that 'partnership is most effective where both sides understand each other through clear dialogue and where decision-making is made through consultation, discussion and honest feedback'. She concludes that the relationship between teacher and assistant 'requires shared values and common goals which are reached by a clear commitment to working together' (Clipson-Boyles, 1996).

Fostering personal relationships

Doyle (1997) describes the 'inclusive classroom' in which 'children and adults are welcomed and belong unconditionally. Everyone in the inclusive classroom community actively encourages participation from all its members.' Such a concept recognises the importance for both adults and children to feel that they are a valued part of the class group so that an atmosphere of support

---

Strategy 5.1 *Involving the classroom assistant in the whole life of the classroom*

Children respond well to the opportunity of seeing the adults in their classrooms as individuals with home lives outside school. Staff can develop personal relationships more effectively by seeking opportunities to join in celebrations with the classroom community.

- A class which celebrates the birthday of each pupil can extend that celebration to include the birthdays of the teacher, the assistant and other adults.
- Special occasions for the adults can also be shared with the class so that a 'certificate' can be issued to a classroom assistant who has just completed a First Aid course.
- The sharing of news at the start of the week can be planned to include a relevant contribution from both teacher and assistant.

---

and shared responsibility is fostered. The team of teacher and classroom assistant can help to foster the caring, sharing environment which children need in order to thrive by demonstrating a harmonious relationship. (Strategy 5.1)

Managing the work of the classroom assistant

It is the teacher's responsibility to ensure effective professional teamwork and to manage the adults working in his/her class effectively. The teacher should support in-service training to ensure that the assistant is aware of key elements of good practice in supporting learning. The teacher needs to emphasise the importance of the learning process rather than over-emphasising task completion or the end product. Moyles's research (1997) confirms the dangers: 'our most significant finding is that, while teachers work from a basis of learning processes, classroom assistants focus heavily on the outcomes of children's activities'. Part of an assistant's induction to her role should emphasise that her work will not be judged on the pupils' output as this can put undue pressure on the assistant to help pupils to complete their work, rather than to ensure understanding of key concepts. (Strategy 5.2)

Strategy 5.2 *Involving the classroom assistant in the planning process*

It is through effective planning and clear communication with the assistant that the teacher can clarify learning objectives, identify the points of focus for an activity and agree the nature of the learning support that the assistant can provide. There should be a general policy within schools that all planning documents should include specific reference to the role of the assistant (where relevant). Teachers can ensure that assistants are involved in the following ways:

- The written weekly plan for numeracy includes details of the activities for each ability group and the key objectives. The assistant is then aware of the key points of focus.
- The Year 4 class teacher includes on the lesson plan the key vocabulary and terminology which she wants the assistant to reinforce with the group.
- The Reception Class teacher always discusses the following week's plan with the classroom assistant at a set time on a given day of the week.
- The teacher takes into account in her planning the assistant's focused observations on individual children, their progress and behaviour.

Practical support in the classroom

The teacher as manager will consider the most effective management of the assistant's time in the classroom. Occasionally, an assistant can be most usefully deployed by preparing resources or photocopying lesson material and suitable time can be planned for these tasks. However, if this means that the assistant is not present during the teacher's introduction to the lesson, the assistant must be clear about the main focus of that introduction so she can seamlessly move into appropriate support for related group work. If the assistant is present during the introduction and plenary, it is important that her role is planned to ensure her active participation. The assistant can:

- join in discussion;
- contribute in mental arithmetic;
- take a role in play reading; or
- report back with her group in the plenary.

But the requirements for the involvement must be planned and agreed in advance. It is the teacher's responsibility to manage the arrangements for group work, including the location of the groups and the nature of differentiated material. (Strategy 5.3)

Strategy 5.3 *Sharing support tasks*

A useful strategy to adopt during the teacher's introduction is for the assistant to carry out focused observation on a pupil or pupils (identified by the teacher) to note behaviour, concentration and understanding and can then report on areas of concern about particular pupils. Alternatively, the teaching assistant could change roles with the teacher, perhaps leading the class in guided reading, while the teacher carries out the observations.

During the introduction the assistant could sit close to a particular pupil experiencing difficulties in numeracy and use a small wipe-clean board for calculations to provide additional help for the pupil.

Feedback

It is vital that the teacher is fully informed of each pupil's progress when that pupil is working regularly with an assistant. The teacher should inform the assistant of the nature of the feedback required and ensure that time is available for reporting back. Often brief verbal feedback is adequate to ensure the teacher is informed of the effectiveness of learning following the assistant's work with a group of pupils. (Strategies 5.4–5.6)

Strategy 5.4 *Managing feedback from the classroom assistant*

The Year 3 class teacher designs a form for the assistant to provide brief, written comments on the progress of the group of four pupils that the assistant regularly takes out of the class for additional support. The form covers a key session in the week when the assistant is working outside the class with the group, and the activity is noted together with comments on particular pupils' successes and difficulties.

Activity: Writing a diary

Pupil	Strengths	Difficulties
Shazia	Grasped the concept of diary writing. Concentrated well. Wrote detailed entries for four days – no assistance. Used word book without prompting	Needed reminding about size of letters and spacing.
Sarah	Understood about diary entries, but could not think of anything to write. Careful handwriting, correct letter formation and size.	Avoided starting. Unable to think of her own ideas, wanted to check what Shazia had written. Said she needed to check spelling of common words. Insisted on erasing a large section of her work because it wasn't right.
Andrew	With prompting was able to write about what happened at school for two days. Good attempt at spelling some unfamiliar words.	Found it difficult to be factual – he wanted to write imaginative entries. Complained that he hadn't done anything to write about – he understood the concept but was not happy with the task.
James	Wrote in sentences with capital letters and full stops. Good attempt at spelling.	Did not seem to understand the task: wrote in the present tense with general descriptions of home and school.

Strategy 5.5 *Using learning management data*

Another Year 3 class teacher identifies specific targets at the start of the week for the pupils the classroom assistant will be working with and asks the assistant to focus on those targets as part of her support and to comment on the achievement of those targets by the end of the week.

Pupil	Target	Attainment/Difficulties
Alex	1. To recognise questions in given texts.	At first some confusion with exclamation marks. By Friday, confident in recognition and able to use appropriate expression when reading aloud.
	2. To turn statements into questions.	Still needs reminding: see work from Thursday.
	3. To use question marks correctly in writing.	Completed the worksheet and creative writing without help.

Strategy 5.6 *Developing ways of managing information between teacher and assistant*

A teacher agrees a form of hidden 'code' with the assistant so that it is clear to the teacher (but not to the pupil) how much assistance has been given with a particular piece of work: work ticked by the assistant in a blue pen means that the pupil has completed the work unaided, a black pen means some assistance and a red pen means that a lot of help was given.

An alternative way of reporting back to the teacher on pupils' progress is for the assistant to keep a daily log recording key aspects to be drawn to the teacher's attention.

(Any form of record keeping is time-consuming and assistants cannot be expected to spend time outside their contracted hours in writing detailed reports. Arrangements should be made for assistants to have some short periods of time outside the classroom to write brief, focused notes for the teacher's feedback. The teacher must then assume responsibility for reading and acting upon such feedback.)

Agreed responsibilities in behaviour management

It is important that both teacher and assistant are clear about areas of responsibility. The assistant needs to know in advance if it is part of her role to intervene to manage misbehaviour when the teacher is present or whether she should leave all behaviour management, outside the pupils she is currently working with, to the teacher. Difficulties can arise if the teacher has decided to ignore a pupil's attention-seeking misbehaviour but has failed to notify the assistant of her 'planned ignoring' and the assistant intervenes because she thinks the teacher is unaware of the misbehaviour. It needs to be agreed whether or not the assistant can give rewards or issue sanctions to pupils without first checking with the teacher. The teacher needs to ensure the assistant is aware of the class rules and school policy and is confident about enforcing them. (Strategy 5.7)

Strategy 5.7 *Sharing the management of behaviour in class*

Ideally the assistant should be directly involved in the lessons when class rules are formulated, as an equal partner with the teacher and pupils in establishing and subsequently maintaining the agreed rules.

Role of the head teacher

Overall responsibility for deployment of assistants in school rests with the head teacher, who will take an overview of all classroom support across the school. The head teacher clearly needs to take a lead in demonstrating respect for all staff in school and valuing their contributions to the learning environment. The head teacher, in planning the deployment of an individual assistant, needs to recognise the pressures placed on any assistant who works across a number of classes/year groups, in a range of curriculum areas and with different class teachers, often in the course of one day. Parents may well question the amount of time their child spends with an untrained assistant, rather than with the qualified class teacher, especially when the pupils are withdrawn from the class to work elsewhere with an assistant. The head teacher needs to inform parents of the very productive and often individualised support offered by trained assistants.

This overview of the work of assistants in the school is an important school management responsibility and merits the same careful, advance timetabling as the planned work of class teachers, since the team work between teachers and assistants needs to be developed and effective learning support must be well-planned. The National Standards for Headteachers (DfEE, 2000a) highlight the importance of heads in leading and managing staff and in the efficient and effective deployment of staff. No specific reference is made to the management of classroom assistants but it is clear that the head teacher's role encompasses the management of all staff in school. (Strategy 5.8)

Strategy 5.8 *Providing information about the employment and deployment of classroom assistants*

Providing information is an important management role. Heads would do well to consider how they could explain to parents about the roles and activities undertaken by classroom assistants.

From time to time it may be useful to review:

- References to classroom assistants in the school brochure.
- Whether a letter to parents (e.g. at the beginning of a new school year) might clarify to them the value of classroom assistants.
- Whether parents, governors and relevant others understand the levels of training undertaken by assistants.
- How assistants are used in the whole life of the school, and what messages their use conveys to outsiders.

School policies

The HMI Review of non-teaching staff in schools, published in 1992, highlighted the fact that although non-teaching staff made a 'significant contribution and their work was highly valued by teachers', their effectiveness was constrained by a number of factors:

> a limited perception, on the part of schools and these staff themselves, of their capabilities and potential; inadequate management and in particular the absence of a job description; a lack of formal or informal appraisal of performance; lack of in-service training; and a shortage of time to perform duties.

Some progress has been made in addressing some of these factors, particularly in the perceptions of the impact classroom assistants can have on pupils' learning and in the provision of more appropriate and widely available training opportunities. However, lack of clear job descriptions and planned duties, the monitoring and appraisal of assistants and the need to ensure adequate time to perform the wide range of duties remain matters for concern in some schools.

The more recent DfEE guidelines (2000b) stress the vital importance of school policies in developing the work of assistants. Planning for the role of assistants needs to start before the recruitment and selection process and should be formalised in a clear job description. The monitoring of the assistant's role needs to be planned and reviewed in regular appraisal. In a school with a number of assistants in post, it may be appropriate to designate a member of the senior management team as responsible for all assistants in school and this person can organise regular meetings of the classroom assistant team. Matters of general concern can then be discussed and the assistants will feel that they have a formal voice within the school. (Strategy 5.9)

Strategy 5.9 *Formulating school policy with respect to classroom assistants*

Formulating policy is a good way to clarify one's own thinking, as well as a way of informing relevant others (such as school governors). A policy about the employment and deployment of classroom assistants might answer the following questions:

- How many assistants are employed in the school?
- What are their backgrounds (e.g. who are qualified, who are trainees etc.)?
- How are they used?
- With what classes/groups of pupils?
- To serve what purpose?
- Specifically, what learning gains are expected from the employment?
- How are assistants to be involved in planning for learning? Is time allowed for this?
- What wider involvement do they have in the life of the school (e.g. are they expected to assist at school events such as the Christmas play)?
- What mechanisms are available for assistants to express their views and observation?
- How do assistants relate to teachers on the one hand and other school employees on the other?
- What behaviour is expected of pupils in relation to assistants?
- Are they involved in continuing professional development (external courses etc.)? When? In what ways?
- Are they included in staff meetings, training days and school-based training?
- Are salary levels appropriate? Are there opportunities for career progression?

Training

Induction training for new assistants is, at long last, being given a high priority so that all new assistants should receive well-focused training and support in their new roles. The National Occupational Standards, which are currently in preparation, will provide a framework for subsequent qualifications and career progression for experienced assistants. The appraisal process can usefully be extended to all staff employed in school in order to highlight personal achievements, set targets and plan training. There should be a clear commitment from senior management recognising the value of appropriate training for all staff. Suzi Clipson-Boyles (1996) provides a strong argument for appropriate training for teaching assistants, noting that 'the quality of support which adults give can have a significant effect upon the quality of learning, but such a responsibility requires guidance'. She emphasises that it is the pupils who ultimately benefit from support from a competent adult and makes the point 'it is to them [the pupils] that we owe a responsibility to work from a sound base of guidance and training'. Within the school there needs to be a culture where training is seen both as an entitlement for individual performance development and as a necessity for more effective working with pupils; schools could then be more accurately considered as 'learning organisations'. However, without a clear career ladder with appropriate remuneration and recognised status for assistants the incentive to pursue further training and development may be lacking. If the role of the assistant is valued then it must be recognised and rewarded. (*See* Strategy 5.9, page 85.)

Initial teacher training

With the role of the teacher constantly changing to meet apparently ever-increasing demands for the profession in the 21st century, with more of a focus on the teacher as a manager of learning in the classroom and with increasing numbers of assistants being employed in schools, it is absolutely vital that the skills necessary for managing other trained and experienced adults in the classroom should be acknowledged and that training should be provided to develop those skills. It is therefore interesting, but a matter of some concern, to note that, in the key 4/98 Standards (DfEE, 1998) for the award of Qualified Teacher Status (QTS), among the many and comprehensive listing of competencies required by the teacher, reference to the necessary skills in working with other adults in the classroom is sparse. In fact, there is only one related standard in Annex A, Section B 'Planning, Teaching and Class Management'.

Moreover, this standard is restricted to the 'Additional standards relating to early years' and requires that those to be awarded QTS must 'demonstrate that they manage, with support from an experienced specialist teacher if necessary, the work of parents and other adults in the classroom to enhance learning opportunities for pupils'. Even this very restricted reference does not relate specifically to work with assistants, beyond the early years classroom. In Section D, a further reference appears in 'Other professional requirements', where those to be awarded QTS must demonstrate that they 'have established, during work in schools, effective working relationships with professional colleagues including, where applicable, associate staff'. This again is a reference, almost in passing and only 'where applicable', to all associate staff and one which does not acknowledge the need to demonstrate awareness of and the skills needed in leading a professional team in the classroom. In a revision of the 4/98 Standards it is to be hoped that this key area in the professional teaching role will be recognised and accorded due consideration.

INSET for established teachers

If initial teacher training is to include preparing teachers of the future for work with classroom assistants, then established teachers also need to be encouraged to recognise the need for appropriate training for them to effectively manage the role of the assistants under their direction. Those who trained for a system of autonomous teachers as the sole adult in 'their' classroom may have found difficulty in adapting to another adult's presence in 'their' territory. They may have found such a presence threatening or unnecessary and may have resisted sharing ownership of 'their' planning, teaching and assessment with another adult. Balshaw (1999) refers to the perception of an assistant as a 'spy in the classroom' and emphasises the need for assistants to feel valued as part of a working team.

Any such negative perceptions by teaching staff need to be addressed and the head teacher must recognise that teachers may be unsure how to manage assistants and may need to develop professional team working skills which were not required in the classrooms of the past. This chapter has suggested some strategies to this end, but the real key is in the attitudes of the teaching staff to the work of classroom assistants (and indeed to that of other support staff referred to throughout this text).

Summary

The skills and learning support demonstrated by classroom assistants clearly fall within a definition of teaching focused increasingly on helping pupils to learn more effectively. The management aspect of the class teacher's role encompasses specific responsibility for planning of pupils' learning experiences: the role of assistants is clearly central to the learning process. Furthermore, a more flexible approach to a review of learning encourages us to recognise that learning does not necessarily need to take place in a large group, in a traditional class setting. The planning can be more flexible to allow pupils to learn in the school library, in the IT room or in a designated classroom area as part of an individualised, planned programme, guided and supported by a range of appropriate adults, trained to provide specialist learning support.

References

Balshaw, M. (1999) *Help in the classroom*. 2nd edn. London: Fulton.

Clipson-Boyles, S. (1996) *Supporting language and literacy*. London: Fulton.

Department for Education and Employment (1998) *Teaching: High Status, High Standards*. Circular Number 4/98. London: DfEE.

Department for Education and Employment (2000a) *National standards for headteachers*. London: DfEE.

Department for Education and Employment (2000b) *Supporting the teaching assistant – a good practice guide*. London: DfEE.

Doyle, M. (1997) *The paraprofessional's guide to the inclusive classroom*. Baltimore: Paul H. Brookes.

Headington, R. (1997) *Supporting numeracy*. London: Fulton.

Her Majesty's Inspectorate (1992) *Non-teaching staff in schools*. London: HMSO.

Mills, J. and Mills, R.W (eds) (1995) *Primary school people: getting to know your colleagues*. London: Routledge.

Moyles, J. (1997) *Jills of All Trades*. London: ATL.

6

■ ■ ■

The special needs teaching assistant

Introduction

At the beginning of this book we identified various groups of people referred to as 'learning support assistants', 'classroom assistants', 'teaching assistants' and so on. Chapter 4 focuses on the trained Specialist Teacher Assistants (or their untrained equivalents) who deal mainly with groups of pupils in Key Stage 1, and who – at least for the present purposes – include nursery nurses. The other group, the focus of this chapter, are those who either assist groups of pupils with special educational needs or who are allocated on a 1:1 basis to an individual SEN pupil. These special needs teaching assistants (SNTAs) can span primary and secondary years and may or may not have backgrounds and training very similar to the support staff dealing with Key Stage 1. This group of support staff are overtly involved in learning and are employed specifically to support learning in classrooms. The most recent major study of this group was carried out by Farrell, Balshaw and Polat (2000).

The backgrounds of special needs teaching assistants

The people who found themselves drawn to this work came from many walks of life. In our sample they were exclusively female and this would be the typical pattern. This is not because men are uninterested in this role (our male laboratory technicians, for example, indicated that they gave – and enjoyed giving – transitory help to special needs pupils (*see* Chapter 8)), but because society prefers women in these relatively intimate roles.

In some cases their career path and training were tightly geared to the job operations they were called upon to undertake. (See Case Study 6.1.) Others had similar educational backgrounds and initial clerical or banking jobs before moving into this field – often, it would seem, to fit work in with family patterns. One had moved from being a laboratory technician to this job role.

Case Study 6.1
Mandy's story

I left school with ten 'O' levels and 2 'A' levels, and have since completed a Diploma in Pre-School Practice, and a City and Guilds Certificate in Learning Support, as well as holding a First Aid at Work Certificate.

I have attended courses on how to teach reading, the literacy hour, additional literacy support, working with children with speech and language difficulties, autism and behaviour support.

I started my working life as a clerical assistant for British Telecom, and then became, successively, a child minder, a playgroup leader, and a 1:1 special needs support assistant before becoming an ancillary.

The job description of a special needs teaching assistant

As expected, the job descriptions in our sample were varied. It was clear that some had been devised a long time ago (this was deduced from the yellowing of the paper on which they were printed and the kinds of reprographic systems used to produce them!) Others were detailed and up-to-date; though we took the precaution of asking our sample to comment on the matches and mismatches between the job descriptions and the realities of the role.

Case Studies 6.2 and 6.3 set out two contrasting job descriptions with notes from the post-holders on the relationship to their actual daily routine.

Case Study 6.2
Job description for a special needs teaching assistant at St Joseph's primary

Responsible to: The head teacher, the Special Needs Co-ordinator (SENCO), class teachers and the school secretary.

Purpose:

- To assist in providing a more effective teaching programme throughout the school by support to the special needs co-ordinator, class teachers and school secretary.
- To assist in providing a smooth administration of the school by carrying out administrative duties.

Key tasks:

(The head and SENCO will determine, within the total hours available, the priority to be given to the following tasks.)

- To give assistance in the classroom to children with learning difficulties under the close direction of the SENCO and the class teachers.
- To participate in school activities and attend appropriate staff meetings and in-service training courses.
- To attend special needs review meetings.
- To assist in the arrangement of medical and dental examinations.
- To assist in the compilation of such reports and records as may be required by the teaching staff, SENCO, head teacher and school secretary.
- Subject to qualification, be a provider of First Aid.
- To supervise the taking of 'prescribed' medicines under the head's direction.
- To care for sick and injured children, escorting them home or to hospital.
- To assist in contacting parents and completing accident report forms.
- To organise and provide (sic) refreshments for school visitors as needed.
- To assist in supervising children at playtimes.
- To set up and record radio and TV programmes for use by teachers.
- To assist in the upkeep and running of the library and resources area.
- To assist and support students from secondary schools on work experience in the school.

The post-holder comments:

The original job description was accurate...In addition I attend SEN planning meetings and am responsible for reporting faults and clearing problems with ICT resources...I do not attend special needs reviews or record radio and TV programmes.

Case Study 6.3
The job description of a 1:1 special needs teaching assistant in Nike secondary school

Responsible to: The head teacher through a class teacher.

Key tasks:

1 To assist the child on arrival at, and departure from, school.
2 To work on individual programmes with the child under the guidance of the class teacher, educational psychologist, physiotherapist, speech therapist etc.
3 To supervise the movement of the child in class and between classes.
4 To help toilet and supervise changing and emptying of appliances where necessary.
5 To carry out specific instructions as laid down by the Medical Officer to ensure the child's well-being.
6 To supervise the child at playtimes.
7 To supervise the child at meal times and give assistance where necessary.
8 To care for the physical welfare of the child, their training in personal hygiene and general safety standards.
9 To participate in school activities and to attend staff meetings and training courses as required.
10 To attend to such other duties as may be required.

The post-holder comments:

She carried out job roles 1, 2, 3, 8, 9, 10 but not 4, 5, 6, 7.

The effectiveness of the job role

Some SNTAs seemed to be content with the ways in which their jobs operated in the schools. Case Study 6.4, the only example – among all the support staff surveyed for this text – where an individual felt moved enough to write a spontaneous piece of prose about the improvements she would like to see in the role. She had typed this up before we met the survey sample and left it with us at the end of the session.

Case Study 6.4 raises a range of significant issues. You might care to consider their implications before moving on, particularly:

- The ethics of the contractual arrangements.
- The reasons why special needs assistants may not be made aware of lesson planning ahead of the lessons.

Case Study 6.4
Kate's paper on improvements in the job role

Greater liaison with the teachers would be a great bonus, so that we can pre-plan for the lessons, be more organised, and find out a bit more information on particular topics (if we are not familiar with them).

We would also prefer it if we were not treated like 'dogsbodies'. Some of us in this role feel that we are frequently ignored or treated like dirt. Obviously, the pupils start to pick up on body language and lack of communication.

When in support for health and safety, it would be a great help if we knew each individual pupil's guidelines, what each pupil is/is not allowed to do, and how to use equipment correctly.

This group of support staff are let down when it comes to having a union. Just recently they (unions) are becoming more popular, but our rights should be just the same as teachers' rights. If we have a problem, we should be able to contact someone who will be able to help us do something about it.

We do not have enough authority. We can't administer punishments, so the pupils know we have no sanctions. They see us just as office staff or helpers.

We are not happy about our pay. Last year I worked 15 hours a week for £105. I was offered another 15 hours weekly, and I thought 'Yes! Double the money'. In fact, that wasn't the case. Each time when you get a new contract your pay goes back to the scale you started on (in my case, four years ago). I now earn £150 less per month than I did! It's disgusting.

The communication between teaching staff and us is quite poor, and needs improvement.

- The possible reasons for poor communication between them and teaching staff.
- The issues of egalitarian treatment between teaching and support staff.
- The lack of proper briefing for these post-holders.

There is no way of knowing whether every detail in Kate's paper is objectively accurate – it is her construction of events. We can say, for example, that some unions (such as the Professional Association of Teachers) have established sections for support staff; though these tend to support the general proposition here of poor conditions of service. However, it is a disturbing tale and one to which we shall return.

Special needs teaching assistants talking about their roles

Our sample of post-holders were very articulate, as one would expect given the nature of their educational backgrounds. They spoke at length about the work that they did, indicating a high level of commitment and enjoyment overall. In the paragraphs that follow we have culled out some of the points that they themselves made about their work as in Case Studies 6.5, 6.6, 6.7 and 6.8.

Case Study 6.5
Jo's story

A good sense of humour is a must, lots of patience and understanding, and a large amount of TLC to share with pupils and staff.

I try to be each child's friend, teacher and confidante: to help each child build their confidence and self-worth. One child I worked with had attention deficit and hyperactivity syndrome and a very sad home life. He found school a very warm and friendly place. Every time I walked into the room his face lit up, which made it a pleasure working with him. It was a great boost to see him a more confident, happy and less naughty and disruptive child when he left primary school. I still hear from him, and he seems to be doing well in secondary.

I started as a parent helper in the school. I often feel the formal role is treated as a 'Jack of all trades'. Some teachers do not like support staff in their classrooms, but over the years I can see this attitude changing.

Case Study 6.6
Mollie's story

Support begins at 8.50 a.m., covers six lessons throughout the day, in any subject, for Years 7 to 9.

The thought of working in a secondary school (after a primary experience) was quite daunting at first, though the skills are much the same.

The most difficult incident has been when a Year 7 boy refused totally to co-operate. I had been advised that if he crawled under tables to avoid help just to leave him. Although he did not hide he did make it virtually impossible for me to support his learning! I used to ignore him for several lessons, and eventually he would come round.

The same boy is now in Year 8 and we have quite a good, positive relationship with only a rare blip.

Case Study 6.7
Carrie's story

For the first half-hour of the school day I have administration and preparation time. If we have parents who need help and support, this is the time when they come into school so some of this time may be taken up talking with them. If I have a problem about which I need to see the head, this is my chance. From then on I follow my timetable...

I wanted to do this job because I wanted to make a difference to a child's life. So many children feel failures if they cannot perform academically. I felt that some of these children needed support emotionally and some behaviour management, before they could see academic success. A lot of time is spent on emotional and behavioural support...

After three years in the post, I am just beginning to see my opinion being sought of what a child's needs are and what help we might give. I am beginning to feel my judgements are valued...

The most difficult incidents I face are when I feel that the tasks set to the children [in my care] are not appropriate. I am just beginning to feel secure enough in my role to be able to say to the teacher: 'I don't think that will work with Freddie', and to come up with an alternative...

I gained a great deal of satisfaction when a parent came to me and thanked me for the support I had given her child and her when a review had come as a shock to her. She had been trying to deny, for three years, that the child had a problem. I went to the review and sat next to her; she agreed with my assessment of the pupil's needs. Later she told me that it helped to 'know that someone who wasn't a teacher' could see her child had problems. Now she accepts support readily...

Case Study 6.8
Sadie's story

...Also, I help run a homework club, which is not just for pupils with special needs. It runs after school and at lunchtimes...

We contribute to learning. We make pupils' lives easier. We establish their weak points and support them when they are having difficulties. We are a sympathetic ear. We can simplify things for them, and explain things differently...

Without the contributions of the special needs support staff the pupils would not move forward and progress as quickly, so we make a difference to teachers' performance...

The pleasures and problems of the SNTA

These case studies have covered many of the motivating factors and satisfactions in the role: the following shortlist sums them up.

- Seeing pupils progress academically and socially.
- Building relationships that are conducive to learning.
- Giving confidence and improved self-image to pupils.
- Providing a background of social and psychological security.
- Supporting troubled parents.
- Being part of a team in a school community.

However, the sample we surveyed were not oblivious to the problems associated with the role:

- Lack of time to discuss individual pupils' progress or needs.
- Lack of status for the role.
- Difficulties in supporting a pupil without making him/her feel 'different'.
- Being allocated to jobs that are not directly supportive of special needs children.
- Not being given adequate information about pupils or schemes of work.
- Poor differentiation of work for special needs pupils by the teacher.
- Resentment by a minority of teachers of support staff presence.
- Non-involvement in curriculum/lesson planning.
- Lack of team identity in larger schools.

Case Study 6.9
Nicki's story

One of the most difficult incidents I have had to deal with happened when a newly qualified teacher was having a great deal of difficulty controlling his classes. He would shout all the time and lose his temper. He would take a child out of the class to admonish, sometimes for very long periods. I was then left on my own with the disruptive class...

I felt very uncomfortable, and in a difficult position as I knew it was not my place to discipline the students. I referred the incident to my SENCO as it happened almost every lesson for a time. She dealt with the matter. But I felt this was an important issue because it seemed to imply that I was not doing my job properly. I could not help the students I was there to look after, because the noise was too loud and they couldn't hear me. I grew to dread those lessons...

The problems outweighed the pleasures in sheer numbers, but not in the over-all 'psyche' of the post-holders. Some further difficulties emanated from the post-holders' views about the nature of opportunities for training and professional development, and it is to this topic that we now turn.

Sometimes, the work that fell to a special needs teaching assistant might be considered inappropriate, as is illustrated by the alarming Case Study 6.9.

In-service training and professional development for SNTAs

Most of the post-holders had received some degree of in-service training. Among these were computer courses, courses on behaviour management, child protection, speech and language and First Aid. Some of the support assistants felt that provision was satisfactory, but that courses tended to be sited a long distance from their work, and that – unlike teachers – they did not get release time. There was no monetary reward for further qualification, which was a dis-incentive. A few even alleged that the current availability of courses was a matter deliberately withheld from them by their managers because 'they could not be spared'. They were invited to most in-house training days for teachers, but they did not always find these directly relevant to their specific needs.

Training would develop the skills required for the role – these are many and various. Our respondents were able to articulate them at length:

- listening skills;
- patience;
- tolerance;
- a sense of humour;
- interpersonal skills;
- communication skills;
- empathy;
- flexibility;
- organisational skills;
- discretion and confidential working;
- teaching/learning skills with which to aid pupils;
- coaching skills;
- ability to analyse needs;
- assertiveness;
- specific knowledge (e.g. of subjects within which their work was located).

What our survey showed was that these post-holders did value training. They would have liked a nationally recognised route to an advanced qualification, one that was known and respected by teachers. They thought that such a course would comprise specific issues such as how to deal with disruptive behaviour, training on various medical conditions, and school-related training. Our post-holders wanted career opportunities: the chance to progress through experience and training into other specialisms – for example, a route into teaching or careers such as speech therapy. Trainers would need to be people who had done the job themselves and could talk from experience and people with specialist skills.

Summary

This was a demanding role. It was one very closely associated with learning and teaching. It brought the post-holders into closer and more prolonged contact with teachers than most support roles. It made them more critical of teachers and teaching than other support staff. It required a range of very specific and valuable skills. Yet it was undervalued by society and, on occasion, even by the schools themselves.

Reference

Farrell, P., Balshaw, M. and Polat, F. (2000) *The management, role and training of learning support assistants*. London: HMSO.

7
■ ■ ■

Managing the special needs teaching assistant

Introduction

In Chapter 6 the view was expressed quite forcibly (mainly but not exclusively through Kate's story, *see* page 93) that SNTAs had some significant reservations about their conditions of service. Despite this, they were not unhappy about the management in their individual schools. Indeed, on a seven-point scale (1 = high) they rated their management in the range 2–4 with an average score of 2.5. This speaks volumes for their school-based managers and for the intrinsic satisfaction associated with this job role.

Managerial practice

Typically, SNTAs met with their managers daily, though there were exceptions and weekly and termly meetings were recorded. It may be that an insufficient distinction was drawn between meetings of a formal nature (e.g. to discuss policy or identify achievements) and the day-to-day encounters about immediate tasks to be completed. Thus the following comments set the tone:

Weekly SEN meeting with SENCO about possible timetable changes or details of specific pupils' needs. Daily as required.

We work in a very small SEN office and the SENCO is very much 'down to earth'. If there is anything important, or even not so important, we all communicate daily at lunch, break, or after school. We have an SEN meeting once a month.

In practice, the guidance given to these post-holders was very varied in its immediacy and intensity, as can be gleaned from a sample of their responses to our survey:

I feel I know exactly where I should be and what I should be doing. I am given information about students and their difficulties.

My management is very effective...problems are sorted out almost straight away...

On the whole, every effort is made to use my skills in particular areas whilst maintaining involvement in all subjects. My SENCO is very experienced and knowledgeable and I believe uses me to maximise the best of my ability.

IEPs give me a basic structure and some guidelines to follow. Sometimes I find it difficult to fit these individual programmes into the daily timetable.

I am usually left to plan my own timetable once I have been given statistics on children I am to support. This is passed to the head for agreement. I do not have any appraisal, which I would like to have. I am not always sure who to answer to as I have three line managers.

The management is ineffective. I often have problems with my statemented child's time, but find it difficult to get help, advice...sometimes I am given a group and the teachers don't know what to do with (the children)...I need clearer planning and instructions.

This rather varied picture demonstrates the complete range of managerial practice from best to worst. In assessing the qualities of an ideal or good manager, however, the post-holders in our survey were quite clear what types of characteristics were effective, as shown in Table 7.1.

Table 7. 1 A good manager of special needs teaching assistants

A good manager should be:

- supportive;
- easy to approach, talk to;
- able to judge the assistant's strengths and work to them;
- a good communicator;
- professionally credible;
- honest;
- available;
- able to delegate effectively.

When assessing the strengths and weaknesses of their current management, similar strong messages arose from the survey. (*See* Table 7.2.)

In the freehand comments made by our respondents on these issues the view was expressed that the post-holders wanted to be made to feel more a part of

Table 7.2 Strengths and weaknesses in managers of special needs teaching assistants in our survey

Strengths

He/she:

provides plenty of suitable work for the SNTA;

delegates responsibility;

recognises a job well done;

is supportive;

is available for consultation;

holds regular planning meetings;

is a good and frequent communicator;

produces a relaxed and friendly atmosphere in the unit;

understands the value of praise for employees.

Weaknesses

He/she:

is too busy;

does not get to grips with problems;

doesn't organise paperwork well;

takes advantage of employees' goodwill;

doesn't maintain continuity in the employee's role;

doesn't plan ahead sufficiently or brief the SNTA.

the school team. They saw better forward planning as a route to this end. The fact that this cluster of responses was made by a group of workers who were basically content with their jobs and had high job satisfaction makes them all the more pertinent.

In the sections that follow we have tried to extract and build on these messages to suggest positive action by managers to ensure the effectiveness of special needs assistants' work.

Extending the work of special needs teaching assistants

Before moving on to the management issues, however, there is a postscript to this consideration of the SNTA role that it is important to add.

While it is unusual to find special needs assistants working with pupils other than those with learning difficulties, there is a small but growing trend (emanating in part from the Government's Excellence in Cities initiative) to place such post-holders with the more able. This is a trend to be welcomed. Very able children, like the least able, have very specific learning needs; and educators have an obligation to meet these.

In the management strategies that follow the language refers to the most common work of the special needs assistant – i.e. those with learning difficulties. However, all the strategies could apply equally to a special needs assistant in the support of an able pupil.

Strategy 7.1 *Forward planning*

Our special needs teaching assistants identified their involvement in pupils' learning as a key role. Yet they felt that their effectiveness was hampered because there was often insufficient forward planning in the school, or planning to which they were party. The first management strategy, therefore, is to look at the role of forward planning, and the part of SNTAs within it, in order to promote pupils' learning opportunities. It may be helpful to use the following questions to explore school practice.

What is the involvement of special needs assistants in:

- long term planning (i.e. syllabus construction, academic year planning)?
- medium term planning (i.e. term plans)?
- short term planning (i.e. for individual lessons, for the week ahead)?

During lessons, can SNTAs draw the attention of teaching staff to difficulties emerging for the pupils in their specific charge?

In implementing IEPs for pupils, are SNTAs:

- afforded an opportunity to contribute to their formulation?
- involved in monitoring their effectiveness?

Does the presence of the special needs assistant inhibit the teacher from working with special needs pupils within the class?

- who monitors these classroom processes?
- how are they monitored?

How do SNTAs convey their knowledge of pupils' strengths, weaknesses and progress to teachers to ensure these are taken into account in future planning?

Do SNTAs have a role in the assessment of and reporting on, pupils and their progress?

Strategy 7.2 *Considering individual education plans*

If the purpose of the special needs assistant is to support a child or group of children with special learning needs of some kind, then the key to unlocking the door of that support is the Individual Education Plan (IEP). For this reason it is critical that SNTAs have a major role in the process that generates and evaluates these plans.

What is the process within the school through which IEPs are compiled:

- who is consulted?
- when?
- how often?

Who compiles the plan?

What chance do the SNTAs involved have:

- to comment on the plan's content?
- to monitor its value as each term unfolds?
- to assess and review the plan and form its next stage?

To what extent are SNTAs involved in:

- meeting with parents?
- hearing parents' perspectives at first hand?
- feeding back directly about children's progress?
- having an input to the school's 'public face' for special needs provision?

Strategy 7.3 *Undertaking self-assessment for managers of SNTAs*

Managers of SNTAs need particular qualities. These have been identified by our respondents on page 100. All those with management responsibility for special needs assistants in the school would benefit from this self appraisal exercise and sharing the outcomes with one another. At the end of this process the senior manager should take whatever action is necessary to sharpen up management for this group of post-holders.

DO YOU...

- provide plenty of suitable work for the SNTA?
- delegate responsibility appropriately? (Give an example)
- recognise a job well done? (Quote a specific incident)

continues

Strategy 7.3 *continued*

- act supportively? (When? How?)
- make yourself available for consultation? (When?)
- hold regular planning meetings? (How often?)
- act as a good and frequent communicator?
- produce a relaxed and friendly atmosphere in the unit?
- understand the value of praise for employees? (Example?)
- organise paperwork well?
- get to grips with problems?
- maintain continuity in the employee's role?
- plan ahead sufficiently and brief the SNTA?
- say you are too busy to deal with SNTAs' concerns?
- take advantage of employees' goodwill?

Strategy 7.4 *Providing appraisal for SNTAs*

Too often among the post-holders in our survey we heard expressions like 'dogsbodies' and 'an extra pair of hands'. These expressions suggested that in some cases, the work of the post-holders was seen more as a way of lightening teachers' responsibilities than as a fully integrated part of the learning team. It was therefore not surprising to find a desire among many of our respondents to have their work subjected to appraisal.

If you do not have one already, use the following questions to plan to put an appraisal system in operation for special needs assistants. If you do have a system, adapt the following questions to review its effectiveness. (You will have local schemes in operation to assist you in answering these questions.)

- Who will conduct the appraisal for SNTAs?
- Who will introduce the system to post-holders and allay any fears?
- How often will the appraisal take place?
- Under what rules and guidelines will it operate?
- What will be its intentions and objectives?
- Who will be party to any outcomes?
- How will any needs identified by the appraisal be met and financed?

Strategy 7.5 *Establishing a professional development structure*

A recognised problem for special needs support staff is that there is no professional development structure available to them and that career paths are limited. It is suggested, therefore, that effective management will attempt to mitigate the worst effect of such a situation. Appraisals (Strategy 7.4) may be the first step in this process. The questions below should help managers review provisions and seek effective support for their post-holders.

- Do newly appointed SNTAs have a proper induction programme to the school? Who runs this? Who else is involved?
- Has the school a mentoring system for SNTAs? Who acts as mentors? How does the scheme work? Is it effective? How does it link (or not link) to appraisal?
- Is there any systematic in-house training of SNTAs?
- Do SNTAs attend the school's training days? All of them? Selected days? None? On what criteria are choices made? By whom?
- Is there a programme of professional development available from the LEA or a similar private provider to which the SNTA can be directed?
- What opportunities are available to SNTAs to gain access to accredited courses and forge a career path? For example, do they attend local Further Education institutions, have membership of organisations like the College of Teachers, or follow Open University course units?
- Does the school offer support for SNTA professional training? Release? Time in lieu? Help with course fees? Nothing?
- In answering these questions, what view have you formed of the effectiveness of your school's management of the professional development of special educational needs assistants?

Strategy 7.6 *Considering what kind of training SNTAs need*

If training has not been a high priority for special needs assistants it may be that their needs are not well known. Appraisal is one management route to finding out (*see* Strategy 7.4), and moving to a training policy is a useful step for managers (Strategy 7.5). However, post-holders may need more immediate prompts to help them articulate their needs. This proforma may help them and you as the manager.

To: SNTAs at Wingate School

The school is interested to try to fulfil some of your training needs. To help us in this process we need to establish what training you feel you would most benefit
continues

Strategy 7.6 *continued*

from, and to have some idea of your priorities. Please identify with a tick which of the following topics you would find useful. Then re-visit the list marking with the numbers 1–5 your top priorities (1 = high).

Behaviour management

Child development

Classroom management

Developing and using IEPs

Developing resource materials

Equal opportunities issues

Legislation and special education

Reflecting on, and improving, your own practice

Specific forms of learning difficulty (which?)

Supporting reading

Supporting basic literacy

Supporting basic numeracy

Supporting specific subject/s (which?)

Working with parents

Other topics (please list them)

Strategy 7.7 *Building the school team with SNTAs*

We saw in Chapter 6 and the early part of this chapter that SNTAs did not always feel part of the school team. The strategies in this chapter have tried to address this issue by: giving post-holders some joint responsibilities with teachers, recognising and meeting their training needs, considering their professional development, and valuing their specific skills and contributions. This strategy gives the manager the opportunity to reflect on the success of this process.

The learning level

To what extent do you think SNTAs are now part of the team that delivers learning in your school?

Are you secure in the view that they are respected by pupils?

Are they valued by staff and treated accordingly?

The school management level

Does the work of SNTAs receive due recognition from school managers (head, deputy, SENCO)? In what ways?

Is there now a professional training and development structure in place that values their professionalism in the role?

Is their work sufficiently acknowledged in the school's dealings with outside agencies (LEA, Ofsted etc.)?

The 'beyond-school' level

Do the key stakeholders from beyond the school gates understand and value the SNTAs and their work?

Have governors been properly briefed? Are policies in place?

Is the SNTA role carefully explained to parents?

8
■ ■ ■

Laboratory technicans

Introduction

Of all the roles identified in this text, that of the laboratory technician is probably the most 'traditional' in the sense that it has been in existence for a long time and most people, whatever their age, will remember them from their own schools. Yet the role has been subject to some changes, and it might be instructive to begin with one lab technician's reflections (Case Study 8.1).

Case Study 8.1
Reflections on the laboratory assistant's role: Jane's story

The typical day starts with me arriving at about 8 a.m. The labs are usually tidy from the day before. The equipment for the first lesson is prepared and put into the labs and I do any photocopying that the staff members have left while they are at their morning briefing.

During the rest of the day I prepare equipment one lesson ahead. It is difficult to prepare any further ahead than that because there isn't enough equipment to go round if practicals require similar items.

The qualities needed for a technician are:

- the ability to work efficiently;
- learning not to panic;
- methodical working practice paced over the day.

My motivation is the thought that a well-prepared practical is a learning aid to all the pupils. Sometimes, when technicians are involved in presenting the practicals, they can make the experiments work better than the teachers can.

The role could be improved by having plenty of equipment, decent storage areas and a well equipped prep room – probably one designed by a technician!

The main contribution that I think I make to the school is bringing about dialogue and involvement between departments. When I first started, most other teachers saw the science technician as a 'dogsbody'. Now they understand that we contribute to the science department and sometimes more widely. The job is developing into more of a 'manager of the laboratory areas' role. At the same time that the role has become more central, the gap in salary between technicians and teachers has increased.

I think the job should develop by technicians sharing goals with teachers and they should help to keep up a well-organised department with good communications that other departments can emulate.

Who are the lab technicians?

The sample of lab technicians who contributed to our survey had interesting educational backgrounds. A mixed group of men and women, they felt that schools were still, in some ways at least, a civilised arena in which to work. For example, one could apply for another job without being sacked! There were strong hints, too, that the school hours were an attraction – even though most of the technicians started work well before the start of the pupils' school day.

Education played a part in their choice of role. Among men, it was not uncommon to find former military personnel – often NCOs – who have been trained on-the-job but who don't have civilian qualifications that can be traded easily. One respondent specifically mentioned a personal school record marred by dyslexia, that was rescued by an electrical apprenticeship in the Royal Air Force. For men, a service background seems to fit well with the organisational qualities needed in this role.

Important aspects of the lab technician's job

Our survey identified a number of roles associated with the job that the post-holders rated as important. They thought that their availability throughout the day was an important quality in the role: unlike teachers, they were not bound by the timetable and could make choices about priorities for their attention. A key issue was maintaining safe working practices, and they often acted as the school's Health and Safety representatives. Surprisingly high on the agenda of their roles was the task of helping pupils. In particular, they found themselves supporting the work of the less able by explaining things and giving extra attention.

Lab technicians were also resource people, and the problems they faced had to do with maximising scarce resources and getting the best learning use out of them. They felt they often spotted problems not foreseen by teachers, and solved them seamlessly before they happened in lessons. They claimed a considerable role in helping, advising and supporting newly qualified teachers – and even went so far as to use the word 'mentoring' in that context.

The issue of resources resurfaced. They often manufactured equipment to save the cost of purchasing ready-made apparatus. They moved things around to get best use. They carried out the 'house-keeping' function of the department. To a lesser extent they undertook administrative tasks like photocopying – even maintaining the photocopiers to keep the system running – a role in which they felt some obligation as science departments are volume users of this kind of material. Other frustrations included the breakdown of PCs, so that lessons could not proceed according to plan.

In terms of problems and disadvantages in the role, there was a feeling that schools were not well resourced for their work. The lack of money led to a 'make-do-and-mend' culture that did not enhance learning, and to a lack of proper space in which to operate. Recent syllabus changes were a problem for them: teachers did not always plan far enough ahead because of these. This meant that apparatus was often not requested far enough in advance, which put pressure on technicians.

Teachers were also criticised in other ways. Time was wasted when the wrong equipment was ordered. But worse, technicians were unhappy that when bad lesson planning or poor discipline meant that items ordered were not used, scarce resources were ineffectively used.

Technicians' communication within schools was not always good. They felt that support staff were often missed out of the chain of communication. Some technicians were not invited to, or did not attend, departmental meetings – which led to a poorer understanding of what was needed from them. They would have liked conditions of service that allowed flexi-time in order to deal with peaks and troughs of demand: examination periods were a significant peak period.

Worst of all was not being invited or allowed to attend training sessions alongside teachers. This was partly because, unlike teachers, there was no supply cover, but partly because the school did not always see the relevance of training to their job functions.

So lab technicians have quite clear views about their contributions to the life of the school, centring around stewarding resources, ensuring efficient operation and availability of equipment, supporting newly qualified teachers, and supporting the work of pupils – especially the less able. Do their job descriptions reflect these roles?

Job descriptions

Tables 8.1 and 8.2 provide two sample job descriptions from our survey of this job role.

Table 8.1 The job description of lab technician Ros

Responsible to: Senior Technician

- To prepare equipment and materials for practical lessons and demonstrations.
- To clear away, wash up and tidy equipment.
- To maintain a safe environment in laboratories.
- To maintain stock control of chemicals and equipment.
- To update the inventory and to list any ordering requirements.
- To arrange photocopying needs with the school office.
- To give practical support in science practical lessons as requested and required.
- To check and maintain general science equipment in a safe and good working order.
- To purchase items from petty cash when required.
- To give assistance to other departments: food technology, art, PE and D & T, when requested, subject to time availability.
- To collect monies from pupils for departmental events.
- To assist on school trips if required.
- To help with organising open evenings.

Table 8.2 The job description of lab technician Bob

(This post is described as Senior Laboratory Assistant. NB: inconsistencies of presentation are retained from the original)

Reporting to: the Head Teacher through the Head of (unspecified) Department

Organising the support services for science teaching in the school.
To be responsible for the standards of work for the other laboratory technical staff and for the suitable allocation of tasks and areas of responsibility.
To be responsible for ensuring that newly appointed technicians are settled into the department and informed about departmental matters.
To be responsible for assisting with the on the job training of junior technical staff complementary to their further education.
Supervising time-keeping and attendance.
Preparing the materials, stock and standard solutions, specimens and apparatus required for demonstrations and practical work. Replenishing re-agent bottles as required.

continues

Table 8.2 *continued*

Setting up and testing demonstration experiments and ensuring that they will work satisfactorily.

Recovery of residues. Preparation of distilled/deionised water.

Sterilisation of apparatus.

Care of animals and plants kept for observation and experimental purposes, both in terms and during vacations.

Cleaning of apparatus (e.g. glassware) used by teaching staff, and by pupils if it is difficult or dangerous.

Reporting items for repair etc. to equipment services.

Maintaining apparatus and equipment in good working order, and carrying out repairs within the capabilities of the post-holder.

Construction or modification of laboratory apparatus.

Assisting in the construction and preparation of audio-visual aids, and maintaining the AVA equipment used by the science department.

Testing new experiments and assisting in devising new practical work.

Safe disposal of biological and chemical residues and other waste material.

Inspection maintenance and correct use of safety equipment.

When trained, first aid treatment of minor laboratory injuries and the maintenance of first aid equipment in the laboratory area.

Operating an efficient system for stocking, storing, transporting and distributing all items used in the science department.

Operating laboratory documentation systems: cataloguing, filing etc.

Making petty cash purchases.

Being responsible to the Head of Science for the maintenance and upkeep of the science laboratories, and advising on any improvements.

Operating and administering stock control and ordering procedures, obtaining quotations, checking deliveries, co-ordinating common stock between sections.

Maintaining a good stock of necessary materials and keeping legal records (alcohols, poisons etc.).

Any other duties which may be reasonably be regarded as within the nature of the post.

A range of slightly unlikely job roles emerged during this exercise and it may be of interest to record a sample of these:

- operate IT for teachers;
- instruct teachers in the use of IT;
- look after supply teachers during the absence of teachers;
- deal with indiscipline of pupils when a teacher is not present;
- assist the school matron;

- sell items to pupils (books, pens, pencils, rulers);
- collect and prepare items from abattoir.

This is the way it is – how would they like it to be?

The lab technicians in our survey were clear about the ways in which their jobs worked in practice, but it was interesting to listen to their commentaries on this, and on how they felt that the job might develop. In Case Study 8.2 we have reconstructed one of their conversations from notes made at the time. It runs as follows:

Case Study 8.2
Conversation with lab technician John

To do this job well I need to be flexible and knowledgeable (sometimes, it seems, about everything in the Universe!). But I am motivated by personal pride in what I do, and the satisfaction I get from the job. I enjoy the job, though I feel that quite a lot of my time gets wasted – which prevents me from giving even more to the school. Teachers could sometimes do more to help themselves, and me – little things, like shutting drawers for example. It would be good to work in new and up-dated labs, and with some newer equipment.

I advance pupils' learning by freeing up teachers' time so they can do more teaching. But, from time to time, I have also taught pupils: for example, a double lesson of First Aid to the Health and Social Care sixth form group. But I would like to extend that aspect of the role, working alongside the teacher in the classroom during practical sessions to support students. I think sometimes the teaching would be more efficient if I had an input.

Technology has made the job more efficient. We have a security radio system now and we have also gained an assistant matron which makes working safer.

At present we are a split-site school, but that will change and should save time and promote learning.

The sentiments expressed here were widespread. Other issues were raised in our dialogues with lab technicians. There was a general view that the role should be more classroom-based, and some post-holders felt that they were used by pupils as a pastoral resource: less threatening than teachers and easier to talk to than parents. One respondent identified a trouble-shooting role between feuding staff members and having to act as go-between and appeaser. Another respondent reported not having a job description at all – this in what was certainly the best-equipped school in the sample and one of the most demanding.

Training for the role of laboratory technician

Our survey revealed a wide range of people drawn into this role. As well as the stereotypical ex-service male, there were females from the health services, people with qualifications such as ONC medical laboratory sciences, nurses/midwives and holders of City & Guilds technical certificates.

On the job training and professional up-dating for lab technicians was capricious. Our survey showed that one technician had had ten days training through CLEAPSE in a four-and-a-half year employment period. A longer serving individual had been on a one-week course and a one-year part-time course in 11 years of service, for which the school provided support in the form of release time, travel costs and fees. But a technician with 16 years' service had attended just five day or half-day events, run by the Association for Science Education.

Some of the reasons for non-attendance at courses were the paucity of provision, inaccessibility of venues and lateness of notification of the events. Some events were useful (though not necessarily related to the immediate role) for example, courses on child abuse, drug awareness and special educational needs. There was some familiarity with courses on National Curriculum requirements on a need-to-know basis. A few courses on management training had been accessed.

Our lab technicians would have liked training to have been compulsory, on the pattern of the training days for teachers; they suggested that accreditation should be attached to courses, and that they should take place in work time. But trainers needed to understand the job roles. There was a need for some means of formal progression from technician to senior technician for those who wanted it (and some did not). In this way they felt that their work would become more professionally recognised.

9

■ ■ ■

Managing laboratory technicians

Introduction

Chapter 8 has already discussed some of the issues that affect the work of this group of post-holders and may have a bearing on their management. Specifically, it has been noted that much of the role is resource-based, that some time is spent supporting individual pupils' learning, and that there may be scope for extending the role in practical lessons to that of teaching assistant.

In our survey, the laboratory technicians we spoke to rated their management highly; on a seven point scale (1 = high) the scores ranged from one to three – a very positive result. The most commonly identified line managers were the Head of Science and the school bursar. Meetings between laboratory technicians and their line managers tended to happen either daily or weekly but the post-holders felt that their managers were always on call for them.

Most policy relating to the role came out of departmental meetings. Specific instructions were verbal or written, and the written communications were often by e-mail. Those technicians who were dual-managed felt that they were effectively managed, though one post-holder commented that the bursar's management was good while the Head of Department was a poor manager. There was a minority feeling of 'being left to get on' by managers. Two of our technicians were managers of other post-holders and their comments on this were interesting:

I have to manage the department and two technicians, and the only measure I have of my efficiency is that I have had no complaints.

(Lab technician Paul)

I manage a team of four technicians. I communicate with them continuously. I am always available to them to discuss difficulties etc. I take a 'hands on' approach and do not ask them to do anything I am not prepared to do. I also encourage them in their personal career development. I am new to the job, so it's early to make an assessment of success. But to date I have received only compliments on the improved service and the organisation of the prep room.

(Lab technician Peter)

Strengths and weaknesses in the management of lab technicians

The lab technicians in our survey had fairly clear ideas about what made for strengths and weaknesses in management. These are listed in Table 9.1.

Table 9.1 Strengths and weaknesses in managing lab technicians

Strengths

- patience;
- being able to smooth over difficult situations;
- clarity of decision making;
- consultative attitudes;
- openness to new ideas;
- open door policy;
- giving a degree of self-management to the post-holder.

Weaknesses

- lack of communication;
- indecision;
- poor organisation;
- autocratic attitudes;
- being too busy.

Translating views of management into reality

So our post-holders had a keen sense of effective management in their specific situations. The need is to turn their aspirations into reality through relevant managerial strategies. Though job descriptions did not feature in the management issues raised by our respondents, a scrutiny of their job descriptions suggested to us that it might be a good place for a manager to begin.

Strategy 9.1 *Scrutinising lab assistants' job descriptions*

In Tables 8.1 and 8.2 we published two examples of job descriptions for lab technicians, along with a sample of other job operations culled from a number of other job descriptions given to us.

Look back over these items.

- Are all the items that feature in this collection appropriate?
- Do they reflect a good use of technicians' time?
- What would you keep and what would you leave out?

Now collect the job descriptions of lab technicians who work in your school. Comb through them to try to establish whether, in your opinion, they reflect accurately the job you want these post-holders to do.

- Which job operations listed there are appropriate?
- What would you remove? What would you add?
- What scope is there for giving your lab technicians more opportunities to support pupils' learning directly?

If you were to appoint new lab technicians and could begin by rewriting the job descriptions from scratch, would kind of people would you appoint, and what jobs would you want them to do?

Strategy 9.2 *Reviewing resources*

One of the complaints of the lab technicians in our survey was that equipment was so poor or in such short supply that it held up their work and made teaching less efficient.

Ask the appropriate department/s to inventory their current stock of equipment. As part of the process there is a need to establish what:

- is new and efficient;
- is old and ineffectual;
- should be written off.

Now ask the same department/s to produce an 'ideal' inventory – what they would need for the work to run smoothly at all times.

Cost the improvements that would need to be made from 'actual' to 'ideal'.

Look at ways of funding the transition (e.g. introducing zero-based budgeting in the school, contributions from the PTA, sponsorship).

Put in place a plan to move the equipment acquisition of the school on during a pre-determined period of time.

Involve governors in the process and elicit their support.

Strategy 9.3 *Freeing up teachers*

One of the things that lab technicians told us was that they supported learning in the school by carrying out tasks that freed teachers to spend more time with the pupils. However, there was little attempt to quantify the extent or the benefits of this process. This strategy asks the stake-holders involved to give some systematic thought to the process.

Ask the teachers and the lab technicians to review the ways in which lab technicians currently carry out functions that free teachers to spend more time with pupils.

Most of the time it is likely to be as a result of lab technicians setting up equipment so that teachers don't have to, or carrying out manual operations to the same end (duplicating, cleaning, tidying, ensuring safe practices in labs).

In what other ways might lab technicians free teachers' time?

- By tracking down resources?
- By using IT to translate teachers' ideas into visual aids?
- By carrying out administrative roles, such as recording marks and assessments?
- By developing short presentations such as safety briefings and taking responsibility for delivering them, e.g. to new groups of students?
- By overseeing homework clubs and similar self-study activities?

What ideas do the technicians in your school develop when presented with this set of possibilities?

Strategy 9.4 *Supporting the less able*

One of the job operations that lab technicians said they carried out was supporting the less able pupils. Some schools might feel that this is an inappropriate role. However, the argument of this text is that – subject to the suitability of the post-holder – the job of supporting learning is one that falls appropriately to support staff of all kinds. However, no member of a support team should be left, or asked, to carry out such a role without specific help and guidance.

- Take steps to establish whether lab technicians in your school are spending some of their time supporting the learning of less able students.
- Make a policy decision about the role of lab technicians in the learning support role for the less able and the functions they might carry out.

- If it is decided to use lab technicians in this way, assess (in consultation with them) the kinds of training they might need.
- Look to in-house training to help them in their work (e.g. a course run by the Head of Special Needs, a short secondment to work alongside a special needs teacher, some discussion about the role with other special needs support staff).
- Discover what training exists for special needs support staff in your LEA or locality. Make opportunities for the lab technician to access training.
- Ask the lab technician to keep records (a kind of reflective log is useful) of his/her contacts with special needs youngsters and how they were assisted.
- Consider the benefits of multi-skilling in this context, and how the principle might be applied to other contexts.

Strategy 9.5 *Supporting practicals*

Most of the lab technicians in our survey felt that they provided a very efficient service in setting up apparatus for practical sessions. They also expressed the view that they had more familiarity with the equipment than most teachers, and were therefore able to make practical sessions work effectively. They indicated a wish to be more involved, alongside teachers, in the presentation of practical sessions.

Consider the feasibility and implications of using lab technicians more often to assist in the presentation of practical work. Here are just some of the issues that might need to be addressed:

- the qualifications of the technician/s;
- the fluency and ability to communicate of the technician/s;
- the benefits/drawbacks of having a second adult present during the lesson;
- the different perspectives that might be offered in some practical work by 'experienced others' working alongside, and under the guidance of, the teacher;
- the implications of using technicians in this way for other job operations they might have to carry out;
- the specific strengths and abilities of individual technicians and where they might make a significant contribution to learning by pupils;
- the potential for role modelling for pupils not intending to make a career in the academic aspects of the subject;
- the potential for role confusion and conflict in less well organised departments and for less secure teachers.

Strategy 9.6 *Clarifying the roles of the lab technician and the newly qualified teacher*

A surprising outcome of our survey of lab technicians was the number of times our post-holders claimed to be involved in 'supporting', 'guiding' and even 'mentoring' newly qualified teaching staff. The exact parameters of this role were not spelt out in any detail, but one suspects that the actual job operations would, typically, include:

- introducing the new teacher to the lab environment of the school;
- setting out the standard ordering and organisational procedures;
- advising on apparatus and experiments;
- induction in safety procedures;
- acting in an affective capacity as a pastoral carer (being less threatening or judgemental than a senior teacher such as a Head of Department).

In some cases it was clear that the Head of Science effectively delegated responsibility for the new teacher to an experienced technician.

A better procedure might be to have a policy and set of procedures for the involvement of lab technicians in the development of new teachers. To this end, a manager might:

- identify as a matter of policy a formal role for the lab technician in the induction of new staff into the laboratory environment and into issues of safety and day-to-day procedures;
- provide some induction time in which these things can happen;
- identify the technician's advisory role in supporting the new teacher's experimental work;
- clarify the duties of the Head of Department in the professional oversight of the new teacher.

Strategy 9.7 *Providing training for the lab technician*

A strong element in the commentaries provided by our sample of lab technicians was a view that training was not provided or was inappropriate to need. It seems that, to satisfy this group of post-holders, some urgent attention needs to be paid to the issue. What follows are just some possible ideas for making training more widespread and more effective.

- Use appraisal, or pre-appraisal exercises, to establish the lab technician's perceived needs for training.
- Consult the Head of Department about his/her view of the training needs of the lab technician/s.

Reach an agreed list of training priorities, which may need to balance training in:

- operating equipment;
- theoretical knowledge;
- resources for learning;
- budgeting and stock control;
- learning support.

Cost the agreed list, and set some time-scales.

Consider the career development of the individual/s concerned: for example, would it be better to provide long-term, accredited training, or short-term training for immediate tasks?

If there is not a tradition of training support staff outside the school, look at the mechanisms and implications for day-time release and cover.

If there is not a tradition of support staff attending staff training days, consider what elements of the training programme might be appropriate to lab technicians.

10
■ ■ ■

The technical officer

Getting the flavour of the job

In Chapter 1 we indicated that the role of technical officers in schools was changing. In so far as such support staff had a history of employment in schools their roles had tended to be confined to setting up audiovisual equipment, maintaining it and undertaking the necessary stock control to keep it running. Occasionally they would instruct teaching staff or even students in its use. The advent of the computer, however, has changed the complexion of the role.

The technical officers we spoke to were clear about the dimensions of their roles and, although drawn from very different schools (primary, secondary, City Technology Colleges) they shared similar job roles and endured similar problems in them. They agreed among themselves that their highest priority was to keep the school network running: without it, learning ground to a halt. That meant that an aspect of the role was trouble-shooting. This was predictable enough. Less obvious was the fact that they were all involved in data analysis – usually the analysis of various elements of the management data on which the school administration depended.

They all shared the view that programming was an important part of the role – this element has a direct bearing on learning. They felt that they were often involved one-to-one with students and the outcome of these encounters was the raising of student achievement. Often, this student contact came as a follow-up to the student's interactions with a teacher. The student would encounter a problem in using the computer or in trying to glean information through it, the teacher would be unable to solve the problem and the technical officer formed a rear-guard in the facilitation of learning through his/her greater expertise. (Interestingly, though we collected no statistics on the issue, both men and women were employed in the ICT support staff roles, and one sensed a growing female involvement, even at the most senior levels, in what might once have been thought of as a male preserve.)

In a way, learning in the ICT area was different from learning in other areas of the curriculum. Conventionally, in traditional subjects the teacher was the expert, the students were the learners and any support staff were there to give specific help at a relatively low level. However, in ICT, teachers and students often learned together. The students were, quite commonly, more at home in the medium than the teachers – it was the support personnel who brought high levels of expertise. The technical officer was required to deliver instruction, knowledge and skills to both teachers and learners.

This expertise was needed in the production of resources as well as in their smooth operation. GNVQs have accelerated this need. Technical officers might deliver formal training for staff to help them cope. They had to have a curriculum understanding, because curriculum was now on-line. New staff were part of their remit – they had to bring them up to speed on the school's IT operations. Technical officers were a vital link in the chain of curriculum delivery (*see* Figure 10.1).

As well as direct support to the learning of students, technical officers were an indirect source of learning because they often instructed the teachers and enabled them to deliver their teaching more effectively. They were responsible for investigating the availability of, and collecting, computer-based resources – so influenced the learning available in this medium. They were involved in discussions about how IT might be integrated into the curriculum.

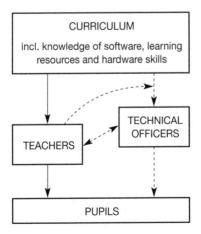

Figure 10.1 The role of technical officers in curriculum delivery

Of course, there were frustrations in the job. Some of these, inevitably, were related to lack of resources. Equipment was expensive, maintenance more so and production of learning resources had financial implications. But cash was not the main concern of the technical officers, especially if they had control of their own budgets. They were more frustrated by staff who did not report faults on the system, so that early trouble-shooting was not possible. They were concerned that teachers often had insufficient training in and certainly insufficient understanding of, the principles of computer-based learning. The Government came in for particular criticism, not because of its lack of financial aid, but because – for example – the government's recognised suppliers of services were so poor. One company, in particular, was named over and over again as being inept and incompetent in delivering on its contracts.

Another irritant for this group of support staff was one that recurs throughout this volume: the failure of other staff in the school to understand, recognise and value their role. Like bursars and others, these post-holders wanted to feel part of the school set-up, to play a part in the provision both of learning and of quality outcomes for students, and to be recognised for their contribution. In many cases (at least in mainstream schools) they were merely 'non-teachers' and that rankled.

Who are the technical officers?

The following case studies reconstruct the CVs of three very different kinds of people who have become technical officers. They are chosen because they are not 'typical' – though we suspect that being untypical in this role is typical!

Case Study 10.1
Technical officer Babs

Until 18 months ago I was employed as a Learning Support Assistant at this same school. I have no previous experience of computer networks, and have had no training. I was asked to take over as network technician when a previous teacher (who had carried out this job) left. I do have a good knowledge of computing, but I have had to teach myself a lot very quickly, mainly through telephone technical help and from handbooks. I can cope with most software problems, but my knowledge of the hardware is limited. We have an RM network, and the company runs courses, but they are too expensive for the school to send me!

Case Study 10.2
Technical officer Tom

I work in a large secondary school that boasts several hundred PCs and a substantial network. I learned my computing in the Army, creating and maintaining data records using bespoke systems and commercial database software. I helped train other military personnel, and completed NVQs in the Army. Since leaving that post, and taking up a school role, I have been studying for a BSc with the Open University, and I provide on-line advice to other OU students on IT issues. I do voluntary work with young people in my free time because I have a commitment to education in its widest sense.

Case Study 10.3
Technical officer Sean

I had a pretty conventional education, gaining a cluster of GCSEs and A levels before reading for a BSc in zoology. I also studied for City & Guilds qualifications in computer electronics and software. My early employment used the technical qualifications, but later I worked in agriculture, eventually combining the two interests selling technical products for a veterinary company. After a period of self-employment designing small and medium-sized Ethernet networks, I took up a school post as ICT Development Officer.

Job description

Just as the background of the technical officers varied widely, so did the job description for people in these roles. We were unable to produce either a 'typical' or an 'ideal' job description from those we collected – mainly because they were so specific to each school's individual need. For this reason, the two chosen to be included in this chapter (shown in Tables 10.1 and 10.2) have been selected for their contrast. (In these job descriptions oddities of grammar and layout have been retained from the originals.)

Table 10.1 The job description of technical officer Boris

Title: ICT project development officer

Responsible to: A member of the senior management team

Curriculum involvement

- advise on the purchase of software for use in the curriculum;
- demonstrate in the classroom the use of various hardware and software;
- evaluate new and existing software for curriculum use.

continues

Table 10.1 *continued*

Pupil and staff involvement

- support and encourage teachers in their use of ICT in the curriculum;
- organise and support training for teaching, support and special needs staff;
- run lunchtime and after school clubs for pupils;
- work with other ICT technicians to upkeep and improve the school's provision.

System development

Maintaining a development plan for IT and to undertake regular reviews of the system taking into consideration issues of:

- connectivity and possible improvements;
- hardware capability and additional requirements;
- software and its accessibility via the Network server;
- develop and implement Internet and Intranet provision;
- availability of non-computer ICT resources;
- liaison with hardware and software suppliers over demonstrations, purchases, repairs and replacements;
- support and initiate ICT developments in feeder schools and other community initiatives.

Administration

- attend and minute all ICT Development Group meetings;
- record usage of ICT facilities throughout the school;
- work with the other ICT technicians to ensure the inventory is up-to-date.

Table 10.2 The job description of technical officer Rose

Title: IT technician

Responsible to: Senior administration manager

- The person will work closely with the IT teacher helping to run, maintain and update a small network and stand alone machines throughout the school.
- Tasks will involve floppy and hard disk management and organisation, and software maintenance. These will include virus checking all disks regularly, backing up the network and adding/removing users from the system.

Specific tasks: weekly

Hard disk management

- virus check on all hard disks;
- checking back-up onto DAT tape;

- moving files and generally keeping the hard disk tidy.

Stand alone machines

- keep all computers updated.

Printers

- check all printers for paper and cartridge quality;
- replace cartridges where necessary and possible.

Specific tasks: occasionally

- keep the network running, repairing or reporting breakdowns and problems;
- add/delete files from the network;
- be part of a team when ordering equipment and when making software/hardware purchasing decisions;
- producing certificates, posters, tickets as time allows and when required by the school;
- advising on database production;
- writing programs to produce reports and analysis.

It would be worthwhile to pause at this point to look at the two job descriptions of the technical officers selected here. You might ask yourself the following questions:

- How do these job descriptions (JDs) compare and contrast to any that operate in your own school?
- How effective do you think each of the JDs cited might be?
- Is there anything missing in these JDs?
- What do they tell us about the roles of technical officers in the learning that takes place in the school?
- How do you overcome issues of relationships between support staff and teaching staff in your own situation?

The work of technical officers

So far this chapter has attempted to reconstruct the roles and relationships of the technical officer post-holders in schools through an analysis of discussions, interviews and conversations. At this point it might be valuable instead to let them speak for themselves. We asked a sample of these post-holders to write freely about their own jobs, and in the case studies that follow this is what they did.

Case Study 10.4
Bring on the computer police?

The first thing to remember is: there is no such thing as a typical day. I'm at work by 8.15 a.m. and am accosted to sort things out even before I get to my office, take my coat off…

Jobs can vary in any given day from being asked to revive a dying Mac, having to try to recover students' work after they have deleted it, or being asked to advise a parent about computers…

One difficulty is trying to make sure we are not seen as the 'computer police'. We have got to exercise control over the system, but sensitively, not allowing that to rule how we see users and our attitudes to them…But we do have to deal with outsiders sending abusive e-mails, or with students who fill boring bits of lessons by trying to 'improve' the school website with more colourful language!

A large part of my job involves multi-tasking: I may go into a study area to check some equipment, but I can guarantee that within moments I will have answered half a dozen students' questions. It is reassuring to know that they believe that even if I can't give an instant answer, I will know by the end of the day!

Most jobs are not planned; try as one might, time-tabled activities will go to pot for immediate problems. Most jobs run smoothly. If they don't, of course, it's definitely always my fault! I am constantly needed, never quick enough, required to be psychic, to repair faults before they happen and so on…But I'm not complaining. I enjoy the job. I particularly like helping students. I relish the fact that a student can come to me with a problem or a query and by coming up with the solution or the answer, I am responsible for moving on their learning. The fact that *they* want to learn motivates *me*.

Case Study 10.5
Busy, busy, busy…but worth it!

The day begins at 8.00 a.m. with strong coffee, followed by a quick visual check of the main servers and a session catching up with my assistant technician and trawling any problems she can't sort out. Then we ensure the previous night's back-up logs are OK and put new tapes in for the next back-up…

After this I begin the first sweep of the day to check all ICT facilities throughout the school. During this time I am entering classes and giving direct support to both teachers and students using a variety of packages and equipment. Once this is over I return to my office and undertake the day's paperwork: catalogues, invoices, adverts for courses etc...Network management, such as setting up new user accounts might come next...

At the start of the lunch hour I open up the IT suite and run the ICT club. This is fully booked every day, and it is a truly rewarding experience to be able to help the students on a one-to-one basis. During my own lunch I am usually required by members of staff to help them with some task or other, and afterwards I have a briefing meeting with the head of ICT.

The afternoon might involve financial paperwork, or chasing up orders and equipment...

Then the day ends with a second session of the ICT club...

One student remarked to me the other day: 'What would the school do without you, Sir? I think it would curl up and die.' That moved me very much and gave me an overwhelming sense of contribution.

Case Study 10.6
Big sister is watching you....

Earlier this week, one of our staff sent two pupils to our ICT area to do some careers research. They ended up missing for the whole lesson, but the teacher was suspicious about whether they had really been on the network for all that time! I was able to give him a print-out that showed that the two pupils had been on-line for a total of 19 minutes out of the 50-minute period. I don't know what they were doing for the rest of the time, and it wasn't my job to find out – but, I guess they are still wondering how the teacher knew that!

The technical officer from Hell: a parable

The essential spirit of the technical officer's role would, it appears from our case studies, be one of helping and of satisfaction through facilitating the learning of teachers and students. Yet other scenarios have sometimes dominated this area of work, as indicated in the parable that follows – which is based upon real events.

There was once a technical officer who was assiduous in his job and meticulous to a fault. He was smart and a good time-keeper. His line manager impressed upon him the importance of careful stock control and the need to steward carefully the school's meagre resources, and left him to do his job.

Now the line manager was a keen individual who was anxious to further the work of the students of this school and wanted them all to value and utilise the power and flexibility that using the media gives to human kind. He put on special courses and out-of-school classes to teach the students to use the various pieces of technical equipment and software that made up this armoury of modern communication systems. He promoted this work and encouraged its wide-spread adoption by other members of staff.

Yet, despite all the best efforts of the line manager, the interest in, and commitment to, technology simply failed to materialise. The students became listless and the staff unenthusiastic. He spent sleepless nights worrying about why this should be and he thought of all the articles and professional papers he had written – papers that had had a profound effect in other schools – and began to call himself at best misguided and at worst a hypocrite.

One day, in the great scheme of education that is called training, the local Further Education College rang to say that they had heard of his great works and would like to place a young female trainee technician in his department on work experience. The line manager was flattered. He agreed with alacrity, pleased that some of the girls in the school would have a role model in this area of work; and he prepared some wonderful multi-coloured observation tools that could be used by the trainee in shadowing his technician. It would be a good way to get her into the thinking of the department.

So it was that she came and shadowed. At the end of her first week the line manager called the trainee into his office and said to her: 'Now rehearse for me all the good practice and attitudes that you have learned with us so far.'

The trainee consulted her observation tools and began:

'I have discovered,' she said, 'that students are an unreliable lot and not to be trusted. They are clumsy and ignorant, and break the equipment and lose the software, and generally are inclined to treat things as if they owned them – which is not true at all. I have ascertained the tightness of the budget and the need never to allow any item to get old with use, or wear out through over-work, lest it has to be replaced; and I understand that the best way of keeping an inventory up-to-date is never to issue anything that is listed on it...'

There was more, and the line manager was – in the popular parlance of time – gobsmacked. He called his technician and said:

'I trusted you with the stewardship of my equipment and you have repaid me by mothballing it. I hoped you would instil in the students a love of using technology, but you have demanded they admire it at a distance like objects in an antique shop. I gave you the opportunity to open minds and you have closed them. Remove yourself from this empire of involvement and never show your face here again.'

After he had got his severance pay, the technician got a job with the museums' service and was happy ever after – or at least until they introduced inter-active exhibits.

130

Learning

Unlike the post-holder in the parable, our technical officers were deeply committed to students and their learning, as was clear in the case studies above. But the extent of that involvement might be even greater than we have suggested.

ICT provides an opportunity for learning to be redefined. The concept of any-time-anywhere learning means precisely what it says: students can access learning materials at any opportunity they may have in any place they may choose. This provides a powerful incentive for schools and for commercial organisations to confine curriculum to software as a means to supporting this process. It is not the moment to discuss how such activities may revolutionise schooling (though you may care to refer back to the Introduction). It is opportune to suggest that technical officers may have a crucial part to play in the process or, to put it another way, an indispensable role in learning. The case study that follows suggests just this.

Case Study 10.7
The role of the technical officer in learning

Zena is a well-qualified young woman with a higher degree in educational technology. Her job is to be intermediary between what staff would like to put onto the website and the finished product. Her skills are in the design of the materials to make them user-friendly. We sat in front of a computer screen while she talked me through the materials that had been generated at that point.

Zena believes that the design of a website like this is important. She is concerned with the ease of navigation around the materials, and with the cognitive problems of learning in this fashion. The site has a consistency that she has built in: in the use and size of fonts, for example, and in the roll-over colours.

Using the materials has not been totally trouble free. Some consternation occurred quite early on for the English department when access became difficult; but the fault was traced to Netscape 4.0 software and was rapidly sorted out. With this technical hitch out of the way, Zena has been free to concentrate on making access pleasurable for the user.

The distance learning website is separate, but accessible, from the main school website, and the Master Class website. The three experimental subjects – English, mathematics and IT – are separate again. Glossaries assist the student with understanding and there are quick routes into them to avoid 'cognition overload'. Students can move freely from the materials into their homework pages and vice versa. All of the content itself is written by departmental experts, either on disk or in manuscript and then Zena transfers it into the chosen formats.

The potential for growth is enormous. In English, the grammar area can have the number and range of topics extended to add, for example, pages on adverbs in the grammar section. Test pages are built in to check knowledge. These tests give immediate feedback to the student via a computerised marking system; and staff can see who has accessed the tests and view their levels of performance.

The mathematics material is a little more tricky to handle at present. The built-in tests exist but have to be multiple choice items with the formulae etc. inserted as graphics. This is due to inadequacies of software at present, but the problems are soluble in the long term.

Zena is now putting Help pages into the system for new users. These, and the materials, link to other departmental pages but are kept separate so that the departmental collections do not get over-long and confusing. A more up-to-date server will eventually be installed and solve some of the more intractable issues. For example, students accessing a page of the materials can print out that page; but they cannot manipulate the text (e.g. respond to test questions) and then print out the result of their own work. Nor can they download a complete document.

As yet the participant students do not have school-owned lap-tops. They are all individuals who have PCs at home, with access to the Internet (those on cable can link in free of charge). They can access the school's own Internet system in this way. This is filtered for undesirable elements, though sometimes this causes irritation. A level students studying slang expressions, for example, may not be able to gain access to material on this because it is filtered out by the system.

Each page has an icon to return the user to the homepage. Frames and tables are used sparingly in the design. The problems of working for long periods on the screen are acknowledged – which is why good design of the web pages is so crucial.

Overall, Zena is optimistic about the technical future of the project. She sees its potential, and looks on system inadequacies as opportunities for devising more creative solutions.

Professional development

Our technical officers were aware of the need for further professional development to help them in roles that are constantly changing within a rapidly developing field. Some training was provided through commercial organisations, mainly about technical issues rather than about their roles in supporting learning. This was sometimes of high quality, but often far too expensive for schools to access even though it was designed for them. Too often it was irrelevant to schools' needs. They also felt that some available training, though potentially useful, was directed more at the teacher who headed up ICT than at the support staff. A major problem in a developing world was a paucity of credible trainers.

It was interesting that, during a conference day that we held to gather some of the information cited in this chapter, the technical officers present set up their own self-help group to continue after our event. They also expressed a desire for the establishment of a Professional Association which could meet their specific requirements.

Our technical officers wanted training to be delivered within school time, to be funded centrally (i.e. by government rather than the school – after all, the Prime Minister had declared his intentions on spreading the computer revolution!), and to have a proper system of accreditation. This last point was seen as a move towards a proper career structure. In-school appraisal systems were useful, but did not deliver any results in the form of training. More opportunities were needed to learn more about network systems and about new hardware and software products.

Conclusion

In line with the overall thesis of this book, we believe that technical officers, like support staff generally, have a critical role to play in schools of the future. This role is not just about supporting the infra-structure of learning, but crucially about direct involvement in the learning that has to be done by both teachers and students. Their direct role in effective learning and the raising of standards in schools is perhaps the clearest of all support staff.

11

■ ■ ■

Managing the ICT technical officer

The views of technical officers about their management

In our survey, a wide variety of management practices emerged.

Technical officers met their managers with variable frequency: at its least frequent, three or four times a term; at the most frequent twice a day. There was an overall satisfaction with their management, mainly because it followed principles described below. On a scale of one to seven (1 = high), the scores for satisfaction with management ranged from one to five across the group surveyed.

One respondent said:

> We have a new head teacher. She is very efficient in her management. Her management of my role is good. She is supportive, and always consults me and discusses with me any plans she has for the future of ICT.

Another painted a different, but equally satisfactory picture:

> When the chain of communication is working properly, management is fantastic; when it breaks down, problems arise. My line manager and the Senior Management Team appear confident of my ability to self-manage, too.

This was echoed by others:

> My manager is not technically-minded and therefore relies on my experience and advice. He is, however, flexible and can be relied on to back me up on any issues that are put to the Senior Management Team. He places a high degree of respect in my position relative to teaching staff.

These views contain the key sentiments expressed about management of this role:

- listening;
- respect; and
- support.

Management styles, however, vary – as the following quotations show:

Most management decisions are discussed with me at an informal meeting called either by me or by the manager.

Management decisions can come from a variety of sources. Mainly, they come through the line manager, but occasionally direct from the Senior Management Team. For example, decisions about the funding of equipment and about the budget tend to come from the line manager. But when I was asked to take on responsibility for helping a local feeder school, the request came directly from the head.

Management decisions are passed both verbally and in writing, either directly from my line manager or in the form of memos from the Senior Management Team. My work is guided by my line manager in the sense that there is a limited budget for ICT and we must commit money to the best advantage, i.e. to bring maximum benefit to the users of the system.

So how did our technical officers see the strengths and weaknesses of those who managed this role? Tables 11.1 and 11.2 set out the answers to this question.

Though the technical officers were generally satisfied with their management in their current posts they were not slow in making a critical assessment of how management of the role could be carried out and improved. They were keen to share with managers the ways that they did their jobs and the decisions that they made. This meant that, when disagreements arose (albeit infrequently), they looked to discussion and analysis of the situation as a way forward – which did not always happen. They thought that managers ought to show high levels of organisational skill, and that – even if they were not experts – they should be prepared to do some homework about IT so that they could engage in intelligent discussion.

An issue of some concern was that of training. Our technical officers felt that they did not really feature in the pecking order of receiving training money. They tended to feel that, in this fast-moving area, schools could not expect them to perform well unless they themselves were given opportunities for professional development. No-one actually used a phrase like 'compared to teachers', but this comparison was always hovering just below the surface of their remarks. Teachers had statutory training time and (as they saw it) quite generous training opportunities. The technical officers did not share these. Sometimes they were included in training days and sometimes not – but training days may not be the most useful experiences for technical officers anyway.

Table 11.1 Strengths in the management of the technical officer's role

- flexibility in approach;
- trust;
- support;
- willingness to listen;
- willingness to learn about, stay up-to-date in, ICT issues;
- conduct of regular appraisals;
- effective communication;
- respect for the technical officer's knowledge/experience;
- willingness to allow a degree of self-management;
- understanding ('The line manager previously did my job').

Table 11.2 Weaknesses in the management of the technical officer's role

- failure of communication;
- lack of availability;
- over-reliance on technical officer by the manager.

Our technical officers craved empathy from their managers: signals that they understood and identified with the constraints and problems of the role. The word 'respect' recurred, usually in a positive context, indicating that managers treated them with respect. Good managers were open-minded and approachable, not requiring intermediaries.

There were some very specific suggestions, too:

> Provision of my own budget for ICT development would release me from the ignorance or lack of understanding of some senior staff. I feel I would then be able to spend the money in the most beneficial manner for all.

> In order to attract more and better qualified and experienced staff into my kind of role managers need to recognise the need to provide a more suitable remuneration package.

Overall, though, this was a group of well qualified people who were satisfied with their roles (if not always with their conditions of service). This satisfaction stemmed from their particular expertise, so that they were essential to the working of the school and the learning of pupils. The essential nature of the role gave them a degree of *kudos* and respect, perhaps beyond that of other support staff in the school. As a result, job satisfaction was high. Management of these post-holders had to be reasonably sensitive because of the indispensable nature of their services.

Managing the technical officer (ICT)

When looking at managing these post-holders it is important to take a lead from their own insights into management: its strengths and failures. In the suggestions that follow we have used clues from the technical officers' own assessments of their management to draw out some possible strategies.

Strategy 11.1 *Assessing your own management of technical officers*

Using the headings supplied by the technical officers themselves, make an assessment of your own management skills. In each case, write a short appraisal of how you think you shape up to the skill listed:

- understanding;
- flexibility in approach;
- trust;
- support;
- willingness to listen;
- willingness to learn about, stay up to date in, ICT issues;
- conduct of regular appraisals;
- effective communication;
- respect for the technical officer's knowledge/experience;
- willingness to allow a degree of self-management.

Overall, how do you rate your management of this group of support staff?

Strategy 11.2 *Examining the job descriptions of technical officers in your school*

Collect the job descriptions of technical officers in your school. If any of them do not have job descriptions this exercise should be seen as especially pertinent.

Look over these job descriptions and try to analyse the job operations listed under the following groupings:

- Items concerned with systems maintenance.
- Items concerned with systems development.
- Items concerned with software and its applications.

continues

Strategy 11.2 *continued*

- Items relating to curriculum.
- Items relating to supporting the learning of students and teachers.
- Items concerned with budgeting and financial control.
- Items concerned with administration.
- Items concerned with keeping up-dated about future developments in ICT.

Once you have analysed the job descriptions you might want to make an assessment of their adequacy for the purpose you think they should fulfil for the school and its mission.

One way to see how effective the job description is in the light of the mission of the school might be to work-shadow a technical officer (by prior agreement) to check on the match between job description and the reality on the ground.

Strategy 11.3 *Looking at the training issue*

One of the frequent complaints of the technical officers was that they did not have adequate access to training. Use the headings below to review training facilities in your school.

What use do you make of appraisal?

How/how else do you assess training needs?

What kinds of training have technical officers accessed over the last year

- Relating to hardware?
- Relating to software?
- Relating to learning through ICT?
- Relating to best practice in other institutions?
- Relating to budgeting for ICT?

How is training undertaken then evaluated?

What kinds of training might your technical officers now need?

Do they access the training days for teaching staff (all, some, on appropriate occasions, how are these defined)?

Is there a budget set aside for training technical officers (how much, how effectively used, how monitored)?

Is there a policy for training these staff?

In summary – what could now be done to improve the training of ICT staff?

Strategy 11.4 *Assessing your own ICT skills*

One criticism the technical officers made of their managers was that they were over-reliant, mainly because they knew too little about ICT and its applications. While you cannot expect to be an expert on every area of school life, you do need (as a manager) enough knowledge of every aspect to make intelligent management judgements. This exercise asks you to review and improve your own knowledge.

How fluent are you in the use of your own computer:

- Word processing;
- Excel;
- Power point;
- Other applications?

Have you read any basic texts on ICT in schools (such as Zanker, *Effective information and communication technology*)?

Have you read any texts about managing ICT (such as Freedman, *Managing ICT*)?

Have you visited other state-of-the-art institutions to see the applications to which ICT can be put?

Do you take an active interest in the IT/ICT related work of pupils?

Do you seek clarification and guidance from your technical officers when you need to?

Do you feel that you have, overall, an intelligent appreciation of the work of the technical officers?

Strategy 11.5 *Examining the technical officers' role in student learning*

The technical officers in our survey told us that they had a significant role to play in the learning of students. As a manager you need to both understand and be able to maximise the effectiveness of that role. This exercise asks you to reflect on the learning-related work of technical officers.

Ask your technical officers to keep a record for a period (perhaps two to four weeks) which lists all the occasions when they give learning support to students or teachers. There is no need for them to name the people they help. They might use a simple proforma like the one overleaf:

continues

Strategy 11.5 *continued*

Date	Duration of assistance	Pupil/teacher	Nature of assistance
1.3.01	13 minutes	P	Explaining how to use Excel to make a bar chart
2.3.01	21 minutes	P	Helping pupil to use a new piece of distance learning software
2.3.01	5 minutes	T	Solving an operating problem and showing T how to self-help next time

Analyse the outcomes of this exercise, e.g. calculating the time spent on teaching/learning, average number of incidents per day and so on.

Now draw out the conclusions from this about the role and training needs of technical officers in the light of their instructional activities.

Strategy 11.6 *Dealing with the technical officer from Hell*

Not all management runs smoothly, and some management tasks are unpalatable.

Look back to page 129, and reread the section headed *The technical officer from Hell: a parable.*

Try to list what are precise dimensions of the problem in this little story.

If you had discovered or inherited such a person in your school, what steps would you take to put the situation right?

What part do you think the line manager should have played in the story? Did he do the right things? What would you say to him?

References

Freeman, T. (1999) *Managing ICT.* London: Hodder & Stoughton.

Zanker, N. (2000) *Effective information and communication technology.* London: Hodder & Stoughton.

12

■ ■ ■

The school
secretary/receptionist

In Chapter 1 it was argued that holders of posts in this cluster were people who could wield immense power in a school, for better or worse. At its worst, a manipulative secretary has access to a range of confidential information and can almost take over the management of a school from a relatively unassertive head. At best, holders of these posts have it in their gift to set a tone for the school that can be a cornerstone in its public image and success. This chapter examines some case histories of school secretary/receptionists and explores the role from their perspectives.

What do school secretaries/receptionists do?

As with many support staff, there is no simple answer to this apparently obvious question. We asked a number of post-holders to provide us with job descriptions. Three of these are reproduced in Tables 12.1, 12.2 and 12.3. Before reading on you would be well advised to study them. In doing so, you should ask yourself the following questions:

- What can you tell from the job descriptions about the size, phase of schooling and type of school that Sam, Mel and Sandy work in?
- What are the overlaps between their roles?
- What are the contrasts in their roles – what accounts for these?
- What background qualifications would you expect Sam, Mel and Sandy to have?

When you have come to your own conclusions about these questions, you will find a brief set of 'correct' answers at the end of the chapter based on information that the three post-holders supplied about themselves. Ask yourself:

- Am I surprised at any of my perceptions of these posts/post-holders? Why?

Table 12.1 The job description of Sam

Post title: School administrator

Responsible to: The Head Teacher

Key tasks:

- To be responsible for controlling the effectiveness of service provided at the school, e.g. building, grounds and catering (seeking specialist advice when necessary), and to manage the budget as appropriate.
- To keep an inventory of equipment and arrange for its maintenance.
- To keep an inventory of furniture and fittings and, when required, to arrange for the repair and replacement of furniture and fittings.
- To administer the teacher support staff, control the appropriate budgets and be present at interviews of such staff.
- To carry out induction training and to assist with other training of teacher support staff.
- To represent support staff, as required, at meetings of the School Management Team.
- To authorise claims from teaching and non-teaching staff (e.g. wages, overtime, midday supervision, supply teachers, teachers' meals, labour in excess of core time, travelling and general expenses).
- To authorise reprographic work.
- To take full responsibility for lettings and the associated budget.
- To monitor all school budgets and assist with the control of teaching and capitation budgets.
- To act as public relations officer for the school.
- To be responsible, when required, for emergency liaison arrangements, including contact with other schools' Education Officers and transport operators.
- To liaise with governors, members of staff and the Clerk to the Governors.
- If appropriate, to act as Clerk to the Governors and carry out tasks listed in that job description.
- With the agreement of the post-holder and subject to qualifications held and the policy of the school, to be a recognised provider of First Aid.
- To assist in carrying out administrative/secretarial/clerical tasks as necessary.
- Such other duties as may be determined from time to time within the scope of the post (which at present include: pupil record keeping, updating and banking of data, checking registers, administering school funds, organising trips, ordering goods, checking deliveries, ordering items of school uniform).

Table 12.2 The job description of Mel

Title: School Secretary

Responsible to: The Head Teacher

Key tasks:

- To provide telephone, reception and messenger services throughout the school.
- To receive, open and distribute incoming mail and to despatch outgoing mail.
- To undertake filing, typing and reprographic tasks to meet the needs of the school.
- To receive incoming goods, check and issue goods as necessary, and sign delivery notes.
- To maintain pupil records on the school management system.
- To record weekly attendance and produce reports for EWOs and form tutors.
- To maintain free school meal entitlement records and medical records.
- To design and produce forms and booklets.
- To assist in the arrangement of medical and dental examinations.
- To provide First Aid, enlisting the support of expert medical help if necessary; to escort sick pupils to hospital or home as appropriate; to maintain personal First Aid qualifications; to ensure completion of accident report forms and notification of parents.
- To assist in the compilation of such reports and records as may be required by the school, governors, LEA or DfEE.
- To provide occasional supervision of the pupils in the resource area.
- To assist with new admissions and intake, maintain new records and complete relevant documentation, and to allocate enquiries to the correct form or track personnel.
- To liaise with outside agencies, e.g. LEA, PTA and EWO.
- To monitor progress of pupils against the targets set in the Administration Team Development Plan.
- To undertake such other duties as shall be required.

Table 12.3 The job description of Sandy

Post title: Receptionist

Responsible to: Not quoted

Key tasks:

- Manning reception office: dealing with enquiries; answering the telephone; making sure all visitors sign and are issued with a security badge.

continues

Table 12.3 *continued*

- Registers: maintaining and checking the admission and school meals registers.
- Money: Counting and banking all monies.
- First Aid: Administer First Aid and TLC; maintain stock in First Aid boxes.
- Photocopying: carry out photocopying as and when required; order consumables as necessary.
- Stationery store: Keep and maintain stock levels.
- Photographs/Fleeces/Sweatshirts: Keep records and order appropriate items.
- Educational visits: booking of buses and venues as requested.

What are the priority roles for school secretaries/receptionists?

Post-holders we talked to suggested that a prioritisation of their roles might look something like this:

- They are ambassadors and first point of contact for the public with the school: they set the tone.
- They have contact with children: they are surrogate mums, administrators of first aid, dispensers of TLC.
- They form the hub of the communications network, receiving, filtering, passing on information.
- They prioritise work load and flow of work for others.
- They act as the buffer between the head, the staff, parents and the public; they see themselves as the gatekeepers of the school, sifting the levels of enquiry, pointing enquirers to the right people, making judgements about importance.
- They provide information, about pupils, budgets, and general answering of queries; these functions share a need for word processing but fulfil very different functions in the running of the school – some more significant than others.

These roles are important, not least for the centrality in which contacts with pupils are held. As hypothesised, our secretaries identified the first priority of the role very clearly as being the customer care issue, or as they put it 'setting the tone'. This is their role from the extra-school perspective. Looking after the children is the same role with an intra-school perspective. These two roles form the pivots on which their job revolves.

What motivates school secretaries/receptionists in their roles?

From what we have seen so far one would suspect that school secretary/receptionists are 'caring/sharing' people. To explore something of this aspect of the role we asked our sample to write about their jobs. We gave them some basic guidance (*see* Note on Research Underpinning), but emphasised that we wanted them to use this only to start their thinking, and that they were free to indicate whatever they thought was important. What follow are some extracts from their reflections.

Lyn wrote:

> *The motivation comes from never knowing what will happen today – a, b and c may be in the plan but most days consist of x, y and z, with a, b and c squeezed in at the end. I think the challenge of keeping everything balanced turns this into a positive rather than a negative job. I feel positive about my job. I know I do it well and that I have strengths in many areas that the head feels he could not find 'anywhere else'.*

Taf wrote:

> *Motivation comes from pride in the school and from job satisfaction. The job is interesting, characterised by variety, the unknown and new challenges.*

Sam wrote:

> *I enjoy my job because it is so interesting. I particularly enjoy the day-to-day contact I have with the children.*

Kikki wrote:

> *I see my job as a challenge...I enjoy helping the children in any way I can.*

These reactions are in many ways so similar to each other, and to others, that they almost appear like repetition. Clearly, this view is at the heart of people who take on the secretary/receptionist role in schools. But why schools? Is there some element of the role that is essentially about the function of a school, i.e. learning?

The secretary/receptionist role and its relationship to learning

Throughout this text we have talked about learning as opposed to teaching. We all learn from others, though those others are not necessarily teachers and do not necessarily 'teach' us what we learn through them. Putting this insight into operation in examining the role of secretary/receptionist we discover that these post-holders report being involved in a significant amount of learning by pupils. We report this in the post-holders' own words first of all, so that the case we are making is not influenced by our own views.

Nicki said:

> Sometimes (rarely) I am asked to supervise a group of pupils in a lesson (secondary school), but I am not very good at discipline. I do try to talk to some of the 'difficult' pupils – ones who try to get out of lessons etc. and persuade them to go back, and ask why?

Jo said:

> I find some cases very distressing; once I had to report to social services that I had seen two burn marks on a child's neck that his brother had made with a lighter...I also found out that they were living in a damp caravan with no money. Both children had hacking coughs and asthma...

Mandy said:

> My role does give me the opportunity to be a second mum/carer to the children (in a primary setting).

Georgie said:

> Much of my day is taken up with assisting the (primary school) teachers...photocopying, maintaining pupil records, dealing with sick and injured children...If a child is feeling distressed or unwell they are usually sent to my office...I particularly enjoy the day-to-day contact with the children and they often stop for a quick chat when they are collecting registers, delivering messages etc.

Taf said:

> I contribute to pupils' learning by keeping the wheels oiled. If records are maintained this assists in the classroom...If pupils are free to call at the office when they are worried or unwell and are treated sympathetically this improves their learning. Assisting teachers with their preparations for lessons and exams also contributes to pupils' learning (independent school).

Linda recounted the following incident:

> One of the most difficult incidents I faced was when we took a child from another school. He came into Year 6 and had many problems regarding relationships with peers and family. He ran out of school on several occasions...The head came into my office one afternoon and said: 'I can't get him to talk to me; will you see what you can do?' I do have a counselling diploma. I wasn't sure about this though concern for the child took over. The incident led to me seeing the child on a regular basis and we felt (as did his parents) that this was a straw for him to clutch at...He seemed to benefit from the support. This incident led to me running a 'circle of friends' for another child...The head would like my role to develop towards counselling pupils...

Experience suggests that these accounts are not untypical of the work of school secretaries/receptionists. They are people who are clearly involved in learning by pupils at a number of levels. In these accounts we can isolate five roles at least:

- Involvement in pupils' learning through the social skills of informal conversation.
- Involvement in learning through providing the administrative underpinning of lessons and examinations.
- Dealing with the 'whole child' within difficult social situations.
- Informal and formal counselling.
- Supervising a class, albeit on an occasional needs-must basis (*see* also Table 12.2 – supervision of pupils in the resource area).

These insights into the learning-related roles of the secretary/receptionist are incredibly important; yet they are not the stuff of job descriptions nor of any formal recognition. Some might argue that they should not be, that they are outside the scope of such employees to handle.

Yet the fact remains, they do emerge in practice as integral to the job. So a more positive approach is to try to establish how such activities might be better developed and managed within schools. This specific issue is really the task of Chapter 13. For the moment we need to take another look at the more 'conventional' secretarial roles to assess what part these post-holders play in the overall life of a school.

How do school secretaries/receptionists see their overall role in the life of the school?

In a group discussion respondents were able to identify a number of support functions. They were even able to assess a priority order to these:

- Facilitating the work of teachers by:
  - photocopying;
  - typing up lesson notes;
  - ordering books and other software;
  - maintaining equipment or seeing to its maintenance;
  - providing relevant information, e.g. about timetabling.
- Making sure administrative processes are in place and carried out efficiently, e.g. dealing with registers.
- Acting as a buffer between teachers and parents: fielding queries and complaints.

- Setting a social and moral example for the pupils through their own behaviour in the school.

- Acting as social worker and counsellor to both pupils and, on occasion, teachers.

So we have to balance the cold print of the job descriptions quoted earlier in the chapter against the living reality of the secretary/receptionist's involvement in both supporting learning and, on occasions, being a source of learning. But it isn't an easy task, and it would not be a balanced picture of the role if its frustrations were ignored. In Case Study 12.1 we report the outcome of a group discussion in the form of a piece of continuous prose, though the views expressed were actually generated by a number of people.

Case Study 12.1
What makes the secretary/receptionist's job difficult?

There is a fundamental problem – a tension – built into the role. It's about pressure really. On the one hand you have the fact that it seems everyone who wants something from you wants it NOW. On the other hand, there are constant interruptions to be dealt with. The phone doesn't stop ringing just because someone is standing talking to you in the flesh. Visitors turn up, often unexpectedly and want rapid attention. First Aid is, by definition, a 'do it now' activity: you can't just ignore a child who is dripping blood.

One aspect of this tension is being expected to do now the jobs that other people should have thought about earlier. It is common for teachers to send photocopying that is needed during the current session: they send it with a pupil and expect an immediate turnaround.

One outcome of this pressure is that doing jobs is a balancing act and often you end up feeling that nothing has been done thoroughly. Job satisfaction can be compromised by this. You buy some files to improve the filing system, which would make life easier and the job more efficient and find you haven't had time to re-vamp the system five months later. Some of the records need careful checking; and things like financial records and registers leave one feeling on edge unless one can make time to recheck them.

In most schools the role is sufficiently loosely defined that it expands constantly and new things get added and new work arrives without warning. The recent changes in the way government deals with schools has pushed up the amount of paper required and form filling often gets delegated to us. Computers actually increase the amount of work overall, because we often have to deal with paper copies as well.

And photocopying just proliferates. Pupils and teachers expect copies of everything...

The secretary from Hell

Of course, not all secretaries/receptionists are the paragons described so far in this chapter. Case Study 12.2 outlines the alternative scenario as reported by one school governor.

Case Study 12.2
The secretary from Hell

She welcomes you with a smile, but the smile is always frozen. Her eyes are unsmiling and there is a blank hostility to the vast majority. To the chosen few, to the elite: 'Welcome'.

The reception area, and the headmaster's private office are her domain. You can access neither unless you get her permission – the office contains confidential material, the headmaster is busy: 'he is working on the budget, on the SDP', on anything so long as it disturbs neither his solitude nor invades her space.

The younger staff all like Cully; she cultivates their friendship and offers a shoulder to cry on when times are bad, but over the passage of time she gains access to personal information that may be traded with the head over cosy cups of coffee. Older staff have become wiser, and treat her overtures of friendship with caution but still they cannot resist her offer: 'Let me type up your CV and application form for you. I can do it in a matter of minutes, it won't take long'. And within a twinkling of an eye, she draws the unsuspecting (or just overburdened) class teacher into her net. Another cup of coffee with the head beckons.

Her present power, though, lies in her friendship with the head. He has only two years at the most before he takes early retirement – her future will be secure if she maintains access and control over all aspects of the running of the school. When the new head is appointed, he/she will need advice and support in the first months, Cully will be on hand, she will become indispensable again … but all that is in the future.

For the present, the governing body needs Cully's attention – her other role is that of Clerk to the Governors. She tolerates the Chairman, but the vice-chair is dangerous; she is asking questions about matters best left alone, those small financial and staff appointment irregularities.

There is a chink in her armour though, she is quite good with the children, especially the young ones. Cully sees all her actions as in 'the best interests of the children'. In her view it is in the children's interests that she acts as their liaison with the head, who, on his own admission 'hasn't been in an infant class for two years'. But the reality is that it is she, not the head, who has the overview of everything that takes place – she has access to all material that passes through the head's hands; she has the head's ear for those valuable snippets of information recently acquired; she sits on SMT; she 'looks after' the new, young staff, and line manages all support staff; she relieves the experienced teachers of the burdens of multiple job applications.

The day ends as it began, the seraphic smile creeps over the face of one who deems the day's work as 'a job well done'.

Conclusion

School secretaries/receptionists deal with the front-of-house jobs, carry the burden of school administration, support and sustain learning, and become involved in pupils' learning experiences. Despite playing such a key role they do not feel valued.

In our discussions with school secretaries we were told very clearly that they were not consulted within the school, that their management was often poor, and that they had little support and in-service training.

These themes continue in Chapter 13.

*

Answers to the questions on pages 141–2

- What can you tell about the size, phase of schooling and type of school that Sam, Mel and Sandy work in?

Sam's school is a rural primary school about to be swallowed by a growing suburb; there are about 120 pupils in the school; it caters for pupils from Year R to Year 6. Mel works in a comprehensive school in a small market town that has its population swollen by a Royal Air Force base. The school is essentially a former secondary modern school of about 600 pupils. Sandy works in a Roman Catholic primary school.

- What are the overlaps between their roles?

Registers, money, reprographics, First Aid and some aspects of stock control are among the common items.

- What are the contrasts in their roles; and what accounts for these?

Sandy's role is most limited in range of functions and this may be partly because it is a less than full-time post, but also because her time is taken up with front-of-house duties and so she cannot undertake the other functions of the role. Mel undertakes a lot of outside liaison work and some direct contact with parents. Sam's post veers towards bursaring functions in that she is buildings, grounds and catering officer and she may attend the SMT.

- What background qualifications would you expect Sam, Mel and Sandy to have?

Sandy followed a two-year secretarial course some years ago, as well as taking First Aid at Work exams. She worked outside the education system before becoming a school meals supervisor at the same school before her current appointment. Sam gained a clutch of quite good O levels at school and then took a BEC National Diploma in Business Studies (with distinction); she spent eight years with a building society where she attended customer care courses, and four years with a medical practice, before this post. Mel worked for a transport company, the GPO and a housing department before her present post, having taken O levels and various RSA certificates; she is now moving on to Open University courses.

13
∎ ∎ ∎
Managing the school secretary/receptionist

In the previous chapter we took an overview of the school secretary/receptionist's role, both in general terms and in particular with respect to its links to the learning process for pupils. The intention of this chapter is to examine how that role is managed, and how management of the role could be improved to provide optimum benefit for the school.

How effectively are school secretaries/receptionists managed?

To our surprise, the response to this question turned out to be largely negative. In a reconstructed group discussion the following points were made to the chairperson:

Case Study 13.1
Some secretaries' views of their management

We don't really feel we are managed at all, we manage our own jobs. In many cases we have created our own jobs too, written the job description and everything. You could say we are the bottom of the heap in that respect. A surprising number of us have a Health Service background at some point in our careers. But once you join a school it's a whole new world. It stops being a job and becomes a way of life. You go out shopping, and every kid you meet is calling out: 'Hello, Miss!' We're everyone's favourite when they need the photocopying, but most of the time they forget we're there.

This rather depressing picture seems to apply to every person in the secretarial range, from the part-time administrator to the Head's PA. We pursued the issue in an individual questionnaire, but little changed. So we asked about the good and bad practice in management as these post-holders saw them. These were the results:

Table 13.1 Weaknesses in the management of secretaries/receptionists

- not really being managed at all;
- lack of communication with the manager;
- being left to one's own devices;
- being consulted and the advice not heeded;
- lack of understanding by management of the range and number of jobs done;
- managers not realising that others are 'swinging the lead', e.g. by taking numerous breaks for cigarettes;
- being left to talk to difficult parents when the head is really present;
- handling stress in the manager;
- insecurities in the manager about his/her own decisions.

Table 13.2 Strengths in the management of secretaries/receptionists

- manager who doesn't interfere with the way jobs are done;
- supportive attitudes generally;
- good sense of humour;
- trust from the manager that you will 'deliver the goods';
- support in difficult situations.

Despite this negative feedback one has to conclude that these post-holders are pretty resilient. Asked to rate their job satisfaction on a seven point scale (1 = high, 7 =low), they averaged 2.4, and only one respondent recorded a score in the negative end of the scale.

A way of exploring the nature of the negativity about management was to ask the respondents what they would like to change about their jobs. The answers ranged as follows:

- additional hours to employ another member of the administrative staff;
- I'd like complete peace on Monday mornings to balance the dinner money;
- more consultation;
- more and better training;

- for teaching staff to be made more responsible;
- more assistance with routine jobs so that I could learn the new computer programs we need;
- incentives to keep the office tidy;
- someone to listen;
- the end of the attitude by staff and governors: 'We are the professionals, you are not';
- pay that is commensurate with the level of responsibility.

The following quotation sums up this set of insights quite effectively:

> It would be useful to be included at some stage in the school management team, as our ideas and observations could be quite useful. At present, the bursar tends to take a defensive role most of the time as he is concerned more with finances. Support staff could, I feel, take a more pro-active role in the school. My role is managed from a crisis/solution point of view, rather than for improvement/updating. We always have to 'make do and mend' as we are at the bottom of the heap for finances. Little time or thought appears to be given to our role in the overall picture of the school.

The time has come to try to pull together the messages of Chapters 12 and 13 and to consider some ways in which the role of the secretary/receptionist can be more effectively managed. So we need to pose a question.

What are the issues arising from the background research about managing this role?

Our survey of the views of post-holders themselves has identified a number of factors in the better management of the role. Among these are:

- clarification of the job operations through a more effective job description;
- capitalising on the commitment and skills of the post-holder;
- recognising the roles of the post-holder in indirect and direct learning by pupils;
- providing time: for reflection, for implementation of improvements in administrative practice, for training;
- clarifying to others' legitimate and illegitimate demands made on the secretary/receptionist;
- overcoming the 'faceless' nature of the post;
- taking on board the insights of this role in the management decisions of the school;

- avoiding the Machiavellian behaviour of the lunatic fringe of post-holders;
- providing a listening ear – the tip of the iceberg of line management.

Some strategies for managing secretaries/receptionists more effectively

Strategy 13.1: *Review the job descriptions of secretarial/receptionist staff*

Ask the post-holders to carry out an exercise in which they produce their job descriptions, and a critical commentary on:

- which jobs they do;
- which jobs they do not do;
- the relative balance of time on each area of work;
- which jobs are straightforward (not 'easy');
- which are complicated and why;
- what would ease any problems identified.

(You will need to stress the openness of the school to listening to the messages they produce, and that accuracy is a keynote of the exercise)

Using the data generated, arrange interviews with each employee to discuss the outcomes. These should be:

- conducted in a quiet place, undisturbed by the phone etc.;
- low-key and reassuring in tone;
- inclusive of the line-manager, if appropriate;
- constructed so that a series of agreed and recorded outcomes emerges (like an appraisal interview).

Take follow-up by action, so that value of the process is stressed. This action should include:

- revisions to the job description;
- clarification of any expectations with the post-holder;
- follow-up communication with staff about reasonable and unreasonable demands, or about areas of responsibility;
- elaboration about the boundaries of the secretarial/receptionist role as they impinge on others (teachers, bursar, other administrative staff etc.);
- provision of identified training/resources that are appropriate.

Repeat at annual intervals.

Strategy 13.2 *Capitalising on the commitment of the post-holder*

The heart of this strategy is to raise the morale of the post-holder. The following suggestions are based on ideas our respondents listed.

- Provide some thinking time, when the secretary/receptionist can work undisturbed on important tasks.
- Ask the post-holder to review their accommodation and material needs: storage space, equipment, systems.
- Negotiate how best to use times when the post-holder is working but the school is not operational (such as teachers' training days).
- Make sure that the post-holder does not have to learn elements of their work, such as new software for school management systems, while carrying out the normal duties of the post.
- Consult about new ways of working if these are likely to affect the post-holder's routine.
- Be guarded about using the post-holder's time on trivia, such as making coffee for visitors: find more efficient ways of doing this.
- Ensure that teaching and other support staff understand the boundaries of the post-holder's role.
- Guard against the post-holder carrying out 'illegitimate' chores for members of staff, such as typing up applications for new posts.
- Confine some of the post-holder's roles to specific times of the day, so that there is a not a constant stream of interruptions.
- Educate other staff to think further ahead.
- Reward the achievements of the post-holder publicly, e.g. in assembly, just as you would those of pupils and teachers.

Strategy 13.3 *Recognising the roles of the post-holder in the indirect and direct learning of pupils*

In learning schools, the whole staff can engage in helping to further the effectiveness of the institution; the behaviour of all staff, and elements of their roles may impinge on pupils' social and other forms of learning. Effective schools will capitalise on this and use the opportunities created.

Many schools use the work of the post-holder as a training ground for pupils, who may greet visitors, issue passes, even answer phones, for a few hours of their school career. This is most effective when there are clear

Strategy 13.4 *continued*

- Survey the 'interruptions' that the post-holder reports as disruptions to their work. Discover whether some of these fall into patterns that could be better controlled through the co-operation of others. Some 'interruptions' may actually be important, e.g. phone calls from members of parent body or the public. Try to redefine 'interruptions' to take account of a scale of importance for such events.

- Ensure that the post-holder is secure with the hardware and software needed to run the post. If not, explore and exploit training opportunities.

- Call in an outside consultant (with the post-holder's agreement).

Strategy 13.5 *Clarifying to others legitimate and illegitimate demands made on the secretary/receptionist*

Sometimes, teaching staff are insensitive to the business of the secretarial staff; sometimes they exploit them to cover for their own lack of forward thinking. Everyone in the school needs to be aware of the boundaries of good practice in enlisting the aid of secretarial staff.

- Produce a list of tasks that it is legitimate for teaching staff to ask secretarial staff to undertake.

- Attach to this list a note of reasonable periods of prior notice for each kind of task.

- Produce a list of prohibited tasks and make sure it is observed.

- Provide (additional) facilities to enable teaching staff to carry out some tasks themselves.

- Review arrangements in the school for carrying out such manual tasks such as photocopying. Explore options such as employing unskilled operatives, or using 'free' labour such as parent volunteers.

- In all communications with staff about these issues, emphasise the value that the management places on the role of the secretary/receptionist

- of the post
- at major events in the school, take no public part

Strategy 13.6 *Overcoming the 'faceless*

schools depend heavily on their secretary/recep... school's life they are yet again just administe... proceedings and are not recorded in the v...

learning objectives for the 'secondment', and when some form of back/assessment is provided.

Inventory the current role of the post-holder in the learning of pupil the tasks undertaken:

- appropriate?
- consciously undertaken?
- properly recognised?
- understood by teaching staff?

Articulate to the post-holder and to other teaching and support staf what these 'learning points' are, and their value.

Involve the post-holder in school-based training along with teache

If the post-holder is used to carrying out supervisory tasks, e.g. to the resource centre, ensure that this happens with teacher sup agree what skills the post-holder can bring to the task.

Build the social learning that is so often a province of the post-h the social curriculum of the school by including it in policies an that it integrates with other related learning.

Where appropriate, provide training (see below).

Strategy 13.4 Providing time: for reflection, for im tion of improvements in administrative practice, for

Time in schools is always at a premium; but unless one invests tin reap the rewards of using time effectively. This is true for th secretary/receptioni and for all posts in the school.

- Send the post holder on a time management course.
- (appraisal) training needs view (see Strategy 13.1) identify the up a training plan and cost it. Begin
- As the post-hol th compare and keep a log of what she actually d
  - what you expect with:
  - what their job desc?
- Use the post-holder's them to do? need doing, that just don activities, or to ide time aside for th

- Ensure that secretarial/reception staff are included in major events in the school's life – invitations to attend prize day, school performances, concerts etc.
- Remember to mention them at such times as the Head's annual address to parents.
- Involve the support staff in such activities as reading at the carol service.
- Do an occasional 'walk-about' of the school specifically to talk to support staff rather than teachers or students.
- Institute a 'Support Person of the Month/Year' award.

Strategy 13.7 *Taking on board the insights of this role in the management decisions of the school*

Exactly how this can be done will depend largely on the size of the school, and the number of secretarial/administrative staff.

- Have a post-holder as non-teacher representative on the governing body.
- Invite the post-holder to SMT meetings often/occasionally for special items/always, but for a single, regular item on the agenda that provides them with opportunities to feed back on issues of concern to them.
- Set up a teacher/support staff liaison group.
- Use annual appraisals for feedback on less urgent issues.
- Link a school governor with the secretarial team.

Strategy 13.8 *Avoiding the Machiavellian behaviour of the post-holder from Hell*

This can be a 'hot potato', because the manipulative post-holder may also be bar-rack-room lawyer; so one has to make sure of one's ground at every step. Luckily, this is a minority event.

- As manager, make sure you know what is going on in the formal, and the informal, communications structures in your school.
- Be aware of the liaisons that develop between the post-holder and influential staff/parents/governors which might begin to look like a wielding of undue influence.

continues

159

Strategy 13. 8 *continued*

- Spread confidential/sensitive information between several post-holders, where appropriate, rather than leaving it all in the hands of one person.

- Take control of your own job – don't delegate functions that are really yours.

- Remember: some aspects of school life (timetabling, control of finances) are associated with enormous power and influence; control who does them.

- Nip in the bud any negative signs; don't let situations drift.

- Perhaps, institute a system whereby some jobs rotate so no one member of the team becomes the 'owner' of them.

- Even before trouble shows, don't be tempted into using the post-holder as a confidante.

- Remember: when you are tired or stressed you are at your most vulnerable to manipulation.

- If you have to act to correct a situation, do it early, do it fast, and do it properly.

Strategy 13.9 *Providing a listening ear*

This is a critical skill for all managers in all situations.

- Provide formal opportunities to listen to the post-holder, e.g. through appraisal, contributions to committees etc.

- Informally, listen to the 'message beyond the message' when there are hints, suggestions or advice about how things might be done differently/better.

- Watch the body language of the post-holder: are there times when this displays disaffection, annoyance, stress?

- Notice how the post-holder deals with others – the stress may only show when you are not there!

- Revisit strategies such as those in 13.2 and 13.4.

14

■ ■ ■

The role of the bursar

(In compiling this chapter my thanks are due to my colleagues Fergus O'Sullivan, Elizabeth Wood and Professor Angela Thody for allowing me unlimited access to their published works. These are credited in the Sources at the end of the chapter. James Welsh supplied additional, and useful, information.)

Introduction

Bursars have a long history of employment in the independent sector, but have been a recent development in the staffing of public sector schools. Private schools frequently used the services of retired military personnel and other professionals pursuing a second career to carry out these duties. The move towards grant maintained schools, and the greater financial independence of public sector schools since the mid-1980s, encouraged the proliferation of bursar posts in the maintained sector. Their emergence on the national scene was not necessarily welcomed, as Case Study 14.1 demonstrates.

> ## Case Study 14.1
> ## The new bursar: Jake's story
>
> When I left the military I thought: 'Well, I've got to augment my income and I'm still relatively young. So I looked around for a job that would use my experience as an organiser and personnel manager. I saw an advert for a bursar post in a grant maintained school. At interview there were several people in similar situations to myself, but I was the fortunate one who got the job. When I started, a month or so later, I wasn't so sure that I was actually all that fortunate. The education profession was not a welcoming milieu. Despite having responsibility for looking after the school's total

> resource – financial and plant – I discovered that I could only be defined as a non-person: a 'non-teacher'. By definition that meant 'lacking status'. At that time there were no professional qualifications available for bursars, no professional organisation and few of us to get together and share problems. I began to realise what it was really like to be a refugee.

So the early bursars were 'new' people in a 'new' profession. But they quickly set to work to carve out a way of working for themselves. Research shows that their duties became wide-ranging and critical to the success of schools: *see* Table 14.1.

Table 14.1 The range of responsibilities undertaken by bursars in schools

Resource Management Function

Administration management

1. Prepare and produce records and returns.
2. Maintain pupil records.
3. Analyse and report trends in pupils numbers, examination results and exclusions.
4. Manage the administrative, clerical and other support functions of the school.
5. Manage legal, public and statutory matters.
6. Initiate and manage change and improvement in pursuit of the school's goals.

Financial resource management

7. Keep accurate financial accounts.
8. Comply with sound principles of school finance.
9. Maximise income through lettings and additional activities.
10. Manage the budget cycle.
11. Analyse costs to ensure value for money.
12. Report accounting, auditing and financial information.
13. Manage cash, investments and credit control.
14. Evaluate and plan the budget.
15. Develop sound financial systems and practice.
16. Develop financial strategy and planning.

Human resource management

17. Keep accurate staff records.
18. Administer personnel remuneration.
19. Follow clear and fair principles of recruitment, retention and discipline.
20. Supervise and deploy support staff.

21. Manage staff contracts.
22. Manage supply staff cover.
23. Appoint and induct support staff.
24. Secure good labour relations through individual and collective negotiations.
25. Appraise and develop support staff.
26. Develop good labour relations.

Facilities and property management
27. Keep records of equipment, furnishings and school maintenance programmes.
28. Ensure the continuing availability of supplies, services and equipment.

Resource management function
29. Follow sound practices in real estate management and grounds maintenance.
30. Ensure the safe maintenance and operation of all buildings.
31. Supervise planning and construction services.
32. Ensure the maximum level of security consonant with the school's ethos.
33. Establish and monitor a site security policy.

Information management
34. Manage information and communication systems.
35. Evaluate management information systems.
36. Develop management information systems.
37. Participate in strategic planning.

Support services management
38. Ensure the adequate and safe operation of school transport.
39. Ensure the adequate and efficient provision of food services.
40. Manage risk/fire control, safe systems of work and medical aid.
41. Ensure conformity with health and safety legislation.
42. Manage school support contracts.

ICT management
43. Keep records of computer hardware and software.
44. Manage maintenance of the school's computer system.
45. Ensure compliance with legal requirements for ICT.
46. Develop the school's computerised administration system.

Marketing
47. Maintain positive relationships among all members of staff.
48. Manage support staff to promote the school positively to all stakeholders.

continues

Table 14.1 *continued*

49. Manage marketing matters.
50. Develop relationships with community and businesses to secure support for school.
51. Create positive relationships among all members of staff.
52. Develop supportive relationships with parents.

Teaching and learning

53. Keep accurate records of learning resources and equipment.
54. Maintain learning resources.
55. Articulate the curriculum philosophy of the school.
56. Teach pupils when required.

What qualities does a bursar need?

There are two aspects to this question. First, what kinds of people (with what kinds of backgrounds) become bursars? Second, what kinds of qualities do they need, once appointed, to carry out the job effectively?

Having talked to many bursars, the following is a representative set of answers to the first question:

> *I worked as an administrator for London Transport for a while; then I thought it would be good to have a change of scenery.*

> *I was a deputy principal for many years, having come up through the ranks of teaching. I began to specialise more and more in the resource area of work. Eventually, I asked if my job description could be rewritten so that I lost the remaining teaching responsibilities and took over the bursar role as a formal status.*

> *My first school post was as a secretary/receptionist in a small primary school. My line manager left, and the job sort of grew from there.*

> *I came out of the finance department at a Local Education Authority. Now I administer a small special school admitting children with behavioural problems for either day or residential care.*

> *When I took early retirement from the bank I wanted to go on working for a while without the sorts of pressures of the commercial world.*

> *I was a teacher, then decided to leave and have a family. Now the family has grown up I wanted to go back into the school environment that I understood, but I didn't want to be a teacher again. So I took a bursar post instead, and use my knowledge of the profession in a slightly different context.*

These backgrounds are fairly typical, though not exhaustive, of the origins of those who take up bursar posts. Educational background has been shown by research to be just as varied. While some bursars come with just a handful of

GCSE or equivalent passes, others have first degrees, professional qualifications or even master's degrees. In the same way, while some have held managerial posts in other professions or occupations, others may have come to the role through clerical posts or even through acting as treasurer for a club or society.

Once in post, research suggests that personal qualities matter; in particular, a high level of personal organisation and efficiency. Indeed, the characteristic of bursars who pass through the MBA course in which we are involved at the University of Lincolnshire and Humberside is that they have to organise themselves, the school, and the staff of the school, as well as those from outside (such as maintenance officials).

Tact and communication skills feature highly in the profile of the effective bursar. The job is demanding. Most put in long hours, but they are hours when there is constant pressure to respond to the varied demands of people and events. Because the job is wide-ranging, but not tightly defined, there is a need for flexibility and energy; and the post-holder must show considerable commitment to the institution.

The nature of the role has caused O'Sullivan *et al.* in the Sources cited at the end of the chapter to rename the bursar 'the school business manager'. One secondary school bursar described it as:

> The ability to 'interpret dreams into reality'.

The relevance of the bursar to learning

Due to the decentralisation of financial management, UK schools in the 21st century are increasingly making strategic decisions about their area of specialisation in order to compete in the open market place. Indeed, as this chapter is being written the Prime Minister is addressing a teachers' union on the proposed increase in the number of specialist schools. In common with schools around the world, UK schools have to decide:

- how they will organise and operate the service they offer;
- the optimum use of the staffing complement in the school;
- how this staff will be remunerated and rewarded; and
- which categories of revenue to pursue to operate the business.

Increasing accountability involves the senior management team in sustaining improvement through setting educational standards and monitoring and evaluating quality. Physical, human and learning resources are measured in terms of impact on standards and quality in order to achieve the best possible outcomes for all pupils.

Research shows that half the schools in the UK now use bursars or their equivalent to administer or manage their resources. Although financial management is a major responsibility, it is no longer the main or only remit for bursars. Many areas of activity previously within the remit of the LEA have now been delegated to bursars, whose duties have expanded to include human resource management, facilities administration, marketing, ICT and control of management information, as well as direct involvement in teaching and learning through record keeping and evaluation. Bursars often lead and represent the other groups of support staff in the school and administer and manage contracts.

As a relative newcomer to school administration and management, the bursar's role in the school is uncertain. Teachers are suspicious of their position but value their contribution. Governing bodies still have no real understanding of the role and many senior management teams and principals have not taken the opportunity to use the bursar to provide detailed management information about resources, marketing opportunities and, more importantly, about student learning and progression. Principals, however, are taking the opportunity to delegate resource administration and management when they are uncomfortable with the role themselves.

Although the majority of bursars are not directly involved in teaching and learning, effective bursars will contribute to school achievement by efficiently and effectively running their schools to enable teachers and senior teaching managers to concentrate on the core business. They:

- create a good quality learning environment;
- manage contracts;
- work well with all staff;
- raise the profile of the school;
- generate extra income;
- analyse and evaluate essential data so that they, the governors and other managers can make decisions based on value for money and pupil achievement.

In practice, bursars may be even more involved in learning than is indicated by this rather bald list. O'Sullivan *et al.* (2000c) describe how bursars became involved in various learning projects in schools (op. cit.: Ch. 11). This outline includes descriptions of how bursars:

- contributed to pupil performance (especially the performance of the most and least able pupils);
- facilitated access to learning out of normal school hours;
- changed the balance of teachers to support staff to improve value for money and efficiency in learning;
- analysed assessment data, thus releasing teacher time;

- identified the need for specialist staff to support learning, e.g. IT technical officers;
- provided alternative scenarios for resourcing learning (e.g. less reprographics, more CDs);
- up-graded library resources for learning;
- improved the job descriptions of support staff to improve learning by pupils.

Work with bursars shows, again and again, that these roles in learning are becoming more and more significant. They are not teaching roles, but they are learning-related roles and schools would be poorer without them.

Bursars, training and professionalism

As one might expect, when bursars began to be appointed in maintained schools, they quickly organised themselves and the National Bursars' Association (NBA) was formed. The NBA is now the country's professional body for bursars and provides 'professional services and programmes to promote the highest standards of school business management practices and professional growth, and the most effective use of educational resources' (NBA materials).

The objectives of the NBA are:

- To represent the views of bursars and allied post-holders to Ministers, the DfEE and other relevant agencies.
- To provide the bursarial perspective on DfEE and government consultation documents.
- To endorse nationally recognised qualifications and to provide, encourage and support professional development and professional recognition for bursars.
- To promote a National Code of Good Practice.
- To provide professional support for members.
- To inform others in the education sector about the interests of those holding administrative posts.
- To develop relevant national and international links.

The NBA is linked with schemes to provide in-service recognition and training through a Licence of the National Bursars' Association up to master's and doctoral degrees. It might well be argued that the pattern established by the NBA is the way in which all support staff roles will develop over the next few years.

Further information

Details about the role of the bursar have been researched at length in the publications reported and listed in the Sources below, and the issues need not be laboured here. Readers with a particular interest in these areas are advised to follow them up using these publications. For the more general reader, the information here and in Chapter 15 will suffice as part of an overview of support roles in schools.

Sources used in the compilation of this chapter

Working papers

O'Sullivan, F., Thody, A. and Wood, E. (2000a) *From bursar to educational resource manager: reengineering a key role in schools for the 21st century – methodological issues and literature review*. Working Paper 37. Lincoln: University of Lincolnshire and Humberside.

O'Sullivan, F., Thody, A. and Wood, E. (2000b) *From bursar to educational resource manager: reengineering a key role in schools for the 21st century – bursars' careers and roles*. Working Paper 38. Lincoln: University of Lincolnshire and Humberside.

Conference papers

Wood, E. and O'Sullivan, F. (2001) 'Site-based school business management: implications for supporting teaching and learning', AERA Annual Meeting Seattle: USA presented at Division 5: School Organisation.

O'Sullivan, F. and Wood, E. (2001) 'Leading site-based management: aligning resources to the learning environment', AERA Annual Meeting Seattle: USA presented at Strategic Change Special Interest Group.

Textbook

O'Sullivan, F., Thody, A., and Wood, E. (2000c) *From bursar to school business manager*. London: FT/Prentice Hall.

15
■ ■ ■

Managing the bursar

Introduction

We saw in Chapter 14 that a bursar's role can be ambiguous: not a teacher, yet a professional; a manager of others, yet often not part of the Senior Management Team. This chapter attempts to help Heads and others look more closely at the role and to facilitate its better management within the school.

Bursars have working relationships with other adults and youngsters in the school. With governors, research suggests their role is mostly formal – often as Clerk to the governing body. According to the same research (O'Sullivan *et al.* 2000c, cited in Chapter 14), relations with teachers were the most strained. Teachers did not welcome non-teaching colleagues. Indeed, most of the bursars whom I have taught at Master's level over the last three years have complained that, for teachers, there is an almost unbridgeable gap between teachers and non-teachers in the school. The language is always perjorative ('we are second class citizens'), and teachers expect a subservience that many bursars, with their professional backgrounds, find hard to stomach. Conversely, bursars often regard teachers as having little managerial skill and as being generally 'inefficient' or 'disorganised'.

It may be that as the role of the bursar becomes better defined (e.g. into the school business manager) respect will grow. Bursars don't seem to have relationship problems with Heads – except in the handful of cases where inadequate Heads treat them as confidantes:

She [the head] broke down and cried on me. I didn't know what to do. It put me in a very difficult position. I became party to all her insecurities. I didn't feel it was part of my job, but I didn't know how to say so.

(Female bursar)

The NBA, mentioned in the previous chapter, has developed National Standards for bursars, against which their professional performance can be measured. These standards also give an insight into the way in which the role might be managed. It seems appropriate to begin with the role that the bursar (or the equivalent post-holder) might play in your school.

One of the national standards looks at key areas of bursarship and identifies them thus:

- Administrative management.
- Financial resource management.
- Human resource management.
- Facility and property management.
- Information management.
- Support service management.

Strategy 15.1 *Reviewing the role of bursar in your school*

Use the list of job roles in Table 15.1.

Ask your bursar to identify the roles that he/she plays.

It may be even better if he/she is prepared to rate each role, on the three-point scale: 1 = very important, 3 = not important.

When this is done, sit down together and try to identify:

- The nature of the jobs your bursar does which are most central in your school.
- How these important jobs relate to the NBA six categories (above).
- What roles are seen as not important and whether this is reasonable in your situation.
- What support the bursar might need to perform some roles more effectively.

Table 15.1 The range of responsibilities undertaken by bursars in schools

Resource Management Function

Administration management
1. Prepare and produce records and returns.
2. Maintain pupil records.
3. Analyse and report trends in pupils numbers, examination results and exclusions.

4. Manage the administrative, clerical, other support functions of the school.
5. Manage legal, public and statutory matters.
6. Initiate and manage change and improvement in pursuit of the school's goals.

Financial resource management

7. Keep accurate financial accounts.
8. Comply with sound principles of school finance.
9. Maximise income through lettings and additional activities.
10. Manage the budget cycle.
11. Analyse costs to ensure value for money.
12. Report accounting, auditing and financial information.
13. Manage cash, investments and credit control.
14. Evaluate and plan the budget.
15. Develop sound financial systems and practice.
16. Develop financial strategy and planning.

Human resource management

17. Keep accurate staff records.
18. Administer personnel remuneration.
19. Follow clear and fair principles of recruitment, retention and discipline.
20. Supervise and deploy support staff.
21. Manage staff contracts.
22. Manage supply staff cover.
23. Appoint and induct support staff.
24. Secure good labour relations through individual and collective negotiations.
25. Appraise and develop support staff.
26. Develop good labour relations.

Facilities and property management

27. Keep records of equipment, furnishings and school maintenance programmes.
28. Ensure the continuing availability of supplies, services and equipment.

Resource management function

29. Follow sound practices in real estate management and grounds maintenance.
30. Ensure the safe maintenance and operation of all buildings.
31. Supervise planning and construction services.
32. Ensure the maximum level of security consonant with the school's ethos.
33. Establish and monitor a site security policy.

continues

Table 15.1 *continued*

Information management

34. Manage information and communication systems.
35. Evaluate management information systems.
36. Develop management information systems.
37. Participate in strategic planning.

Support services management

38. Ensure the adequate and safe operation of school transport.
39. Ensure the adequate and efficient provision of food services.
40. Manage risk/fire control, safe systems of work and medical aid.
41. Ensure conformity with health and safety legislation.
42. Manage school support contracts.

ICT management

43. Keep records of computer hardware and software.
44. Manage maintenance of the school's computer system.
45. Ensure compliance with legal requirements for ICT.
46. Develop the school's computerised administration system.

Marketing

47. Maintain positive relationships among all members of staff.
48. Manage support staff to promote the school positively to all stakeholders.
49. Manage marketing matters.
50. Develop relationships with community and businesses to secure support for school.
51. Create positive relationships among all members of staff.
52. Develop supportive relationships with parents.

Teaching and learning

53. Keep accurate records of learning resources and equipment.
54. Maintain learning resources.
55. Articulate the curriculum philosophy of the school.
56. Teach pupils when required.

Once you have looked at the results in Strategy 15.1, you could revisit the outcomes from a different perspective by using Strategy 15.2.

Strategy 15.2 *Planning professional development for bursars*

- Revisit the job role exercise in Strategy 15.1.
- Ask the bursar for which roles he/she feels most equipped, and for which he/she would welcome more access to training.
- Develop a prioritised list of training needs for the bursar.
- Implement a strategy for assisting the bursar to access the identified training at appropriate times.
- Consider affiliating the school to the NBA to take advantage of the professional information available through this medium.

Strategy 15.3 *Turning dreams into reality*

Whether or not the bursar is, formally, a member of the senior management team of the school, he/she has considerable responsibility and power.

In the previous chapter we mentioned that some bursars saw their role as 'turning dreams into reality'.

This is a laudable ambition, but the first question has to be: whose dreams?

Find an opportunity for the senior management team and the bursar to 'share their dreams'.

What emerges from this? What vision does this session identify for the future development of the school? In particular, how will these dreams shape the developing/learning of the pupils?

Turn the dreams into an agenda. Empower the bursar to attempt to implement the resource elements of that agenda.

Strategy 15.4 *Improving the understanding of the bursar's role*

We have established in this chapter and in Chapter 14 that the role of the bursar is sometimes misunderstood and may even be resented.

Consider the ways in which the role of bursar might be better presented in your school:

- to governors;
- to parents;
- to teaching staff;

continues

Strategy 15.4 *continued*

- to other managers (especially middle managers);
- to pupils.

Is the role described in the school brochure?

Are there potential areas of conflict with other staff? What are they? How could they be resolved?

Are there opportunities to celebrate the role and its successes (e.g. when a new classroom is opened or a new facility is made available)? How? Through a letter to parents? A school newsletter?

Does the bursar report to the governors? How often? In what format?

What else could be done to profile the role more positively?

Strategy 15.6 *Developing the role of the bursar as manager*

Bursars are often the managers of other staff of the school, most frequently of some or all of the support staff.

How well equipped by experience or study is your bursar in the business of management and leadership in the school?

The use of some appraisal time might be devoted to exploring this issue. The following notes, based on the national standards for bursars, might help focus attention of the major issues:

To what extent would a) you and b) your bursar rate the bursarial performance in the school against these headings:

- professional leadership;
- sound management of the support staff/services;
- improved standard of learning leading to improved attainment;
- high quality support for teaching staff;
- improved team spirit among all staff;
- effective budget procedures;
- good premises management;
- sound health and safety practice;
- good external relations;
- effective appraisal for managed staff;
- sound decision-making;
- good communication;
- effective self-management?

As a postscript to this chapter, it is worth noting that O'Sullivan *et al.* (op. cit.: 199) conclude that the bursar who has become the school business manager is a pro-active site manager:

Such bursars would have the opportunity to operate in a leadership capacity as they would be members of the senior management team and hold designated responsibility for the school's support staff teams. They would, therefore, contribute to setting the ethos and policies of the school and communicating them to their staff. They would also lead the implementation of their staff development to enable them to operate as effective individuals working collaboratively with all staff in the school.

16

■ ■ ■

Parents and other voluntary helpers

Introduction

In Chapter 1 we discussed the 'Mum's Army' debate that racked education a decade or so ago when the government of the time suggested that courses should be run for Specialist Teacher Assistants. But the real Mum's Army has been with us far longer and its members are not the trained personnel of STA fame, but the many voluntary helpers used by schools. They are, almost exclusively mums, and many (though not all) are motivated in the first instance when their own children reach school age. Some see involvement in the classroom as a way to keep some contact with the child and some control over, or at least some knowledge of, their schooling.

These remarks should not be interpreted in any sense negatively. In Chapter 2, we noted that in many areas of the world, especially the USA, the use of volunteers in classrooms is viewed as a huge advantage to the education service. This is the stance that will be taken in this chapter, too. However, the degree of value to be extracted from this group of classroom assistants depends entirely on how well they are managed. As the group with the least training (if any) and the least well defined roles, this is the group for whom effective management is vital. This chapter explores whether they get the management they need and what could be done to maximise their potential. Here we need to begin by looking in detail at who they are and at what schools ask them to do.

Who are the parents and volunteers operating in schools?

In our sample, though we were able to trawl only a small number of such volunteers, what stood out was the variety of backgrounds of the people (all female) who acted as volunteers (the term we shall use to describe their role). These are some of their stories.

Case Study 16.1
Mag's story

I attended a small town grammar school and came away with nine O levels and two A levels. In the 1970s I went to a city Polytechnic and read for a Higher National Diploma in Business Studies, writing my dissertation on computerised data processing. After gaining the award I stayed in the city, working first as an accounts clerk at a local company and later as a production control technician with the City Council.

I was promoted to a more senior post with a neighbouring Council and then again within the Council. Personal circumstances took me from the North of England to the South at this point and I again worked in the local Council offices, and later in London.

I started my school involvement only just over a year ago.

Case Study 16.2
Rita's story

I had a conventional education at the local High School and then a Technical College. I trained as a nurse, working for a short period in a Psychiatric Unit before deciding on a career change. I joined the Police Force and after training, became a WPC carrying out uniformed duties in an Eastern county. I was involved in solving crimes related to retail theft and received an award and commendation for bravery for arresting an armed man involved in a bank robbery.

From this role I moved to become a detective constable working with the Regional Crime Squad, investigating drug trafficking and kidnapping, which involved a lot of covert operations. Throughout my police career I went on a vast array of courses on topics from driving to electronic surveillance techniques.

I got involved helping in a reception class in 1998.

Case Study 16.3
Ann's story

I collected a mixed bag of educational qualifications in my younger days ranging from CSE maths, needlework and French, through O levels in English and German, to A level in British Government. I also collected a lot of music qualifications: grade 8 piano, grade 5 music theory and grade 8 singing.

My earliest employment was as a chambermaid in a Ski Lodge, but I moved on from there to be assistant manager and relief manager for a hotel group. I tended to be most attracted by the catering side of the business, and subsequently held four catering manager posts.

In my spare time I am conductor of a youth orchestra and train children to sing. Naturally, in school, I look after quite a few aspects of the music.

Case Study 16.4
Caz's story

I am 36 years old and have three children of my own. I do voluntary work in school, which may mean listening to reading or mounting pictures – it's very varied.

I attended a Catholic school and got the usual cluster of O levels and then studied typing at evening classes. After school I worked in a shop demonstrating musical instruments and then at a service station for several years.

The most interesting job was as a trainee medical photographer in a hospital, which involved photography, exhibition display, reception duties and so on. My husband was keen to emigrate and start his own business, and this we did in 1994. But I was homesick and eventually, though we enjoyed life abroad, we returned to England and I started my voluntary work in school.

What do volunteers do to aid learning?

As part of our survey we asked our sample of volunteers to supply us with copies of their job descriptions. Only one respondent claimed to have a job description but was unable or unwilling to supply a copy; none of the remainder had job descriptions. There is no doubt that the jobs they did were, in practice, various but we had to reconstruct them from other information that they supplied.

Here is some of the evidence we compiled about the roles of the volunteers in their own words:

I don't have a job description for my role as a parent helper. Guidance on what I am expected to do is given by the relevant staff member that I am working with at the time. This is in the form of verbal instruction. What I actually do consists of any of the following. First, I listen to readers; the teacher will have told me where to work and explained how to record information and what I should aim for the pupil to achieve. Second, I have been involved in preparing for the school concert and had to listen to the narrators practise and given them help. Third, I sometimes sit in on music lessons where I both observe and participate if appropriate. In every case I think briefing in the individual situation is necessary.

I help in an infant/nursery school where I am assigned to the IT room with different age groups during the course of the time I am there. With reception children I assist a paid classroom assistant, who tells me what the learning aims for the time are. We work with groups of about nine or ten children.

I help with Years 5 and 6. When I go in I have no idea what I will be doing that day. I quite like it that way because it makes the work more varied. I often work with a group who don't need long term specialist help but are struggling with one specific problem or misunderstanding, such as one idea in maths. My job is to provide a bit more practice, on a small group or 1:1 basis, when the teacher doesn't have time because the rest of the class has moved on.

On arrival each day I would go into the reception class and sit among the children during registration. Then the teacher tells me about what the children will be doing, or which children need help. I work with one child or a group, but it could be on maths, language, topic or art and craft. The most able children will be given supplementary work by the teacher, but when everyone has finished there is 'choosing'. At the end of the day I help the children tidy up before home time, and I will pick on what else needs doing (such as cleaning the painting area). I may take two or three children out for extra reading; and the teacher and the paid assistant will be doing the same, which means children are heard more often.

I work in the afternoon and arrive for registration. The teacher may have collected reading records together for those children who have not yet been heard, or who have been absent ill for a while and so on. I work listening to readers, maybe in the classroom, or in the corridor outside. The child and I chat about the book, I check on their observation and memory skills, and listen to them read...some will read small books with three or four words to a page – in which case I try to get them to read the whole book. Those who are on more advanced books are encouraged to read three or four pages. If they have difficulty I ask them to break up words phonetically and to pursue clues from the pictures on the pages. Advanced readers need to be reminded to use punctuation and intonation and to listen to themselves. I record the child's progress.

What emerges from these accounts are several factors of considerable interest.

First, the work of these volunteers is central to the learning being undertaken by pupils: the tasks they carry out are – at least in part and in every case – learning-related tasks.

Second, there is little systematic control and guidance exercised over this through job descriptions; there is some word-of-mouth direction by the teacher at the time.

Third, there is no pre-planning for most volunteers: they turn up not knowing what to expect.

Fourth, they may work under the direction of a teacher or under the direction of a paid assistant: in the latter case they may be one further step removed from any planned management of their work.

Fifth, some of the tasks they carry out are quite sophisticated, involving actual 'teaching' (for example, reread the last quote, on page 179), and recording of pupils' progress.

Sixth, in most cases they have received no training for these roles.

Of course, we know from experience that there are schools – even primary schools – that resist voluntary help. We know that there are some that use volunteers but only for manual tasks such as duplicating worksheets and cataloguing the library. We are aware of schools that grade volunteers into those who do manual tasks only and those that carry out class-based functions. But we have no reason, and no evidence, for doubting that volunteers are not only widespread in primary schools especially, but that many of them do undertake the kinds of roles described in the quotations above. Nor are we arguing against this. Our thesis is this: that it strengthens the case of this book for improving the training and management of volunteers.

The value of volunteer help in the classroom

We asked a sample of volunteer helpers to reflect on what they saw as the value of volunteers and Table 16.1 encapsulates their reflections.

Table 16.1 The value of volunteers

- They give children confidence (working with children 1:1 or in small groups boosts their morale).
- They provide close supervision that can give children a sense of achievement.
- They can make up for lack of support from home.
- They signal to children that adults other than teachers are interested and involved in schools and education.

- They may provide specific and targeted support for children with a particular (learning) problem.
- They help with social skills.

The specific contribution of volunteers to children's learning

So far we have discovered who the typical volunteers are and what they are likely to do when they come to school. But we need to ask: Why is this useful? The views of the volunteers themselves are shown in Table 16.2. The views are all very positive, but that does not mean that volunteers in our sample did not have some views about problems and disadvantages.

One shared concern was that schools did not have, or did not allocate, adequate space for volunteers to carry out their tasks. Since much of the work was about learning, one might have expected the spaces in which the work took place to reflect the quiet area needed by children to concentrate. We have all seen volunteers squatting in corridors listening to readers, the pupils' eyes swivelling from text to passing distractions just like those of fans at a tennis match following the flight of the ball from one end of the court to the other.

The second issue they raised was that of lack of planning. This meant that they could not prepare ahead, but also that they were often diverted in their work, mid-way through carrying out one task, to look after another. Such a way of managing their time was unsatisfactory for the pupils involved and unsatisfying for the volunteers.

The third issue was one of training – or lack of it – and we revisit this at page 191. As one respondent put it:

> Training has been verbal, while I would welcome written guidance whilst acknowledging that teachers do things individualistically too.

Table 16.2 The value of voluntary help in schools: volunteers' views

We assist learning. ('There would be no point in doing this job unless there were a contribution to children's learning.')

We are able to use our specific strengths and experiences as a way to benefit the young.

We can simplify activities for some children so that they make quicker progress than they would in the regular class without personal attention.

We can give access to expertise that may not be available in the school (e.g. in IT).

continues

Table 16.2 *continued*

We can give children access to different teaching styles (e.g. group work and individualised learning); 'some children find it difficult to concentrate in class but will work great in a small group'.

We can free up the teacher to do things of a specialist nature with smaller groups of pupils.

We can undertake lengthy and burdensome tasks such as hearing children read.

'You find that some children will relate better to a volunteer than to a teacher.'

The problem of training

Volunteers are widely used. Typically, in our sample, the schools involved had five or six regular volunteers sometimes as many as twelve or even more. This represents a significant input of time into the school. Since we have established beyond any reasonable doubt that much of this time is learning related, one might expect the volunteers to receive some systematic briefing about children's learning.

This was not the case. There were in-house instructions given about what to do and how to do it on particular occasions (such as when conducting school visits), but none of the volunteers in our sample knew of any training available specifically to them. They did not think that their schools would support them if they wanted to train: they are considered too short-term an investment to warrant spending the school's money.

Our respondents thought that there should be written guidelines and codes of practice for volunteers but, though one believed that such a code did exist in her LEA, she had not been able to obtain it. None of the volunteers we talked with had received written instructions. They all felt that some general guidance in the form of briefing about how children learn would be useful.

The respondents picked out issues from their daily work that would benefit from training. They knew that boys and girls responded differently to reading but did not know why, nor the scale and nature of the problem. They were often thrown by educational jargon and acronyms. They did not understand their responsibilities in respect of poor behaviour by pupils in their care. They were concerned about safety issues and wanted guidance in sensitive areas like working 1:1 with pupils, that might hold inherent dangers.

This group felt that training would be most appropriate in-house. None said they were invited to training days; but they felt that the sort of training given to specialist teacher assistants might be the right kind of activity for them.

It would seem that, with this group, training is a particularly critical issue.

The limitations of the concept

In this chapter we have addressed issues only as they relate to volunteers as they commonly exist: in other words, to the widespread use of parents (mainly mothers) to undertake both learning related and manual activities in schools, usually primary schools.

In Chapter 2, however, it was noted that other kinds of volunteers exist: specialists from the community who could make occasional contributions, senior citizens who have experience and time and who could help on an informal basis and so on. This is a topic that will be revisited in Chapter 17. For the moment it is enough to raise it as a consideration. If the suggestion is accepted it implies a more widespread and flexible use of volunteers and opens the way for a more extensive use of both men and women in secondary as well as primary contexts. Of course, one would have to put in place the essential security checks and vetting procedures required by such a scheme and it is important to recognise the sensitivities implied by this way of working.

If the suggestion is to be realised, however, it throws into even sharper relief the matter of training discussed in this chapter and the matter of management of the role that is the subject of the next.

17

■ ■ ■

Managing volunteers in schools

Introduction

It will come as no surprise to readers of the previous chapter that this group of volunteers had very disparate views about their management. There was little evidence in our survey to suggest that they were managed effectively. Such a discovery highlights the importance of this chapter in changing practice. We asked the respondents in our survey to rate their management on a seven point scale (exactly as we did for specific groups of paid assistants discussed in this book). The result was a spread of scores from one to seven (1 = high).

How are volunteers managed?

Line management is usually carried out by the class teacher who might also (but incidentally) carry out another role such as year group co-ordinator. Occasionally a paid non-teaching assistant would manage the role. There were no formal meetings to discuss either principles for the role or specific tactics for the sessions; all the management, without exception, was carried out on an *ad hoc* basis on the day at the start of the relevant lesson. There was absolutely no pre-planning about how these post-holders might be best utilised.

Though the statements made above are all rather negative, this does not mean that our respondents were necessarily as critical of their management as we have been. One, whose management was a described above, commented:

It works well because I feel I am trusted.

However, not everyone agreed:

I don't feel that I am particularly 'managed' at all. I'm told that I am a big help but not whether I'm being as effective as I might be or whether the language I use is correct.

There were some instances of 'defensiveness' about the school's failure to manage:

Being a parent governor (as well as a volunteer) means that I am (already) privy to management decisions and discussions.

This comment misses the point. We are not discussing generalised management information here, but the tactics and strategies needed to organise the learning activities in a specific class on a specific day, and knowing these far enough ahead in order to prepare (when necessary).

Asked about strengths and weaknesses in management of the role, the post-holders we surveyed were vague. They constantly referred to being 'trusted', and drew the conclusion that if they were trusted with children, and with knowledge of some children's learning problems, then that was a management strength. Conversely, they tended to reject the notion of weak management because the teacher and/or the Head were 'approachable', which meant that they could be consulted if necessary. However, they did feel that they sometimes needed more information about the children in their charge and that there should be written guidance for volunteers about their role.

There was a half-hearted attempt by the post-holders we surveyed to construct a picture of an ideal manager, and the result appears in Table 17.1.

Table 17.1 An ideal manager of voluntary classroom assistants

The ideal manager will:
- provide information to enable the volunteer to do the job properly;
- give clear instructions;
- trust the volunteer to do what is required;
- be accessible;
- listen to the volunteer;
- forge good relations with the volunteer;
- offer help when needed.

While the material in Table 17.1 is sound enough in principle, it falls well short of effective management. It describes the best end of the continuum of management as volunteers experience it: on an 'as and when' basis, and without forethought. It ignores the major questions that are dealt with in the strategies that follow.

Managing volunteers

The underlying question we have to answer is this: In principle, should the management of volunteers be the same as, or different from, the management of paid support staff?

This text takes a clear and unequivocal line.

Volunteers undertake essentially similar roles to those carried out by paid support staff. Some may be confined to duties of a purely manual or administrative nature – in which case their roles are comparable to aspects of those carried out by school secretaries/receptionists. But usually they carry out learning-related roles (even 'teaching' roles) comparable to the work of specialist teacher assistants/classroom assistants and special needs teaching assistants. In either case, to ensure the quality of their work and maximise its impact on pupils, the role needs to be managed efficiently and effectively, and to be contextualised in the whole operation of the school. Nothing less than this is adequate.

For these reasons, we have included here a number of strategies for managing the role of volunteers in schools that attempt to meet these ideals. In this we are encouraged by an HMI survey and its conclusions drawn from a national sample. The only reservation we have in reproducing the following quotation is that this survey used data collected in 1989–1990 – and there has been no improvement since!

> *Voluntary helpers undertook, under teachers' supervision, virtually any practical task, including mounting and displaying children's work; hearing children read; supporting group activities such as baking, art and craft and story writing; and helping to supervise swimming. They ran the school library, organised toy fairs and bookshops, helped with administrative tasks, assisted with extra-curricular activities such as gardening, chess and drama, and repaired and maintained equipment and books. Volunteers often assisted with educational visits...The substantial majority of non-teaching staff made a significant contribution and their work was highly valued by teachers. However, the effectiveness of many was constrained to a greater or lesser degree by factors which included a limited perception, on the part of schools and of these staff themselves, of their capabilities and potential; inadequate management and in particular the absence of a job description; a lack for formal appraisal of performance; lack of in-service training; and a shortage of time to perform duties.*
>
> (HMI (1992) *Non-teaching staff in schools.* London: HMSO, pp. 10–12)

Strategy 17.1 *Constructing a policy about the use of volunteers*

The first step in utilising volunteers effectively has to be to make conscious decisions about whether and how they should be employed in your school. To this end, the first strategy here asks you to construct a policy – for scrutiny and approval by the governing body – about your use of volunteers. Some headings are attached to start you thinking about key issues, but they are not intended to be exhaustive and cannot be specific to your situation.

- Do you wish to use voluntary help at all in your school?
- What is your rationale for its use? Would there be any problems in using volunteers, e.g. objections from staff?
- If you do intend to use volunteers, do you envisage their roles as being of a purely manual/administrative nature, or classroom-based?
- If classroom-based, what criteria will you use to allocate them to specific classes?
- What functions will classroom-based and non-classroom-based volunteers fulfil?
- How will you vet their suitability? (You need to think about a range of issues from police checks to whether or not you interview potential volunteers.)
- Once appointed, how will they be inducted? When? By whom?
- Will you operate any 'rules of engagement', e.g. volunteers not to operate in classes in which their own children are present? Will you allow 1:1 working or small groups only?

(Strategies 17.2, 17.3, 17.4 and 17.5 may also generate data to be included in this policy.)

Strategy 17.2 *Writing guidelines for volunteers*

In our survey, we discovered that almost all our volunteers would have welcomed written guidelines to help them in their roles. These, however, did not exist. This exercise asks you to consider what you might include in your guidelines and invites you to pursue your emergent outline to a fully fleshed out document.

Some possible areas for inclusion in written guidelines for volunteers

- The mission and vision of the school.
- The school's expectations of volunteers and its rationale for their work (*see* Strategy 17.1).

continues

Strategy 17.2 *continued*

- Types of volunteers and the job roles (*see* Strategies 17.4 and 17.5).
- The criteria for acceptance of volunteers.
- Range and limits of duties and responsibilities.
- Arrangements for the management of volunteers (*see* Strategy 17.3).
- Actions to be taken in specific circumstances, e.g. emergency First Aid, incidents of behaviour management.
- Guidance on specific activities, e.g. how to listen to readers.
- Support available to volunteers (*see* Strategy 17.7).

Strategy 17.3 *Managing volunteers*

All parties have thrown up problems and inadequacies in the management of voluntary help in schools. It is clearly an issue that needs to be addressed with vigour. The headings below offer some starting points, and you should add your own to accord with your own circumstances.

Who will have **overall** responsibility for managing the school's volunteers?

How will that management operationalise the school's policies? (*See* Strategy 17.1.)

Who will have day-to-day **line-management** duties in respect of any individual volunteer?

How will line-managers be selected and briefed for the role?

What will be expected of the line-managers?

How will the school provide for the pre-planning necessary to make the work of volunteers effective?

How will the work of volunteers be:

- mentored?
- monitored?
- appraised?

What arrangements will be made for the volunteers to access any training they need, or that is identified through appraisal? (*See* Strategy 17.7.)

What will be the processes for moving unsuitable/ineffectual volunteers out of the role or into more suitable roles?

Strategy 17.4 *Generating job descriptions for volunteers*

Volunteers in our survey (and in the HMI survey of a decade ago, quoted above) were disadvantaged because they did not have adequate job descriptions. Though unpaid, they carry out specific roles; thus they have expectations of themselves and others may have expectations of them. They needed reassurance that what they were doing what was what was required. If the title 'job description' sounds too formal for a volunteer role, then some other description might be used (outline of duties; guide to tasks). But the principle of generating a job description remains, and this Strategy raises some key issues.

- In advertising for volunteers or dealing with those who offer their services spontaneously, how will the school spell out the contractual nature of the relationship between itself and the volunteer? What are the obligations on each side? How do these promote the school's mission?
- Will all volunteers in the school have the same roles? (*See* Strategy 17.5.)
- If so, can you construct a generic job description for them all?
- Would it be better to have a generic element applicable to all, and a specific one tailored to each individual?
- What would go into the generic element?
- What kinds of specific elements might you construct?
- Who will be party to these job descriptions?
- How will they be used (e.g. in appraisal)?

Strategy 17.5 *Considering different kinds of volunteer role*

Much of what has been said in this chapter has implied that schools and school managers of volunteers have considerable flexibility in utilising volunteers. Volunteers may be found who fulfil either long-term or short-term roles, and they may have classroom-based or non-classroom-based responsibilities. This Strategy suggests that you use the list below to think through:

- The kinds of volunteers who might be available to you.
- The kinds of volunteers you might wish to use from this menu.

(You might use the outcome of this Strategy to inform your thinking under Strategies 17.1–17.4 and 17.7.)

Possible roles for volunteers

- hearing readers;

continues

Strategy 17.5 *continued*

- special needs support/able pupil support;
- ICT support and specialist instruction;
- subject-specific support and specialist instruction;
- being a visiting speaker/expert;
- conducting story time;
- supervising games;
- sports coaching;
- library duties;
- secretarial/reception support;
- running a school shop/tuck shop;
- taking assembly;
- cleaning, tidying, display work and general manual activities;
- others (add your own list).

Strategy 17.6 *Making space*

Our volunteers complained that they did not have suitable spaces in which to operate. This was partly because they were undertaking learning-related tasks and they felt (correctly) that learning had to happen in a suitable environment. The following suggestions may help to focus attention of some important factors about space.

- Identify the types of volunteer you will use and their total number (Strategy 17.5).
- Identify the policy for their utilisation (Strategies 17.1 and 17.2).
- Carry out a space audit in the light of these decisions:
  - Who will work in the classroom, and not need specific accommodation?
  - Who needs to extract small groups or individuals? Where might these groups go?
  - What spaces already in existence are not being used effectively? Are suitable for change of use?
  - Is there a space for volunteers to have a 'base'?
  - Will volunteers use the staffroom? What are the advantages and disadvantages of this arrangement? For them? For the staff?
  - Is there provision for notice-boards and similar facilities?
- How will confidentiality operate within the space-related decisions you have made?

Strategy 17.7 *Training for volunteers*

Our volunteers were strongly persuaded that training should form part of their role. Of course, some members of the teaching profession might feel threatened by this, believing that their teaching roles are being usurped. But the simple logic is that, if volunteers are carrying out learning-related activities – and they are – then they should be given the information they need to do this effectively. That means: training. This text also takes the view that, while in-house training is important, the training of volunteers should not be confined to these experiences. This Strategy poses some questions to focus attention on the kinds of training that might be suitable for volunteers.

Have you put in place suitable induction procedures for volunteers?

Do you hold briefing sessions for new volunteers on critical issues such as listening effectively to readers?

Are volunteers made welcome to attend (suitable) staff training events in-house?

Are volunteers encouraged to look at LEA and other courses that might bolster their work?

Does the school offer tangible support for volunteers who wish to train?

Does the appraisal system work, and does it identify the training needs of volunteers?

Does the manager of the staff in-service training have an extended responsibility for volunteers? Does anyone?

Does the school policy for volunteers include the requirement to keep a log of training undertaken by volunteers as part of the school's quality evidence, e.g. for Ofsted?

Is there any mentoring or counselling that encourages able volunteers to advance their professional and career development through access to training?

18
■ ■ ■
School governors

Introduction

School governors, though unpaid and not technically, or in the public's view 'support staff', form the one group of people statutorily charged with responsibility for the quality of learning in schools. Of all the unpaid personnel who support the learning of our young people in schools, school governors have the highest profile in the community and wield most power within the institution. This higher profile and greater responsibility resulted initially from the Education (No. 2) Act 1986 with subsequent Regulations regularly redefining governors' roles. During the last decade governors' responsibilities have increased markedly. They must, therefore, have a place in a book about supporting learning.

There are different kinds of school governor or routes to governorship:

- staff governors (non teaching staff);
- parent governors;
- co-opted governors;
- appointed governors (by the LEA and others);
- foundation governors (in voluntary controlled schools);
- the Head (if s/he chooses).

Governors are a legally required group of persons who support and assist the Head in the day-to-day management and leadership of the school. The law also provides for teacher governors, but their special situation is not the subject of this chapter.

The governing body system can be fraught with difficulty, not least because, in the eyes of some educators and school managers, those lay persons charged with the task of giving appropriate advice in many cases lack the professional knowledge and wisdom so to do. However, the various guidance documents issued by the government at regular intervals (DfEE, 2000) rehearse at length the various and varied duties and responsibilities of governors. This chapter considers the on-the-job role of governors; listens to what they have to say about their role; discusses their views on ways in which they contribute (overtly or covertly) to the learning of students; and discovers whether, in their opinion, they are valued, can act as a 'critical friend', or are merely in place because that is what current legislation requires regardless of the real preferences of schools.

The voice of the governor

The first encounter with the governing body is difficult for many new governors:

I have just received my first communication from the LEA since being co-opted as governor. I've had a quick look at it all, and the whole lot might just as well be written in Greek!

I was completely overwhelmed. I didn't understand much of what they were talking about. I didn't understand the jargon they used. I was introduced, but no-one really bothered to involve me. I felt a nobody. I wondered why I was here and why I had subjected myself to this torture.

Contrast this view with that of an experienced governor in Case Study 18.1 – a vice-chair, someone who had been involved in the world of education for 30 years, but never an educator:

Case Study 18.1
End of a perfect day: Delia's story

One bright sunny day when all was well with the world and I had plans for a quiet day, the phone rang. I had been wary of the phone ringing during the previous weeks (before, during and after Ofsted inspection), but not today. It was the Head and my peace was about to be shattered: 'You know I have to write to the parents explaining about the Inspection? And you know I have to say how the school is going to respond to the issues identified as *'Key Issues for Action'*? Well, I've started the letter but can't get beyond the first five lines. Will you write it for me?'

And of course, I said: 'Yes', and off he went, back to the peace and solitude of his study. And then I thought: 'What have I let myself in for? Should I even be doing this? Isn't it his job? And what if it all goes pear-shaped and I'm left to answer on Judgement Day?'

> I wrote the letter, and even though I say it myself, it was a good letter, and infinitely better than any he would have written. It passed through the governing body scrutiny, they changed a few typographical errors, praised him for his fluency and clarity of speech. Only he and I knew the truth – that he was either too scared or too incompetent to do the job for which he was paid.

This last example is perhaps an extreme, but it does illustrate with some clarity the responsibility that *may* fall upon the shoulders of an experienced governor. Other common experiences are well illustrated in conversation with a parent governor who both visited the school in her role as a governor and as an unpaid (almost full-time) classroom assistant:

> *I work mainly in Key Stage 1 and most generally in Jane's class. I come in most days of the week to 'help'. I sit with the children in groups, I work with any child who has a specific difficulty – not the statemented child, he has his own one-to-one assistant. I've been doing this for a year now and really enjoy it.*

> *Last month Jane asked me if I would like to take part in a course run by the local authority which was designed to help people who supported reading to do so more effectively. It was a two day course, which I found thoroughly absorbing. When I went back to school I was able to work with those children who found reading difficult and apply the knowledge I'd gained. Working with these pupils on a one-to-one basis, every day for about 20 minutes at a time, improved their reading; it gave me a really in-depth insight into the way classrooms are organised and work and I felt that I had made some small contribution, as both a governor and a parent-helper, to the learning of those half dozen children for whom I had responsibility.*

Role satisfaction is apparent in this last extract, with the parent helper seemingly able to switch roles – from governor to parent-helper – as the occasion required.

What do school governors do?

Jacqui Smith, Parliamentary Under Secretary of State for School Standards, in the foreword to *A Guide to the Law for School Governors* states:

> *As a governor you have a key role to play in helping your school provide the best possible education for all its pupils … governing bodies (have) a specific responsibility for helping to raise standards … . There can be no more important task than helping to raise standards for our children. You play a crucial part in that task.*
>
> (DfEE, 2000b).

School governors are charged, then, to raise standards in schools which is clearly a learning-related (but not a teaching) role. The ways in which they personally fulfil their role will differ from individual to individual. Some governors can at best be described as 'sleeping partners' in the charge to 'raise standards for our children'; but the great majority are genuinely active and fulfil their roles to the best of their ability. So what are these roles?

Again, best advice can be obtained from consulting the various government publications:

- *A Guide to the Law for School Governors* (DfEE, 2000b);
- *Guidance on Good Governance* (DfEE, 1996);
- *Roles of Governing Bodies and Head Teachers* (DfEE, 2000a).

Other useful sources of information are:

- *The School Governors' Yearbook 2001* (Adamson Books, 2000);
- *Trigger Pack for New Governors* (National Governors' Council, 1999);
- The National Association of Governors and Managers.

For the purposes of this book, and its concern for the role of support staff and their management in contributing to student learning, we shall pause and consider the governors' role in relation to the curriculum. Governors and the governing body are required to ensure, for example:

- that the curriculum is balanced and broadly based;
- that the National Curriculum is implemented;
- that there is agreement between the head teacher (who has drafted the curriculum policy) and the governing body;
- that the school has a sex education policy;
- that religious education is provided in accordance with the school's basic curriculum;
- that they ensure compliance with the law relating to special educational needs.

These are only examples, but before looking at some of these 'job roles' of governors in more detail, mention must be made of some other responsibilities that governors have in the management of the school. At most schools, the governing body has delegated responsibilities for finance and inappropriate management of this can seriously hinder student progress and school performance. It also either employs the school's staff or has the employer's main responsibilities, and is the link with and into, the local community. Because of central government initiatives, delegations of powers and the thrust for accountability at all levels of society, the role and responsibility of the governor increased immensely in the past decade and shows no sign of abating in the near future.

One governor was forthcoming in her assessment of her role: *see* Case Study 18.2.

> ## Case Study 18.2
> ## Brenda's story
>
> I have been a governor for nearly six years now, serving two schools but not at the same time. I take the role very seriously and it does take up much more time than ever I would have anticipated. I find that because I have been involved in education for all of my married life that I 'get put upon' – at least I did with the first head. What he did not want to do or understand he gave me to do or read. I remember him saying to me that he hadn't got the time 'to wade through 88 applications for a KS1 post' and that it would be best if I did the first sort. I took that role very seriously because I felt that I owed that much to the applicants, but … was that really part of my role? Should I have taken the responsibility? I squared my disquiet with the thought that perhaps it was in the interests of the applicants that I took on the responsibility. Was it not better that an intelligent, informed governor sift the information on the forms and relate it to the stated criteria than leave it to the head who had no interest in the outcome. After all, he was retiring in two months and had no interest in the appointment.

At this point you may find it helpful to read through this Case Study (18.2) and consider:

- was Brenda right to take on this job?
- would you have made the same decision?
- how would you have proceeded had you disagreed with the head's demand?

Do governors have a job description?

Unlike paid support staff (school secretaries/bursars, laboratory assistants), school governors have no prescribed job description. It is true that all governors are issued with a plethora of documentation; from central government, local government and the school which they serve, and it is from these that the expectations of governors' roles and duties may be culled. An effective governing body is one which, among other things, utilises the skills and expertise of its various members to the best advantage of the school. The head teacher, as a good manager, will welcome skilled contributions but at the same time will coax less sure governors into areas in which they feel a modicum of security. Good relationships between governors and the head are essential – the relationship should be viewed as a partnership, in which each person undertakes those roles ascribed by law to the benefit of all students in their care.

Table 18.1 What are the priority areas for school governors?

First and foremost, governors must fulfil those functions prescribed by law (see *Roles of Governing Bodies and Head Teachers* (DfEE, 2000a)).

The governing body must do its work efficiently.

The governing body functions as an 'incorporated' body.

Governors execute their responsibilities collectively.

Increasingly, governors are utilising some 'independence' within the governing body, i.e. specific tasks may be assigned to a committee or group of governors or even to an individual governor.

Responsibility for decisions that may be made in its name, rests with the governing body.

Good teamwork is a prerequisite.

As an individual governor one's priority area probably rests within one's personal expertise, as shown in the quotations that follow.

Ben's story:

> *My abiding requirement is that there should be equality of opportunity within the school – not just on paper, but in everything the school does. It's all very well to have an 'equal ops' policy, but if its only appearance is in the week before an Ofsted inspection, then it counts for very little. We must be seen to be fair. We must not be majority ethno-centric, and a book depicting a child who is black or in a wheelchair must not just arrive a week after the black pupil or pupil with disabilities does. It must be ongoing, not positive discrimination, but equal treatment. Try getting that message across to teachers in a rural school.*

Jo's story:

> *I have done a lot of research into the education and support for able students; I was able to work with the head in drawing up the school's policy. I appreciated being able to pass on some of the knowledge I had collected through talking to able youngsters across all Key Stages.*

James' story:

> *As an accountant, I am on hand to advise and participate on the school's finance committee. My input is valued.*

Governors' expertise in specific areas is generally viewed as a bonus for the school and its management. But governors cannot just exercise their chosen areas of interest. They have a duty to ensure compliance with the National Curriculum, to set targets for pupil achievement and together with the head teacher, the local education authority and central government share the responsibility for the curriculum. In order to see how governors actually performed these tasks, we asked a sample of governors to take time to consider their role in students' learning, and through a small questionnaire probed these issues in more depth (*see* Table 18.2).

Table 18.2 The role of governors in the support of student learning – a questionnaire

1. To what extent do you, as a governor, contribute to the **learning** that takes place in your school? (Please give one or more examples to illustrate the points you make.)

2. How, and how deeply, are you, as a governor, involved in compiling (as opposed to approving) policies that relate directly to **pupils' learning** in the school? (E.g. curriculum policies, or policies that deal with access to learning such as IT policies.)

3. Are the governors in your school involved in the school's target setting. If yes, how do you make yourself aware of pupils' **learning and learning needs** in order to do this?

4. Governors are the 'guardians of quality' for the school. What steps do you take to inform yourself about the **learning** that happens in classrooms?

5. How much input do your governors, as a governing body, have in setting the criteria for selection of teaching staff?

6. How far do your governors, and the governing body, take responsibility for tackling any **learning** issues that occur in the Action Plan following an Ofsted inspection?

7. Do you feel any conflict in your governing body between the teaching professionals on the one hand and the governors on the other in making decisions about issues relating to student **learning**?

8. Does your school have a strategy for drawing out the best from individual governors within the context of supporting student **learning**?

9. To what extent do you feel that you, as a lay governor, can make real and valid assessments of the **learning** that is taking place within the school? (Specific and detailed examples would be helpful.)

10. How does your governing body take decisions at meetings to ensure the best possible outcomes for students' **learning**?

11. What situations with respect to **student learning** provoke conflict between the school governors and the professional educators? (Examples would be helpful.)

Finally,

12. The purpose of this investigation is to explore how governors can be best used in **learning contexts**. Is there anything else you can add about this topic?

What follows are some of the comments made by governors in response to the questions in Table 18.2.

To what extent do governors contribute to the learning that takes place in school?

We asked this question of governors across all phases. Bob said:

> We get feedback on all LEA and internal reviews, including observation statistics for all staff. Curriculum and targets are on each agenda.

Heather, a secondary school governor, responded:

> As a lay governor, nothing directly, but as a part of the whole structure I am an integral part of decision making as regards learning policies ... governors provide an excellent overview and responsibility for the education provided to children at our school.

John's response was:

> I have been involved in drawing up the short list of applicants for teacher appointments ... and have been part of the interviewing panel to help ensure the appointment of suitable staff who will enable good learning amongst pupils.

He also noted that he 'supported every initiative to obtain the very best financial and material help available to ensure a good learning environment'.

Jean's first response was perhaps most typical:

> I am the governor responsible for overseeing English in the curriculum. I visit the school during school hours to discuss with the Head and relevant staff the philosophy and practice adopted, and sit in on some of the lessons.

Her second response indicated a certain surety of approach:

> At governing body meetings I sometimes challenge the head's views or reports – not in a critical way, but in order to present a possibly different viewpoint. I like to get underneath the words if at all possible, to see what is really happening.

One primary school governor, Anne, had built up excellent relationships with most teachers in her school, but with one in particular. Anne's contribution to the learning that took place was to have a prominent part in a production that coincided with an Ofsted inspection:

> It had been planned for months that this celebration would take place on that specific Monday; what luck it turned out to be the week of Ofsted. Although I have no experience of drama whatsoever, I undertook to be with the teacher whenever there was discussion about the assembly presentation or during the practices. In order for it to have validity in the eyes of Ofsted we had to incorporate those 'speaking and listening' elements required in the National Curriculum. Together the teacher and I hammered out the relevancy of each stage of the drama with these headings in mind; I refined them and had them to hand for the inspectors on the day. My contribution to the learning of these children was my expertise and experience of the subject

matter which the teacher lacked. But our personal relationship was such that it was a partnership, it was successful, commended by Ofsted 'as showing an acute awareness of other faiths', and in the process gave much enjoyment to the children.

Are governors deeply involved in compiling (as opposed to approving) policies that relate directly to pupils' learning?

Responses from those governors to whom we spoke indicated (as one might expect) a variety of practice. As noted above, one governor was able to co-operate with her head on the drawing up of the school's (new) policy on able pupils. Other governors noted:

Not as much as one might.

We write none. The Head is the prime author of policies.

The governing body merely 'rubber-stamps' policies.

The policies are largely drawn up by the Head and her staff, discussed with the chairwoman, presented for modification in the governors' meetings and then with editing, approved.

We act as the 'eye for the lay reader' to avoid education jargon. The policy content regarding pupil learning is written by the professional teachers.

Our curriculum committee acts on our behalf. It reads through new policies, challenges definitions, asks for clarification where there are ambiguities. Before the policies are presented to the curriculum committee they have been discussed with staff at staff meetings.

I am chair of the school 'Effectiveness' committee, and we, in liaison with staff debate and decide policies to be presented to the full Governing Body for approval (or not) by vote. ... Initially curriculum policies are drafted by the staff but have to be approved by governors prior to adoption.

Because of my expertise in mathematics and science my personal input has mainly been in informal discussion with the Head.

Are the governors in your school involved in the school's target setting? If yes, how do you make yourself aware of pupils' learning and learning needs in order to do this?

From some responses it is clear that teacher governors 'are rightly involved'.

Yes, we are involved closely with departments and are guided by them in setting targets. We defer to their professional judgements but are by no means a 'rubber stamp' for ultimate decisions. After all, we are the ones held accountable for such target setting and it is in our own interests to ensure that targets are challenging but attainable, if the curriculum works effectively.

In many instances it seems that the main consultation is between the head teacher and the Chair. One other response highlighted an interesting anomaly:

> *Performance targets for SATs appear to be set somewhat arbitrarily by the LEA adviser and with **seemingly little regard to the professional judgement of the Head** (emphasis not in the original).*

In other schools, as with policies, the school's target setting appeared to be the head teacher's domain with governors 'informed' at a governors' meeting.

*Governors are the 'guardians of quality' for the school. What steps do you take to inform yourself about the **learning** that happens in classroom?*

> *The consequence of any learning done in the classroom should be visible in the behaviour, demeanour and social conduct of pupils.*

> *The results of official testing are available for governor perusal. This I do.*

> *I visit the school relatively often, attend social occasions and watch lessons from time to time.*

> *Each governor at this school is attached to a specific department of learning and we have good feedback from teachers within that department. Governors are invited to attend and take part in actual lessons within their particular 'link' subject.*

> *Heads of department report regularly to the full governing body to explain subject targeting and policy.*

> *Our school has just started a programme of focused governor visits which will give us opportunities to observe the learning that is taking place.*

> *The school has an 'observational day' once a month.*

> *I have to make a report back to the governing body about my visit to the school and give a good account of what I have observed. This makes me think about what I have seen.*

> *I have a fair bit of time to myself and I volunteer as a parent helper on a regular basis.*

Although the issues that we have considered so far relate to the learning that takes place in school, our questionnaire considered the role of governors when setting the criteria for selection of teaching staff. Governors in schools with delegated budgets have responsibility for selecting and managing staff – the Head, deputy, teaching and non-teaching staff – and unless there is a failure by the candidate to meet the staff qualification requirements, where the school is an LEA school, the LEA will appoint the governors' choice of candidate. Our sample of governors were asked:

How much input do your governors, as a governing body, have in setting the criteria for selection of teaching staff?

Appointing the right teachers may have a significant effect on pupils' learning. John noted that his governors had a great deal of input, and that the members of the staffing committee set the criteria in consultation with the Head and Chairwoman and these were then discussed by the whole governing body. Anne, by contrast, felt that in one school where she had been a governor, the criteria were set by the Head but that, because of his devious methods of presentation and discussion, governors felt that *they* had set the criteria. Other governors noted:

> *We had a very large input when we recruited a new Head; for other appointments, the Head drafts a framework which is then discussed by the staffing committee.*

> *The governors are the appointing officers. We have a real opportunity to set the criteria for staff appointments, e.g. staff qualifications; pay range; personality qualities, skills etc. The Head is present, and all decisions should be made with her agreement.*

> *We sit on appointment panels and give our input to the head teacher and head of department which is considered during a selection process.*

> *The criteria are generally negotiated between head teacher and governors involved with the appointment.*

> *There would generally be a representative governor on all but the most junior selection panels.*

The last issue to be addressed that deals directly with the learning that takes place in school was that of trying to gauge whether or not governors had real input into the learning issues that arose as the result of an Ofsted inspection. The overwhelming conclusion drawn was that head teachers and staff took responsibility for responding to these learning issues – although as can be seen in the comments which follow, one governing body faced the issue head-on and took their responsibilities very seriously.

How far do your governors, and the governing body, take responsibility for tackling any learning issues that occur in the Action Plan following an Ofsted inspection?

In most responses it was apparent that governors relied heavily on the head teacher and staff to respond to 'learning issues' identified by Ofsted in Action Plans. They saw their role as one of monitoring, that the issues were being addressed, and that they received this information through feedback by the Head at governors' meetings. Two governors, though, felt that their schools and governors were more pro-active than this:

> *Ofsted reports are studied in depth by all governors in liaison with the head teacher at a full meeting. Areas of concern are highlighted and agreed. These are then written up as the 'Action Plan' and are reviewed through the year as appropriate.*

> *An overall responsibility for ensuring that Ofsted recommendations and requirements are acted upon lies with the governing body, a responsibility taken very seriously, not only by the whole body, but also by those governors who have a specific responsibility for the particular learning issues involved.*

****

The second part of our questionnaire looked at those issues whereby the role of the head teacher in drawing the best from his/her governors was paramount (the management of governors by head teachers is addressed in Chapter 19).

As has been noted at page 192, for the most part governing bodies are comprised of lay persons. Given that there is a charge on all governors to 'determine a policy for delivering a broad and balanced curriculum' and upon the Head to 'draw up the school curriculum plan within the overall statutory framework and the policy framework set by the governing body (DfEE, 1996: 7), we set out to discover from our sample of governors the answer to the question:

Do you feel any conflict in the governing body between the teaching professionals on the one hand and the governors on the other in making decisions about issues relating to student learning?

One governor responded:

Teachers' professional judgement and expertise should be assumed to be beyond reproach until evidence to the contrary is forthcoming. Only then should more direct involvement by governors begin.

Another admitted:

I don't think there is any feeling of conflict, because it is not apparent to me that we make any direct decisions about issues relating to student learning. We listen to what the Head tells us, and yes we do have input into teacher appointments, we try to spend the school's budget wisely, but do we actually make decisions about student learning? Only indirectly I suppose. And since we are guided by the Head, I guess in the end we do what he, and the staff, think we ought.

Heather's view was that in her school 'we have found a balance which works for our school'.

Given that one governor at least had reservations about her input to support student learning, the following question is of particular relevance:

How do schools draw out the best from individual governors within the context of supporting student learning?

Governor support of student learning, on a one-to-one basis or with groups, was commonplace within the classroom. One governor (John) noted that in his school:

Some governors with specific abilities attend the school to help the classroom teachers in the teaching of certain subjects.

This is an interesting response; unlike the parent governor in Jane's class (see above) who undertook training in order to 'improve the reading of those children she was assigned to', in John's response there is specific mention of helping the classroom teacher in 'the teaching of certain subjects'. This is something of a political minefield and an issue at which some teaching unions would bridle instantly – but a word of caution before one leaps into immediate controversy: many governors (co-opted, LEA, parent) are themselves teachers, or have been in the past. Is 'helping the classroom teacher in the teaching of certain subjects', then, such a controversial issue? Is it not, after all, only making best use of the governor's expertise?

Other governors noted that they helped with reading, were charged with the care, control and learning of a small group on a field trip or used their professional work-time expertise (e.g. as a producer for a theatre company) to help with the end-of-year school production. In Heather's school:

> Governors are expected to take up training as and when appropriate ... regular 'Inset' days are in place at school when all governors are expected to take part. Governors on sub-committees are required to take training as appropriate.

Heather's response highlights an issue that emerged throughout our discussion with governors about their role in supporting student learning – the issue of training. Responses such as: 'We are directed to the right training courses by the Chair after consultation with the Head', and 'All governors are encouraged to undergo training under the link scheme' indicates that well managed schools take the issue of governor training seriously. But all too often, it appears, there is a lack of direction – governors may receive a manual of courses on offer by the LEA and will choose which course to attend, but give no rigorous thought to questions like: 'Is this going to benefit the school?' or 'How will this improve my understanding of student learning?' Governors *need* to up-date their knowledge if they are to remain effective within the school setting, and fully understand those issues that affect, among other things, student learning. Managers must ensure that governors, as well as the professional teaching staff, are able to access good quality training both initially and throughout the time they serve the school.

Away from the prescribed issues of governors' responsibility, our questionnaire asked the respondents to reflect on their personal thoughts and opinions about the roles they had undertaken. We asked:

To what extent do you feel that you, as a lay governor, can make real and valid assessments of the learning that is taking place within the school?

What we had not anticipated was the number of governors who were, or had been, involved in education. Thus, when we asked whether real and valid assessments of the learning taking place within the school by lay governors was possible, responses such as: 'As an educator of long standing, the term *lay* does not really apply in my case' resulted.

John, who has been involved in teaching at some time in the past, felt there might well be some conflict, not least because:

For a lay governor who in most cases will be in employment with many demands on his/her time, lacking in most cases the expertise needed to give an accurate judgement, the responsibility rightly and appropriately rests with the staff and the Head. Governors can only keep a watching brief!

This clearly presents a dilemma both for the governor and the head teacher. The Government charges governors with a responsibility to 'conduct the school with a view to promoting high standards of educational achievement' (DfEE, 2000: 5.2), and yet as one head noted when asked the parallel question:

The validity of some governors' assessments may be at best questionable.

A parent governor with no experience of a professional association within the classroom noted:

When I became a parent governor I made a personal commitment to make myself aware of this aspect of responsibility. I think my opinion is valid because I have taken all opportunities to make myself better informed via training and liaison with the staff.

Governors *can* make valid and real assessment of the academic learning that has been achieved by students in school by noting students' performance in national tests; by comparing the school's results with other schools in the areas across the country. Positive comments made by governors in this context included:

Comparisons with the performance of similar students in similar situations can be a useful guide to the level of learning that is taking place.

Much more difficult to assess though, is progress made in the affective domain – good behaviour, positive attitudes to school and each other, a healthy regard for the equality of opportunity that should be open to all, etc.

The assessment of learning both in class and in the social sphere is many faceted. The teacher governors, staff governors, parent governors and Head have together a professional and personal interest in ensuring the best possible outcomes for pupils' learning. We asked governors:

How does your governing body take decisions at meetings to ensure the best possible outcomes for students learning?

One response highlighted the role of the group of people mentioned above: teachers, staff, parents and Head, and indicated that the 'considered advice of this group is rightly given weight, and only after due consideration are decisions made'. Other comments included:

Governors from time to time bring to the attention of the committee some aspect of concern, e.g. SATs results; social behaviour so that good and bad outcomes are recognised and approved or otherwise.

We read and discuss all relevant information available (first-hand from heads of department who are invited to meetings when needed).

On the issue of conflict between school governors and the professional educators, those governors we spoke to were reluctant to provide examples. One governor summed up his role thus:

> *The most appropriate role for a lay governor is to ensure that all staff have at their disposal the very best physical, material and financial resources that can be provided, so that their professional expertise can be used for ensuring that the very best pupil learning can be achieved.*

One governor, however, was prepared to be more explicit:

> *At this school the conflict (if that is the right word) is usually budget-related. In particular, our school is continually having money pared from our budget by the LEA without justification or consultation. As a consequence, we have to make budget changes and face staff who have less money available for books and equipment.*

By contrast, head teachers, when asked a similar question felt that the greatest areas of conflict are those issues that involve the governor's family. Many governors feel unable to withdraw from a situation that personally affects them and their family. This aspect was confirmed by a governor with many years' experience, as told in Case Study 18.3.

Case Study 18.3
Teri's story

I sat back and listened to the discussion which involved one parent becoming overheated in relation to proposed vertical grouping of YR and Y1 for the forthcoming academic year. The Head gave sound, logical reasons for the decision – in effect, because of the planned admission limits, there was no alternative. The parent, on the other hand, didn't want his Y1 son educated 'with all the new babies'. I intervened in the end, the Chair having not, and pointed out quite forcefully that the good of the school, the education of all those children for whom the Head and governors had responsibility, took priority over his wishes for his son. He had, in effect, to divorce himself from his micro vision and look at the broad picture. That was one more enemy I notched up.

This chapter has suggested that governors have a critical role to play in several aspects of learning in schools – and may conduct those roles either more or less 'hands on'. To be genuinely effective in supporting learning, however, these roles have to be managed. The management issue is addressed in Chapter 19.

References

Department for Education and Employment (1996) *Guidance on good governance.* London: DfEE Publications.

Department for Education and Employment (2000a), *Roles of governing bodies and head teachers.* London: DfEE Publications.

Department for Education and Employment (2000b) *A guide to the law for school governors.* London: DfEE Publications.

National Governors' Council (1999) *Trigger pack for new governors.*

The School Governors' Yearbook 2001 (2000). Ely: Adamson Books.

19
∎ ∎ ∎
Managing school governors

Introduction

In *A Guide to the Law for School Governors* (DfEE, 2000) Chapter 5 deals with, among other issues, the relationship between the governing body, governors and the head teacher. It highlights the issue succinctly: 'In a well-managed school, the head and governing body will work in close and balanced partnership' (para. 6). This must be a necessary criterion for a school to be successful. A good Head will keep her/his governing body informed of all the main aspects of school life, will see the governors as 'critical friends', able to offer a balanced and informed, but secular or lay, view of the way the school is being run to the benefit of its students.

As Chapter 18 indicated, not all governors are well versed in the world of education. Others may have their own agendas for undertaking the role – Bradbury (2000: 36) recalls his earlier research (Bradbury, 1998) involving six chairs of governors, that in some chairs' opinions ambition was a motivator 'providing grounding for career advancement':

> he's using (being a governor) as a political step... he wants to get on the Council.

On the other hand, one chair remarked:

> She showed an interest in moving education forward; I think that's what she saw as her remit.

One role of the Head, then, is to manage this disparate body of what Thody (1999: 38) calls political servants or more likely, public servants. Another role is to ensure compliance with all statutory requirements and to raise the profile and achievements of the school. Where the Head and governing body work together in harmony, these demands and aspirations are much more likely to be achieved.

Management strategy

In order to investigate ways in which head teachers manage their governors, a sample of Heads was approached and asked for examples of their management strategy (*see* Table 19.1), using a semi-structured questionnaire.

Table 19.1 The role and management of governors

(A) Learning

1. To what extent do governors contribute to the learning that takes place in your school? (Please give one or more examples to illustrate the point you make.)
2. How, and how deeply, are governors involved in compiling (as opposed to approving) policies that relate directly to pupils' learning in the school? (E.g. curriculum policies or policies that deal with access to learning such as IT policies.)
3. Governors are involved in the school's target setting. How do they make themselves aware of pupils' **learning and learning needs** in order to do this?
4. Governors are the 'guardians of quality' for the school. What steps do they take to inform themselves about the **learning** that happens in classrooms?
5. How much input do your governors have in setting the **criteria** for selection of teaching staff?
6. How far do governors take responsibility for tackling any **learning** issues that occur in the Action Plan following an Ofsted inspection?

(B) The management of governors

7. What strategies do you use, as Head, to maintain the balance between the teaching professionals on the one hand and the governors on the other when making decisions about issues relating to student **learning**?
8. How can you draw out the best from individual governors within the context of supporting student **learning**?
9. To what extent do you feel that lay governors can make real and valid assessments of the **learning** that is taking place within the school? (Specific and detailed examples would be helpful.)
10. How do you, as the head teacher, manage the decisions taken at governing body meetings to ensure the best possible outcomes for student **learning**?
11. What situations with respect to student learning provoke conflict between the school governors and the professional educators? (Examples would be helpful.)

Finally:

12. The purpose of this investigation is to explore how governors can be best used in **learning** contexts. Is there anything else you can add about this topic?

Outcome of the questionnaire

With respect to curriculum and learning, the Head has the responsibility to determine, organise and implement an appropriate curriculum for the school. This must include the National Curriculum. The role of the governors is to ensure that the National Curriculum *is* implemented and that the whole curriculum is 'balanced and broadly based'. Thus we have a scenario where the senior professional in the school, the full-time Head, the principal adviser on issues of education, school policy and policies, and the school's management, is, in effect, overseen by a part-time, lay governing body, some of whose members may only have limited knowledge of the institution and its workings, of the education system in general and curriculum in particular. This is not a criticism of governing bodies, or their members – it is a statement of fact: some governors are very knowledgeable, some are not. Bradbury (2000: 36) describes it thus:

> There was evidence of some governors who just want to see how it all works, perhaps attending only one or two meetings and then not being seen again: ...one gentleman that was on came to one meeting and that was it, gone, never saw him again.

Head teachers, then, have the unenviable task of drawing together a committee with disparate experience and encouraging them to work together for the good of their chosen school, and its pupils in delivering effective learning.

Before taking on the contentious issue of whether or not governors can, or should, be involved in learning, a glance at one Head's response to the role of the governor indicates from the start the potential minefield that is the governance and management of schools today:

> I query the reason why some parents put themselves forward for the role of governors. The 'hit squad' representative is a danger to staff morale ...

This Head's view is countered by another primary Head:

> Despite the problems and misconceptions and 'politics' of managing relationships with a Governing Body, I truly think their challenge and outside perspective helps us to provide better learning, because we are not allowed to shut ourselves away from wider views.

To return to the issue identified above – that of the role of the governor in overseeing that the National Curriculum and its assessment procedures are properly carried out within school – we asked a sample of heads to what extent governors contributed to the learning that took place in school (*see* Table 19.1). A rural primary headteacher responded:

> Governors contribute to the learning in school through their questioning at meetings of school achievements;
>
> They involve themselves to find sponsorship to improve resources for pupil learning;
>
> They support staff in classrooms as voluntary teacher support.

Another primary Head said he utilised governors' particular strengths or knowledge to enhance learning, but that, at the time of writing, this was an area that was under-exploited.

In one secondary school, St James's, it appeared that governors were more formal in their approach to understanding the learning that took place in school.

They have close liaison with managers via curriculum groups ...

When this issue was followed up in a tape-recorded interview it became apparent that new systems were being put into place:

The chair and vice-chair are observing in classrooms next week – they are breaking the ice so as to speak – in order to form a closer link between the governors and the teaching in the school ... After that there will be eight governors involved in the faculties. They will be given a clear remit, discussed by the governors.

Previously, informal contact had been the norm at St James's, with an alleged reticence among the school's governors to observe lessons and teaching because they felt that 'although they had wanted to be involved, they did not have the necessary knowledge'.

The above interpretations of the question are examples of direct classroom contact. Another head teacher answered more indirectly. She concentrated on the way in which governors' questioning made her aware of the need to explain and justify her decisions. She felt it stimulated more self-evaluation than might otherwise occur, and she gave as an example the questioning of her SDP priorities. She felt it was challenging the interpretation of issues from a different viewpoint. Some possible approaches by which heads might manage the role of governors in learning are shown as Table 19.2.

Table 19.2 Successful management strategies to enable governors to contribute more to the learning that takes place in class

- Keeping governors informed of new teaching/learning initiatives at all times.
- Keeping curriculum issues and target setting high on the agenda of governors' meetings.
- Keeping open the opportunity for governors to attend staff meetings at which curriculum issues are being discussed.
- Offering governors the opportunity to attend staff training days where training in aspects of the curriculum is taking place.
- Exploiting governors' specific curriculum interests.
- Ensuring that each curriculum area is supported by the most knowledgeable governor in that area.
- Encouraging governors to visit classrooms, not as 'inspectors' but as observers.

continues

Table 19.2 *continued*

- Encouraging governors to talk with the (observed) class teacher so that misunderstandings may not arise.
- Ensuring that time is available at governors' meeting for good practice to be shared.
- Giving governors feedback on all LEA and internal reviews, including observations by senior staff.
- Ensuring that there is close liaison between heads of department, year group heads, heads of Key Stages and the governors.
- Arranging for heads of faculties/departments/key stages to give a short appraisal of their targets of achievement to the full governing body.
- Ensuring that governors are kept informed of measures to remedy weaknesses, e.g. where there is underachievement by boys in Key Stage 1, the teacher gives a written or verbal report each term.
- Ensuring that good relationships and close links exist between staff and governors.

Managing relationships between heads and governors

When dealing with the management of governors, the Head's role is more tenuous than when dealing with teaching staff. The Head is responsible for the internal organisation, management and control of the school; the governors for promoting high standards of education within the school. The Head (and senior management team) are the professionals; those charged with the responsibility for promoting high standards are lay people. We asked our group of heads how they maintained the balance between the teaching professionals and the governors in making decisions about issues relating to student learning.

We noted earlier that 'in a well-managed school the Head and governing body will work in close and balanced partnership' (DfEE, 2000b). Some heads to whom we spoke confirmed this:

> *Work closely with the chair of governors and as a preliminary sound out plans and possible changes. Keep governors well informed of plans, procedures and developments of the curriculum.*
>
> (Joanna, head of St Mary's infant school)

> *The full and rational sharing of information about the school's work and progress in teaching and learning. Using opportunities to clarify roles in managing, governing teaching and dealing sensitively with overlap.*
>
> (John, St James's community school)

Alternative strategies included discussion by the Head with the school's professionals in the first instance, with their collective wisdom presented to governors for their comment and discussion. Jenny, head teacher at a small rural primary school, St Faith's, said:

Curriculum issues are generally better discussed with staff first – then governors' views sought to complement/challenge.

Decisions tend to be led by initiatives from the teaching staff and can be enhanced by informed governor input.

(Dominic, St Saviour's community primary school)

Those heads that we questioned all appeared to have good relationships with their governing body. Consequently, we were able to draw up strategies that minimised potential conflict between staff and governors over the issue of student learning: Table 19.3.

Table 19.3 Successful management strategies to maintain the balance between teaching professionals and lay governors on issues relating to student learning

- Sharing information about the school's work with the governing body.
- Giving governors full regular reports of all that has happened in terms of teaching.
- Celebrating the school's achievements with the governors.
- Discussing with staff those curriculum issues that are to be presented to the governing body.
- Ensuring that when issues are discussed there is always a *suggested* proposal for action.
- Offering governors with particular expertise the opportunity to participate in, e.g. writing policies, or reviewing existing documents.
- Being clear about the rationale of staff views when presenting these to the governing body.
- Making full use of the expertise of those governors who are qualified teachers. (Value them as friends rather than see them as potential critics of the school's management and its policies).
- Valuing informed governor input.
- Having a clear understanding of the role and responsibility of governors, i.e. their terms of reference.
- Clarifying the roles relating to head teachers and governors – there is overlap and this may be a sensitive issue.
- Involving governors in staff/governor meeting for School Development Planning each year.
- Ensuring that governors observe good examples of the 'practice' before they present their report to the others.

Head teachers were also asked how they managed their governors in order to draw the best from individuals within the context of supporting student learning (Table 19.4). Once again, the good relationships between those head teachers that we questioned and their governing bodies became apparent. Jenny spoke for all in her response:

> *Know about individual strengths. Governors' interests and biases. Work closely with the Chair of Governors.*

Table 19.4 Management strategies to draw out the best from individual governors within the context of supporting student learning

Suggested appropriate action may include:

- Ensuring that governors specialised skills are known and utilised;
- Ensuring that governors with specific skills are encouraged to join the appropriate committee;
- Encouraging less confident governors and guiding them to areas of the curriculum where their skills will be valued;
- Ensuring that those governors with a curriculum responsibility are well informed and that they have an accurate understanding of the area;
- Linking governors to faculties and allowing governors to report back to the full governing body;
- Giving full update on curriculum developments to committees;
- Utilising the skills of the chair to ensure that curriculum responsibility is evenly spread among governors;
- Directing governors to the *right* training course.

Governors and learning

The most visible ways in which governors supported student learning was through representation on committees and by undertaking classroom observation. Both these activities may give cause for concern to teaching staff and head teachers if not handled sensitively. However hard both the head teacher and the governors try to maintain good relationships with the staff, teachers can feel threatened by the presence of a governor during observation of lessons. Jenny notes that in her management of governors, she feels that she has to be assertive if inappropriate governor intervention causes problems. This can be a real issue, with the National Association of Governors and Managers (2001), in discussing the issue of governor visits, suggesting:

> *A formal visit is a significant act, which affects the governing body's relationship with staff and pupils.*

(NAGM, Paper No. 43)

Visiting a school allows governors 'to get to know the school, so that we can carry out our responsibilities as governors' (ibid.). This is sound advice. In a well run school the management of visiting by governors will cause little problem to the Head and/or senior management team. Teachers, on the other hand, may feel threatened; they may feel that their professionalism is being challenged; or that governors may make comments to the Head that will prejudice their position in the school. These issues, and many others, need to be considered sympathetically, both by the Head and the governing body.

What can management expect governors to learn from their visits to school?

A visit by a governor may last for half an hour, it may be that the school has pre-planned visits which take a whole day. A governor may:

- 'drop-in' on the classes (courtesy requires that teachers are told this may happen);
- stay with a class for a session, i.e. pre-break, or for the morning;
- sit with the children listening to their responses and gauging their participation in the lesson, looking at behaviour patterns;
- actually join in with class responses, contribute within a group situation; and
- contribute a skill by participating in the teaching of the class with express permission of the teacher involved.

I'm not an extrovert and I'm not that keen on drama, but the youngsters (Y6) were rehearsing for their presentation in assembly. They hadn't got it quite right. From the back of the room I could see where the problem lay; fortunately, the teacher walked in my direction and I had a quiet word with her – she agreed she was so 'close' to the production she couldn't see the problem. Between us, together, we sorted it out. And it all gelled. Yes, I did take on a teaching role; and no, it didn't diminish the teacher in the eyes of the students. They were used to me; the kids knew that their teacher and I were good friends. We enjoyed the kids' success together. The assembly was a success ... and of course, I was there to see it. Governors are always invited to the 'special assembly', as are parents.

(Liz, co-opted governor at a large city primary school)

From the above synopsis of how governors' visits may be conducted, and the extract of conversation with one governor, it is clear that difficulty may arise. From the governor's point of view, visiting is essential – only by visiting can a governor become truly informed of what is happening in his or her school. Local authority guidelines and government dictates may be essential reading but they are no substitute for hands-on experience. The key to successful governor visiting, then, is expert management of the situation by the Head. Table 19.5 enumerates some possible strategies for handling school visits by governors.

Table 19.5 The headteacher's perspective on managing governor visits

- A head teacher must ensure that any framework drawn up by the governing body regarding visits is consistent with the ethos and daily management of the school.
- Details of the governor's visit should be agreed with the Head (or his/her delegated staff member) in advance.
- A lay governor can *never* assess a lesson.
- A governor *can* make an assessment of students' behaviour in class; the quality of their listening; their participation in discussions; the amount of work generally undertaken; the extent to which there are a range of styles of teaching and consequently learning that can be recognised.
- The remit for a governor to judge what is happening in class has to be different, pertinent and appropriate to the governor's observation. It is different from that of a senior manager, head of faculty or an inspector.
- Governors' faculty or class visits should be done with a clear and agreed remit, questions and focus.
- Governor visits should be spaced so that teaching staff do not feel overly burdened by them.
- Over-zealous governors need to be diverted from visiting too regularly.
- It is vital that a governor should 'judge' a school visit on the basis of what is in the best interests of all the students in school – that governors leave their personal aspirations for their own child at home.
- It might be considered advisable, in some instances, that governors do not sit in on classes in which their own child is being taught.
- Some governors have no benchmark or framework for their views once personal preference or values have been discounted and sometimes the validity of some governors' assessments may be at best questionable. This is an issue with which a manager has to come to terms.
- A governor can make a real and valid assessment of the learning that is taking place in a lesson if the identified learning objective stated at the start of the lesson is matched in what the children are doing at the end of the session.
- Time should be made available for the governor to talk to the Head about his/her thoughts about the day.
- Reports to the governing body should be made as soon as possible after the visit. In order to avoid controversy, the Head might deem it wise to discuss with the visiting governor his/her report in advance.

Governors' views of learning and teaching

Most of the suggestions noted above indicate the positive role of the governor in taking soundings about the learning that is taking place in the classroom. But the follow-on management issue for any head teacher to consider is: What about feedback to the staff member concerned? To the Governing Body? And ultimately (via feedback to the governing body, through teacher and staff governors) to the school as a whole? We asked this question directly in one instance. In this secondary school, feedback was given to the teachers, and to the governing body upon which four senior staff sat. When these teacher governors gave feedback of the meeting to the staff as a whole, the lesson observation report was fed in.

During discussion with the head it emerged that:

- the governors spoke to the observed staff for about 30 minutes;
- good practice was highlighted;
- issues that had arisen were the subject of discussion;
- a report was put into a format for the governing body that had been agreed with the staff member;
- the Head also received feedback from the governors.

Heads have to have strategies for dealing with negative comments from governors. Those which emerged in this research are shown as Strategy 19.1.

Strategy 19.1 *Dealing with negative comments by a governor*

'Mr X delivered a terrible lesson. His class was quite out of control. No one took any notice of what he was saying – he talked for all the lesson. I could have done better myself.'

- Describe the steps you would go through in your debrief with the governor.
- Describe how you would draw from him/her the justifications for such statements.
- Could you defend the teacher's action/lesson given that you had not been an observer?
- What steps could you take to ensure that neither the school's reputation nor that of the staff member suffers because of this governor visit?
- What could you do if you suspect, or know, that there may be some justification in the governor's observation?

Inevitably, conflict will arise between governors and the professional teaching staff. In a well managed and well run school such instances will be rare – but we asked a group of head teachers whether they could define likely areas of conflict. We wanted to discover what strategies they had for dealing with conflict, and methods they might employ to diffuse difficult situations.

What situations with respect to student learning provoke conflict between the school governors and professional educators?

The head of St Mary's primary school (Joanne) noted as potential conflict areas the idiosyncrasies of parental opinion and the effect these can have upon parental perception of the benefit of schooling to their child. Given that parent governors may be targeted either directly, or through 'gate-gossip', it is essential that governors understand the Head and management team's thinking. The Head gave examples of past controversial issues:

- parents had had difficulty in understanding the school's reading policies when their children started school;
- parents found it difficult to understand why the school staggered intakes for pupils;
- parents found it difficult to understand why class organisation (e.g. mixed age groups) changed from year to year.

Joanna's view was confirmed by other Heads to whom we spoke. Dominic felt that personal prejudices played a significant role in conflict areas and cited both religious and sex education. In primary schools (and his school is a county primary) governors have a duty only to decide whether sex education should be included in their school's curriculum, and if so, what it should comprise and how it should be organised. Clearly with this example, there is potential for conflict between the professional educators and the school governors. (A similar situation would not arise in a secondary school, where sex education is mandatory.) Where it arises, conflict has to be defused. Table 19.6 summarises some of the ways in which this might be tackled.

Table 19.6 Strategies for defusing potential conflict between professional educators and governors on issues that may affect student learning

- Ensure that potential conflict areas are presented to the governing body in clear terms and are jargon free.
- Ensure that governors receive full and frank reports of the teaching and learning that take place in the school.
- Enhance the role of the parent governors; they are vital communication links between the school's governing body and the parents in cases of 'gate-gossip' or occasional parental dissatisfaction.
- Be pro-active on behalf of staff when governors make seemingly unrealistic demands upon them, e.g. extending length of parents' evening beyond endurable limits.
- Institute (but keep control over) a programme of governor observation.
- Speak privately and confidentially to those governors who insist that their view of student learning is the 'correct' view.
- Speak privately and confidentially to those governors who view their presence in classrooms as that of an inspector.

- Engage in meaningful discussion about student learning with the chair of governors.
- Entrust governors with particular curriculum area responsibility with full knowledge of the school's progress or failings in their subject area.
- Give full access of information to governor scrutiny (apart from that designated as confidential).
- Ensure that all governors view the whole picture and do not let personal (own child) benefit impinge upon the good for the school as a whole.
- Take advantage of good quality training on this vital issue. Although there may be cost ramifications do not confine the school to the (often generic) training offered by the LEA.
- Seek out professional governor trainers.
- Institute a governor training day if at all possible.
- Offer governors the opportunity to attend staff in-service days when curriculum is at the heart of the training day.
- Team a professional educator with a lay governor to attend quality training. This reinforces good relationships within the team.

In a school where governor observation currently operates, or where plans are in hand for such observation, the dominant management strategy has to be one in which the visit has a clear objective. We asked head teachers with long experience of governor observation for their advice:

I ensure that governors have a copy of our proforma lesson plan upon which the lesson objectives will be written. Governors can use this as an aide-mémoire as they sit in and watch the lesson in progress. Our lesson plan has detailed instructions which the governor can be taken through – we have the lesson theme and teaching objectives; National Curriculum reference; we move through the teacher's objective to the intended outcomes for pupils. Governors can be taught how to observe.

Give the governor detailed instructions, direct his/her observation.

Suggest that the governor may wish to observe a student or group of students for a specific length of time. Surreptitiously the governor can note detail of time-on-task; concentration span; boredom threshold and so on.

Suggest that governors actually talk to pupils, quietly and at appropriate moments, during the lesson. From this they should be able to gauge how much understanding has taken place, whether students show enthusiasm for the subject matter, how they respond to teacher questions, and how polite and co-operative they are. Governors can make meaningful assessments of learning from these kinds of observations.

Once governors have had experience of working to the school's lesson plan, of watching the fruits of the planning in progress in class, as a group they become more informed. They can recognise the 'plan' throughout the school, whichever class they are observing and can now ask themselves: 'Are these pupils achieving these objectives?'

As a long-term strategy, theory has to precede the practical application of the gover-
nor sitting in the class. That has been the strength in this school.

Thody (1999: 40) welcomes the possibility that governor involvement in teaching and learning may become more significant in the future. She suggests that
the present concentration on administrative tasks should be replaced by a concentration on teaching and learning. In her ideal world 'Every agenda item at
governing body meetings should be assessed for its contribution to teaching
and learning. Every governor should be educated in lesson observation and
be able to evaluate and monitor teachers.' And given that the 'governors' legal
responsibility is to ensure that the National Curriculum is delivered to standards laid down by the Government', there is a logic to this suggestion. How
can governors fulfil this responsibility without treading the muddy waters
between professional educator and lay governor?

Do lay governors have the knowledge and expertise to make real and valid
assessments of the learning that is taking place within their school? Chapter 18
gives examples of governors' perspectives on this issue and this chapter has
taken up this issue from other perspectives. Joanna's response, below, highlights present day practice, as opposed to Thody's vision of the future.

Lay governors can achieve a real and valid assessment of pupil learning as they gain:

- *an overall view of pupils' interests in lessons, through their reactions and*
  responses to the teacher;

- *an overall view of pupil behaviour;*

- *the opportunity to see if the identified learning objective stated at the start of the*
  lesson is matched in what the children are doing at the end of the session; and

- *if the children are working confidently.*

The micro-political and macro-political issues of school governance: who manages whom?

One further issue has revealed itself, and needs to be explored with some
degree of rigour. Within the context of this book, there are distinctions both
within the content of the roles under discussion and their management. For
the most part, the support staff whose roles have been subject to scrutiny have
been paid members of the school or the LEA. They have rules of engagement;
the majority have, or should have, job descriptions; they have line managers;
they are members, in effect, of a hierarchical structure. The exceptions to this
rule are two-fold: parent (voluntary) helpers and governors.

Despite being unpaid, the 'volunteer' force falls within the category previously described – they, too, are part of the hierarchy of school life. But
governors are not. The relationship between Head and governors, for all the

fair words written upon the subject, *can* be one of division of power. And therein lies the dilemma. New legislation (September 2000) spells out the respective roles and responsibilities of the governing body and the Head. Within the context of governors' contributions to the learning that takes place in school, the government sees governors as 'fulfilling a largely strategic role' (DfEE, 2000a: 2) in which *they* decide what they want the school to achieve and how they expect the school to reach their targets. *Governors* set aims and objectives; *they* set the targets; *they* agree the curriculum policies; *they* have a monitoring and evaluation role to assess whether or not the priorities are being met. By definition, then, the Government perceives that governors *do* have a significant role in determining, within the national guidelines, what is actually taught in their school. The head's responsibility is to formulate and implement the policies and to lead the staff towards achieving the learning targets set for the school.

Heads and senior management teams are, by contrast, the professionals in the task of educating the nation's children. The DfEE document *Roles of Governing Bodies and Head Teachers* is explicit in its terminology, and describes the Head as the 'lead professional'. However, with constantly changing legislation redefining the roles and responsibilities of both governors and head teachers, the locus of power becomes a shifting commodity, both as a general concept and within the teaching/learning parameters (*see* Figure 19.1). The hierarchical nature of schools becomes less clear, under threat even; visions may become blurred – and the power, in effect, is apparently reversed. Governors, on paper at least, hold most of the cards.

The Government attempts, through some of its publications (e.g. DfEE, 2000a) to play down the reality of this reversal of power in the daily life of schools – within that part of school that comprises the teaching/learning that takes place. When talking about the strategic role of the governing body (DfEE, 2000a: 2), it notes that governors should take advice from the head when:

- setting suitable aims and objectives;
- agreeing policies, targets and priorities;
- monitoring and reviewing aims, objectives, and whether the policies, targets and priorities are being achieved.

Roles of Governing Bodies and Head Teachers goes so far as to explain the allocation of major responsibilities of governing bodies and head teachers in a clear Annex (A). While it states that the list is not a comprehensive list, a cursory glance highlights the inescapable fact that the governing body responsibilities exceed, or equal, those of the head teacher in each of the categories detailed ('Secular Curriculum', p. 12.)

So is there a correlation between central control as seen since the advent of the Education Reform Act (1988) and the increase of governors' power? Is the reality that the Government *is* seeking to control the learning that takes place in

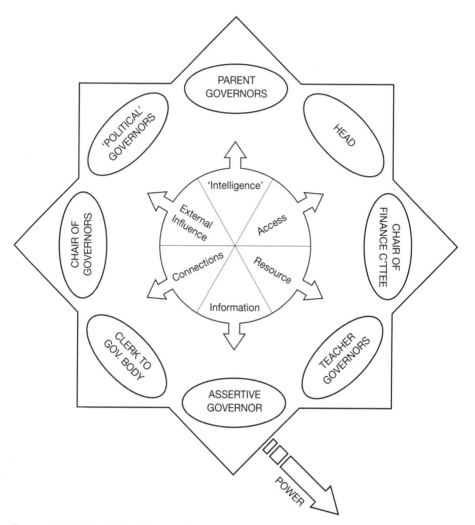

Figure 19.1 The shifting locus of power on governing bodies

schools through the back door by setting up power structures within the nation's schools whereby the role of professional teaching staff is diminished? While the writer may argue that there is evidence to suggest such a scenario, some practitioner Heads suggest otherwise.

Head teachers, particularly those in the first years of headship point to a perceived increase in the power and status of Heads in general, as well as those aspects which relate to learning – they see Heads as the instruments through which Government was 'doing its school improvement and change'. One cited the level of consultation between central government and head teachers; head teacher training; the face-to-face contact with senior ministers at conference level; the reality that, 'Now, we are listened to'. As an example she indicated that there had been some misinformation published by the LEA in relation to her school and its teaching and progress. She challenged this:

> I actually wrote direct to the DfEE; I sent the Director of Education a copy; our grievance was upheld; we were listened to. My personal impression is that this illustrates they are dealing direct with the schools and cutting out of the middle-man, the LEA.

On a personal level, another head teacher felt that, over the issue of the locus of power between Head and governors, the personality of the Head was the key whether one was dealing with general issues or matters of the curriculum. For her, management and communication skills were all important and she indicated that, in a very short time, with careful but firm handling, she had turned her governors around. Under the previous régime, the school's staff had felt a grave concern over the governors' apparent power over what was taught in the school; now, through her own inter-personal skills, the situation had resolved to become more of a Head/governor partnership. She also raised the issue that individual governors – the dominant governor in Figure 19.1 – should not be allowed to overawe other members of the governing body on teaching/learning issues. This was particularly relevant when subsequent decisions impacted well upon the governor's own child/child's class to the detriment of the greater good. The Head, as the senior professional should take the initiative and call a halt to any discussion that falls outside the governing body's remit. Strategies for power-sharing are outlined in Table 19.7.

The perception of some Heads then is that, far from increasing the power of governors over Heads, present Government strategy is directed at reducing further the role and control of the Local Education Authority; that the future for the teaching and learning that takes place within a school lies in the *sharing* of power between governors and Heads; that with the power behind heads of the governing body, the LEAs will become an anachronism. Local authorities will, like old soldiers, 'fade away'.

Table 19.7 Management strategies to enable an equitable sharing of power between head teachers and governors within the context of presently constructed central guidelines

- Clarify potential areas of conflict in advance of governing body meetings.
- Discuss potential areas of conflict with the Chair of governors.
- Ensure, where possible, that decisions made by governors are made in agreement with the Head.
- Good personal management and communication skills between Head and governors can help diffuse potential areas of conflict.
- Ensure that the Head's report to the governing body is detailed enough to allow governors to make rational and informed decisions.

continues

Table 19.7 *continued*

- Ensure that the vision for the school is a shared vision, owned by governors, head teacher and staff alike.
- 'Always be "one-step" ahead of governors, be seen to bend on occasions and then you can set the tone.'
- Be wary of the governor who sets the tone through ignorance rather than knowledge.
- Ensure that only those areas which fall within the remit of governors are allowed to dominate discussion during governors' meetings.
- Accept that there will be a variety of opinions, not all of which will coincide with the opinion of the Head. In a well run school this should be seen as a strength.
- Remain aware of the legislation as it affects relationships between Heads and governors.

The head teacher alone has the overview of what goes on in the school. No-one else has that knowledge – once shared with governors, there is a sharing of power.

Conclusion

Managing governors to ensure that they have a role in learning in the school and to secure its effectiveness and appropriateness means taking some bold steps. Heads have to:

- recognise and acknowledge the role and how it works;
- provide access to the information that governors need in order to carry out the role effectively;
- negotiate and define the exact nature of the role within the particular institution (e.g. in setting up protocols for classroom visiting);
- provide training and encourage access to external training that will equip governors to carry out the role with greater insight and incisiveness.

Allow the governors to exercise their role and to fulfil their functions as critical friends.

References

Bradbury, P. (1998) 'School governors as providers and agents of change: the problem of authority', Paper given to the Eleventh Annual Conference of Psychoanalysis and the Public Sphere, University of East London, January.

Bradbury, P. (2000) 'What do school governors want?', *Education Today*, (50) 1, 35–43.

Department for Education and Employment (2000a) *Roles of governing bodies and head teachers*. London: DfEE Publications.

Department for Education and Employment (2000b). *A guide to the law for school governors*. London: DfEE Publications.

National Association of Governors and Managers (2001), 'Visiting the school': Paper No. 43.

Thody, A. (1999) 'From political servant to community democrat: an impossible future for English and Welsh school governors?' *Education Today*, 49 (1), 37–44.

Postscript

■ ■ ■

This book has been about support personnel in schools – paid and unpaid – about their roles in supporting learning by pupils and students and about the management of those roles. Each role has its distinctive characteristics; deployment of the post-holders varies from school to school. Yet all the groups discussed both in more detail in the main text of Part Two and in outline in Chapter 1 – *all* of them share a single characteristic: an involvement in the learning of young people in the school. The degree and nature of that involvement may vary from role to role, or from school to school across an individual role, but learning remains at the heart of the support process.

Nor, if our construction of the way schools should be envisioned and managed, could it be otherwise. Schools are fundamentally about learning. They are not fundamentally about teaching, though teaching may happen in them and may result in learning. They are not fundamentally about socialisation, or citizenship or vocational skills – all of those things are important but they are outcomes of learning. New technologies and new social and political agendas emphasise the centrality of learning. A school – every school – should be a learning *locus* and a learning organisation. Schooling and learning are inextricable in a way that schooling and teaching are not.

If this is true, then all the members of a school are partners in a learning enterprise. The effectiveness of that enterprise depends upon the skill with which it is managed. Hence a major concentration of this text has been about managing the roles that support learning, not merely attempting to describe them, however precisely. We have tried to produce a text for practitioners – support practitioners as well as teacher, Head and management practitioners.

Of course, there will be a minority in the teaching profession who will react negatively to a text like this – who will feel that, rather than enhancing their status as professionals, it will undermine it. The truth is: nothing written here does, or is intended to do, that. But paranoia is not susceptible to logic.

What we hope will inform and hearten the majority of opinion is the thought that, if all the good practice collected for this volume were to be implemented, then the value of schools as learning institutions would rise beyond measure.

Index

■ ■ ■